T0320801

Business Ethics for Better Behavior

Business Ethics for Better Behavior

Jason Brennan, William English, John Hasnas, and Peter Jaworski

OXFORD
UNIVERSITY PRESS

OXFORD
UNIVERSITY PRESS

Oxford University Press is a department of the University of Oxford. It furthers
the University's objective of excellence in research, scholarship, and education
by publishing worldwide. Oxford is a registered trade mark of Oxford University
Press in the UK and certain other countries.

Published in the United States of America by Oxford University Press
198 Madison Avenue, New York, NY 10016, United States of America.

Library of Congress Cataloging-in-Publication Data
Names: Brennan, Jason, 1979– author.
Title: Business ethics for better behavior / Jason Brennan,
William English, John Hasnas, Peter Jaworski.
Description: New York, NY : Oxford University Press, [2021] |
Includes bibliographical references and index.
Identifiers: LCCN 2021013377 (print) | LCCN 2021013378 (ebook) |
ISBN 9780190076559 (hardback) | ISBN 9780190076566 (paperback) |
ISBN 9780190076580 (epub)
Subjects: LCSH: Business ethics.
Classification: LCC HF5387.B745 2021 (print) |
LCC HF5387 (ebook) | DDC 174/.4—dc23
LC record available at https://lccn.loc.gov/2021013377
LC ebook record available at https://lccn.loc.gov/2021013378

DOI: 10.1093/oso/9780190076559.001.0001

Hardback printed by Bridgeport National Bindery, Inc., United States of America

Contents

1

Why Do Good People Do Bad Things?

Basic Lesson: Most of us are disposed to be good, but we often make moral mistakes. Good ethics education can't transform bad people into good, but it can help decent people of goodwill to avoid mistakes.

We've never met you, but we already know a lot about you.

We know that it matters to you that others see you as trustworthy and honest.[1] We know you care about your reputation. We know that when you read about business scandals, or when you read about people in history doing horrible things, you think, "I wouldn't do that" or "I'd know better."

We also know that despite all this, you probably tell little white lies every day.[2] Perhaps you tell someone an unflattering shirt looks nice or claim you're busy when you just don't want to accept an invitation. In high school, you probably lied to your parents about significant things. You probably cheated on a test or a paper.[3]

Yet we also know that you're a good person overall. You think lying, cheating, and stealing are wrong. You probably barely remember doing these things, and you probably don't intend to do them again.

What's going on?

We're Built for Ethics

Suppose we ask you: *Who* taught you be an ethical person? You'd probably answer that it was your parents or guardians, your friends, your religious leaders, your teachers, and your mentors. You're not entirely wrong, but you're not entirely right.[4]

Consider instead notorious serial killer John Wayne Gacy, who killed at least thirty-three teenage boys in a six-year period. It's not like his mom forgot to teach him that killing is wrong. Nor would it have helped much had he read some ethics books or taken an ethics course.

For what it's worth, Gacy had a business degree from Northwestern Business College. We don't know if they required ethics courses back then, but

Business Ethics for Better Behavior. Jason Brennan, William English, John Hasnas, and Peter Jaworski, Oxford University Press.
© Oxford University Press 2021. DOI: 10.1093/oso/9780190076559.003.0001

we know that they now expect graduates to be able to "understand and analyze ethical behaviors in the business environment."[5]

The problem with Gacy was deeper than that. He was a psychopath. His brain was wired differently than yours.[6] You empathize with others. When you see others suffer, you feel a little of their pain. For various reasons, the parts of the brain responsible for empathy don't work the same way in psychopaths. They feel no compunction against or guilt about lying, cheating, or manipulating others. A few, like Gacy, will even torture and kill victims. Still, most psychopaths behave much like the rest of us do, even if they feel differently on the inside.

Gacy's brain, and others like his, tells us something about ourselves. Unlike Gacy, we are *wired* for morality. Morality is part of what makes us human. Gacy was human too, but abnormal.

Human beings are biologically *weird*. We're the only species that cooperates with strangers—with unrelated members of our species—on such a large scale. Some other apes and cetaceans live in small pods, say fifty members or less, of unrelated individuals. But bees, ants, termites, and wasps, the other species that manage to cooperate on our scale, only do so because they are all related. A giant ant nest consists of a mom and her million babies, forming a superorganism.

This kind of cooperation is possible in part because we are wired to understand and to care about right and wrong. Cooperation requires that people know and live by certain common rules. It requires that we be willing to do our part even when no one is watching, and that we be willing to punish wrongdoers even when punishing them doesn't benefit us personally. Over millions of years, we've evolved to be disposed to do just that.[7]

To illustrate, consider what economists call the "ultimatum game." In that game, we randomly assign two people to two roles, a proposer and a responder. The proposer gets, say, $100. She can then propose to split the money however she wants with the responder, $100 for her and $0 for the responder, $50 each, or anything in between. The responder hears the proposed split, and then can say either "yes" or "no." If the responder says "yes," the players both get the proposed split. If the responder says "no," both players get *nothing*.

Now think of how perfectly selfish people, who care only about themselves and are indifferent to others, would play the game. The proposer would offer $99 for herself and $1 for the responder—the bare minimum to incentivize the responder to say "yes." The responder prefers $1 to nothing, so he'd accept it.

But in reality, around the world, even when *lots of money* is at stake, the proposer usually offers the responder something closer to an even split. And the responder will normally *reject the offer* if the split is too unfair, even if that means he loses lots of money, and even if the other player is someone he doesn't know, can't see, and will never interact with in person. Around the world, proposers are disposed to play fair, and responders are disposed to punish a stranger at their own expense for not playing fair. Pure self-interest can't explain how people play this game.

Further, the behavioral economist Dan Ariely has conducted a number of experiments designed to measure when people will be honest and when they will cheat.[8] When Ariely gives experimental subjects the chance to cheat for, say, a $2 payoff per instance of cheating, he gets high rates of cheating. Now, what happens if he changes the payoff from $2 to $10? It turns out subjects cheat *less*. (Note that Ariely carefully controls the experiment to ensure that the higher payoff doesn't make students more suspicious they'll get caught.)

Most people are willing to tell little white lies on the margins, but they don't tell big, hurtful lies quite so easily. They might steal pencils or notebooks from work, but they don't steal laptops. They might be callous or cruel to someone at lunch, but they wouldn't kill him or her, even if they could get away with it. They might cheat for $2 a pop, but not for $10 or $20. What seems to be going on is that we put limits on our self-interested behavior.

Some cynical philosophers, economists, or lawyers say that we behave well only because criminal or civil courts threaten to punish us when we don't play by the rules. On the contrary, we constantly have opportunities to cheat each other in small ways or out of small amounts, amounts so small it wouldn't make sense to ask for a court to intervene. Consider: If Starbucks defrauded you of $5, you wouldn't sue them. Even if you win, *suing them* costs you more in time and effort than you'd expect to get back in winning.[9] Yet Starbucks doesn't do this kind of thing. Part of the reason is that they benefit from being seen as honest. Part of the reason is that the people working there don't like ripping off other people.

Morality is part of what makes us human, much like the capacity for language.[10] Your parents, guardians, teachers, friends, and mentors didn't teach you to care about right and wrong so much as they helped you apply and refine your basic moral sense. They helped you understand how to use your moral sense in context, and reinforced your efforts to do so. But if you didn't already have an innate desire to do the right thing, no amount of schooling, reading, or lecturing would fix that.

So, Why Aren't We All Angels?

If morality is part of what makes us human—if we have evolved to be moral—then why aren't we all "angels"? That is, why don't we always do the right thing for the right reason?

We all hate lying, cheating, and stealing, and we all condemn the great wrongs of history. We admire people who keep their word and stand up against injustice. We feel outraged when others are wronged.

Yet most of us are only *pretty decent* overall. Most good people commit small wrongs. Sometimes good people do terrible things, things they never intended to do.

Part of the problem is that although we're built to be moral, we're not built to be *perfectly* moral. In the same way, your shoulder has evolved to throw rocks and spears, but it's not like we'd all be ace pitchers or star javelin hurlers if only we practiced more.

There's also a catch: If you're surrounded by people who care about morality, it's to your evolutionary advantage to *seem* more moral than you really are but to bend and break the rules a bit here and there. If people reward you for being virtuous, it can help you to fake being more virtuous than you are. Indeed, you might even trick yourself into thinking you're more moral than you are. We'll return to this point in chapter 7.

The deeper answer to "Why aren't we all angels?" is: It's complicated. There is a mix of factors at work. We care about morality for its own sake to some degree. But we are all also selfish; we might care about a few people (our spouses and children) more than ourselves, but we care about ourselves more than we care about others. And selfishness isn't the only thing that influences or corrupts our behavior. Sometimes we face bad incentives and take the bait. Sometimes, we are conformists who don't know how to say "no" and don't even realize saying "no" is an option. Sometimes, we operate on autopilot; we act but are unaware that anything morally significant is at stake. Sometimes, we suffer from self-deception and so trick ourselves into taking shortcuts. Sometimes, we don't have the willpower to resist temptation.

The truth is that bad behavior is not all one thing. The thing we call our mind is less like a finely tuned engine created by an expert engineer and more like an old engine hot-rodded with lots of different, somewhat incompatible parts. Our brain is a mix of different modules evolved for different purposes. Producing better behavior requires us to take a look under the hood. Once we know how the moral engine works, we can determine how to upgrade it—or choose better roads—to get better performance.

The Nobility of Business

"Business ethics? Isn't that an oxymoron?"

You've probably heard that bad joke. It's a bad joke not just because it's overdone—like asking a cashier if an item is free when it doesn't ring up—but because it's not even making fun of the truth. Businesspeople and business are not especially unethical.

Still, business people get a bad rap. Business has a PR problem.

Our university has both an undergraduate business school (MSB) and a "school of foreign service" (SFS). We sometimes ask our business students to describe the stereotypes of students from each school. Every year, we get the same answers: MSB students are competitive, hard-working, and ambitious, but driven by dollars. SFS students are lazier or more relaxed, but they all want to "save the world."

A recent Gallup poll asked Americans to evaluate how ethical they thought people in various professions are. Although few people thought businesspeople in general are bad, they nevertheless rated bankers, business executives, and especially advertisers much lower than nurses, police officers, doctors, and even auto mechanics.[11] If it makes you feel better, they tend to rate politicians—the very people who are supposed to regulate and control business—even lower.

On TV and in movies, businesspeople are the go-to villains. The next five big dystopian novels will probably depict a world ruled by cold-blooded corporations and heartless CEOs. The media reports every big business scandal, which makes it easy to recall such scandals, which tricks your brain into thinking these behaviors are more common than they are.[12]

Part of the problem might also be that society's expectations of business keep going up. Perhaps businesses and businesspeople are more ethical today than fifty years ago, but social expectations increased even faster.

Part of the problem is simple prejudice. Researchers Amit Bhattacharjee, Jason Dana, and Jonathan Baron find, in a series of experiments, that most people subscribe to what they call "anti-profit beliefs." Most people believe that profit-seeking "is necessarily in conflict with beneficial outcomes for consumers and society."[13] You may have heard of studies in which subjects are given identical résumés, but one has a "black-sounding" name while the other has a "white-sounding" name. People routinely rate the "black" résumé as weaker than the identical white résumé—which indicates prejudice against blacks. Similarly, Bhattacherjee et al. ran a series of experiments which showed that people automatically assume that for-profit businesses are more harmful and less beneficial than otherwise identical nonprofits.

Many business ethics textbooks tell the same basic story. They write as if normal, day-to-day business activity, and the profession of business itself, is at best morally neutral and at worst somewhat morally suspect. They say ethics puts *constraints* on business. Business ethics is mostly a list of "do nots." They say that if businesspeople want to exercise their "social responsibilities," they have to "give back" by donating to various philanthropies or running their business with an eye to promoting various environmental, political, and social causes.

Some of those points are correct. But they miss something, something we'll be careful not to miss in this book, and something you should not lose sight of when you work full time in business: Normal business activity is a good thing. Most businesspeople serve the world just by doing business.

Economist Deirdre McCloskey says we can summarize economic history with one sentence: "Once upon a time we were all poor, then capitalism flourished, and now as a result we're rich."[14] She isn't kidding. Five thousand, two thousand, even one thousand years ago, nearly everyone everywhere lived in what the United Nations would now call "extreme poverty."[15] Yet in the past two centuries, there has been tremendous economic growth. On average, the global standard of living has increased by a factor of at least 20 in the past two hundred years.[16] The average person living in England today is about forty times richer than an English person living one thousand years ago.

People often say money can't buy happiness. They say it can't buy love either. But economists Betsey Stevenson and Justin Wolfers find that around the world, the richer a country is in absolute terms, the happier its people tend to be, and the more likely they are to say they felt loved and respected.[17]

The Marxist philosopher G. A. Cohen notes that money is like a ticket, and there are things we can do if we have a ticket but not otherwise.[18] Thus, to have money is to have an important kind of freedom. The average person today has more real options available to her about what kind of life she will lead, whom she will be, and what she will do at any given moment than at any time in the past.

We owe this to business, to commercial activity, to economic growth. The wealth we enjoy did not exist fifty years ago, let alone one thousand years ago. In 2019, the United States alone produced something like 50 percent more than the entire world's economic output in 1950, and close to eighty times the entire world's economic output in 1000.[19] Wealth has been *made*, not just moved around. Even if all of the wealth that existed in the world in 1000 had been distributed equally among everyone then alive, the average standard of living would have been worse than that of Haiti or Malawi today.

We'll return to this point in chapter 2. Business can be and usually is a noble profession. The average businessperson serves society simply by doing business.

But along the way, businesspeople can fall into traps, where they serve themselves at the expense of society. Further, one trap that businesspeople are especially prone to is thinking that "I'm serving society" or "I'm doing philanthropy" can somehow compensate for dishonest or wrongful behavior.

An Initial Problem: Isn't It All Relative Anyway?

American K–12 schools routinely teach students that there is a distinction between facts and opinions. For instance, they might say that "Hitler was Chancellor of Germany in 1943" is a fact, while "Hitler was evil" is an opinion. Facts, they say, can be tested and proven true or false. Opinions cannot.

But perhaps inadvertently, what the schools end up doing is presenting an extremely controversial philosophical position as dogma.[20] To illustrate, consider this distinction:

1. *Normative statements* evaluate a thing. For instance, "Hitler was evil," "Happiness is good," "Racism is wrong," "Black lives matter," or "It's wrong to punch babies for fun" are normative statements.
2. *Positive statements* describe a thing without evaluating it. For instance, "The universe is about 6,000 years old" and "The universe is over 13.7 billion years old" are both positive statements, though at most only one of them can be true.

American schools teach students that normative statements are all just "opinions" that cannot be proven true or false. Or they'll say that your opinion is true for you but not for me, whatever that means. But, hey, that's just, like, your opinion, man.

Now, it is true that people from different countries, cultures, or religious traditions sometimes, as a result of these different backgrounds, have different beliefs about what is right and wrong, good and bad, or virtuous and vicious. A person raised in Sweden is more likely to advocate free speech than a person raised in a theocratic or communist society. People sometimes claim that because peoples beliefs about right and wrong vary across cultures, then the truth about what is right and wrong, good and bad, virtuous and vicious must culturally determined—that what a particular culture believes to be right or good *is* right or good for that culture simply because they believe it so. This view is called "ethical relativism" or sometimes "cultural relativism." An extreme form of ethical relativism is ethical subjectivism, in which "culture" is reduced to one person, so that what's right and wrong varies from person to person; whatever you believe is right is right for you.

Many students come in prepared to accept ethical relativism, perhaps because they've been taught to do so, or perhaps because they've been told that relativism is somehow more tolerant. But upon reflection, they might find the view uglier and less reasonable than they anticipated. Consider the following hypothetical exchange between Martin Luther King, Jr., and a random racist.

MLK: "Racism is wrong! Everyone should be treated with respect and as equals regardless of the color of their skin. Black lives matter."

RACIST: "Um, no. You see, in our society, we believe that blacks are inferior to whites. Ethics is relative. What makes something right or wrong is what society believes. Look, I have an opinion poll right here that shows 99% of Americans advocate racism and hold that black lives don't really matter."

MLK: "Oh, my bad. I guess racism is right after all. I'm mistaken."

This exchange is absurd. No one, especially not Martin Luther King, Jr., would think an opinion poll settles the matter. He wouldn't have thought that people believing racism is right *makes* it right. But the ethical relativist is committed to saying that King is wrong and the racist is right. If ethical relativism is true, then whatever a culture believes is right for that culture. This implies that racism in the 1960s American South was right, and Martin Luther King was wrong. Absurd.

You can make a similar counterexample for ethical subjectivism, the theory that what makes an action wrong for you is simply that you believe it's wrong. Imagine King tells Hitler it's wrong to murder Jews. If ethical subjectivism is the correct view, Hitler could respond, "It's wrong *for you* but not *for me*, simply because I believe it's right to do so." Absurd.

It's true that people disagree about ethical issues. But the mere fact that people disagree tells us little about whether there's an underlying truth.

Disagreement is boring. People disagree about all sorts of things—whether evolution happened, whether free trade tends to be efficient, whether vaccines work or cause autism, or whether the Earth is older than six thousand years—about which we have overwhelming evidence for one side.

It's true that you cannot prove ethical statements true or false with scientific experiments or observations. But then you cannot prove any of the following statements true or false with scientific experiments or observations either:

1. $2 + 2 = 4$.
2. If many carefully controlled and replicated scientific experiments provide evidence for X, then X is probably true.
3. An act is right for people from a culture just in case people from that culture believe it to be right.
4. There is a distinction between fact and opinion.

This isn't a knock on science, by the way. It's perhaps a knock on your K–12 teachers, who may have taught you bad philosophy. Our point here is that many statements or theories are not testable by the methods of physics or biology, but they are clearly the kinds of things that could be true or false.

Sometimes apparent moral disagreements between cultures are merely apparent. Consider four sets of examples:

Business cards: In different cultures, there are different ways one is supposed to hand others a business card. In Japan, one should hold a business card out with two hands, and the person accepting it should take it by the corners with two hands. In Korea, one should exchange cards while standing, and you should give a person your card with your right hand. In the United States, you can exchange cards with little formality.

Funerals: At one point in history, the ancient Greeks burned their dead fathers and would have thought it repugnant to *eat* them during a funeral. Supposedly the Callatians would eat part of their dead during a funeral and would have thought it repugnant to burn them.

Obscene hand gestures: In the United States, sticking up one's middle finger expresses something obscene. The OK sign expresses, "OK." In other parts of the world, the OK sign expresses something obscene.[21]

Eating: In some places, eating loudly with one's mouth open is disrespectful. In others, eating quietly with one's mouth closed is disrespectful.

At first glance, it may seem like these differences in norms reflect real differences in right and wrong. But on second glance, we see something more interesting. Every culture mentioned here agrees on a fundamental moral norm: *Show respect for others and do not show disrespect.* But then each culture develops a different *ritual* or *language* for showing respect. These rituals are called "etiquette." They imbue certain actions, gestures, and behaviors with symbolic meaning, which then communicates respect or disrespect. After all, it's not written into the fabric of universe that the middle finger means something obscene. Etiquette varies from place to place even though the underlying moral norm—that we should express respect for people and avoid expressing disrespect—is universal.

Many psychologists have investigated whether—regardless of what philosophers think—ordinary people regard morality as relative or not. It turns out they don't.[22] Rather, they presuppose that moral statements are not mere matters of opinion and are not determined by cultural or individual attitudes. Instead, they think that certain conventions—such as not chewing with your mouth open or addressing people by "Ms." or "Mr."—are just that, conventions which can vary from place to place. They think other obligations, such as a duty not to hit people at will, are not conventions and have to be observed everywhere. So, although people disagree about some of the content of morality, they nevertheless agree that morality is not a mere social convention which can be changed by fiat.

What This Book—And Ethics Courses—Can Do

Many professional degree programs require students to take an ethics course. Why?

A cynical—but partly true answer—is to protect their own reputation. When someone like Bernie Madoff (Hofstra University 1960) or Raj Rajaratnam (Wharton 1983) is exposed for high-stakes fraud or insider trading, the media turns around and asks why business schools didn't teach them ethics. There's something frankly silly about that; it's not like Madoff or Rajaratnam would have done the right thing if only they'd spent an extra semester reading ethics cases. (Rajaratnam was required to take an ethics course at Wharton.) But if professional schools offer ethics courses, then, when their alumni do something wrong, they can at least declare it wasn't their fault.

Let's cut past that and level with you about what this book—and any ethics course you take—can and can't accomplish. It can't create goodwill where there isn't any, or make bad people see the light. It can't give you some sort of step-by-step algorithm for calculating right and wrong in every situation. It can't replace the wisdom that often comes with experience or the enthusiasm that often comes with youth.

No worries. Here's what this book—and a good ethics course—can do: It can help clarify what right and wrong are in the context of business. It can help people of goodwill develop a common moral language that makes it easier for them to work together rather than talk past each other. It can reduce moral confusion. It can shine light on the "hard cases." Better yet, it can show that solving hard cases isn't as important as you might think. It can show you how people who do the wrong thing often had no intention of doing so and had every intention of doing the right thing. It can help you see why normal, good people fall into various moral traps. It then can help you see how to avoid those traps.

In short, this book is meant to answer three basic questions:

1. What counts as right and wrong in business?
2. Why do normal, decent businesspeople sometimes do the wrong thing?
3. How can we use the answer to these questions to get ourselves, our coworkers, our bosses, and our employees to behave better?

Our goal is to use the best available resources from multiple academic fields, including economics, political science, philosophy, management, sociology, and psychology, to help you live up to the high standards you probably already have for yourself.

We want to help you learn to navigate the kinds of problems you're most likely to encounter, to help you resolve them or, better yet, avoid them in the first place.

We will then help you diagnose what went wrong, asking both what makes the behavior wrong, and why a morally decent person might act in such a way. We then end with practical guidance—taken from economics, psychology, and management theory—about how to structure business activity to avoid the problem in the first place.

Notes

1. http://josephsoninstitute.org/surveys/.
2. Saad 2011; see Ariely 2013.
3. http://josephsoninstitute.org/surveys/; McCabe, Butterfield, and Treviño 2017.
4. Jason Brennan thanks his colleague Ed Soule for the idea behind this section.
5. https://nc.edu/career-programs/business/business-administration-degree/.
6. https://www.sciencedaily.com/releases/2013/09/130924174331.htm.
7. Simler and Hanson 2018.
8. Ariely 2013.
9. Stringham 2015.
10. No, we don't mean to say that the small minority of people who lack this capacity aren't human; nor would we say that psychopaths who lack a moral capacity aren't human. We're making a significant generalization that has explanatory power; but like most things in nature, there are variations on the rule.
11. Brennan 2016. https://foreignpolicy.com/2016/11/10/the-dance-of-the-dunces-trump-clinton-election-republican-democrat/.

12. http://www.oxfordreference.com/view/10.1093/oi/authority.20110803095436724.

13. Bhattacharjee, Dana, and Baron 2017.

14. McCloskey 1991: 1.

15. Maddison 2007.

16. Ibid.

17. Stevenson and Wolfers 2008.

18. Cohen 1995: 58–59.

19. Schmidtz and Brennan 2010: 122; and

20. Corvino 2015.

21. https://www.globalsecurity.org/military/library/report/1997/arab_culture/f9gestur.pdf.

22. See Nichols 2014 for a review.

2

The Business of Business Is Business

How Businesses Serve Society

Basic Lesson: There is a division of labor in modern democratic societies. The main way businesses serve society is by producing products and services people want at prices they can afford to pay. A good business exercises corporate social responsibility simply by delivering its core service. There is a role for charitable giving and other causes, but having a well-crafted corporate social responsibility campaign is no substitute for ethics.

CSR Is Not Business Ethics

In 2018, FedEx's social responsibility page began like this:[1]

Deliver It Forward.

With networks that span billions of people across six continents, delivering is our business. It's also our responsibility to deliver the resources that improve the lives of those we serve.

When we help businesses access new markets, they grow and create jobs that boost standards of living in their communities. Investments in safer and more sustainable transportation improve our own footprint and make our communities more livable. A more connected world sparks innovation when shared ideas, goods and technologies interact to transform how we live and work.

We believe a connected world is a prosperous and sustainable world. And we aim to deliver that forward.

Notice FedEx's basic message: The way we are socially responsible, the way we give back to society, is by doing what we do, by providing our core service, which we sell for profit.

Business Ethics for Better Behavior. Jason Brennan, William English, John Hasnas, and Peter Jaworski, Oxford University Press.
© Oxford University Press 2021. DOI: 10.1093/oso/9780190076559.003.0002

Now consider the 2017 social responsibility campaign of agricultural giant Archer Daniels Midland (ADM). It begins:

> At ADM, sustainable practices and a focus on environmental responsibility aren't separate from our primary business: they are integral to the work we do every day to serve customers and create value for shareholders. And so as our business grows and evolves, so has our commitment to sustainability. That is why we have set ambitious sustainability goals for ourselves—and why our colleagues around the globe are achieving, and in many cases, exceeding them.[2]

ADM claims to have the "mission" of "turning crops into products that meet the world's growing and vital needs for more food, more energy, and a healthier environment."[3] ADM has a wonderfully detailed social responsibility campaign—*ADM Cares*—dedicated to forming "strong roots," "strong bonds," and "strong communities;"[4] ADM says it wants to "improve the quality of life in our communities today as [it] create[s] a better future tomorrow."[5]

A naïve person might think, "ADM must be a more ethical company than FedEx. Look at all the wonderful charities and environmental initiatives ADM supports. If I dig into their webpage, sure, FedEx does that stuff, too. Still, FedEx seems like they're taking it easy on themselves if their main message is 'We exercise social responsibility by simply doing business.'"

Business ethics textbooks sometimes reinforce such attitudes. But we have to be careful here.

ADM donates to various charities and works on sustainability. But it's also a deeply unethical business, so much so that economists regularly use ADM in textbooks when teaching students about the various ways government can be hijacked to serve special interests.[6] As law professor Jonathan Adler says, "ADM has perfected the art of rent seeking as well as . . . any other company in America."[7] "Rent seeking" is a technical term that refers to a person, firm, or organization trying to manipulate the legal environment for its own benefit at the expense of everyone else. ADM lobbies for a large range of socially destructive tariffs, subsidies, and predatory regulations. For instance, as of 1995, nearly half of ADM's profits came from subsidized or protected products; for every $1 of profits ADM's corn sweetener products earned, consumers lost $10 from predatory subsidies and tariffs.[8]

For the past few decades, business ethics textbooks and business ethics professors taught that being an ethical business includes and involves providing financial support to good causes, focusing on all "stakeholders," and ensuring one is environmentally sustainable. For the sake of argument, let's assume they are right.

Nevertheless, we must be cautious. Unethical businesses often use moral language and language of social responsibility to disguise their bad behavior.

Corporate social responsibility (CSR) is all the rage. The basic idea behind CSR is that companies ought to "give back" to society—usually by donating some of their profits to various social, environmental, and political causes.

But let's be clear—CSR may be part of ethics, but it is not the whole of ethics. Nor is it the most fundamental part of business ethics. It is at best a secondary consideration. A business can have a wonderful CSR program and still be deeply unethical. CSR does not *compensate* for dishonesty, fraud, corruption, or predation.

Instead:

- *Primary business ethics* is about *how* you make your money. Do you make money in an honest, fair, and open way, free of coercion and exploitation? Does your product or service create value for your customers, without forcing third parties to bear your costs?
- *CSR* largely focuses on what issues or causes businesses support, and on what businesses do with the money they've made. Do they reinvest or distribute all their profits, or do they donate some of it to charitable or political causes?

You can have exceptional primary business ethics without exercising CSR, and you can have impressive CSR despite being unethical. Enron became a business built on fraud and deception, but it had robust CSR initiatives. Conflating CSR with ethics is an example of the type of moral confusion that can result in bad behavior if one is not careful.

FedEx's core argument—our core for-profit service is the way we serve society—may strike you as a little too easy. On the contrary, FedEx has exactly the right message. *The most important social responsibility of business is to ensure the world is genuinely better off with that business performing its core function than without it.* The main way ethical businesses serve society is by producing products and services people genuinely want at prices that they can afford to pay.

Those who think this is an *undemanding* moral standard are fooling themselves. Making profit by offering a product or service others will want to buy, when given a real choice, is tremendously difficult. That's why so many businesses, such as ADM, try to make profits through *other* means.

A Division of Labor, Including Moral Labor

There's a big gap between saying "This cause is important" and concluding that "*You* should do something about it."

It's important that enough people grow food. That does not mean you personally need to grow a garden, be a farmer, or contribute to farming causes. It is important that enough people research and practice medicine. That does not mean you personally need to volunteer at a hospital, become a nurse or physician, or contribute to medical research. It's important that children and adults alike be educated, but that doesn't mean you need to Teach for America, become a scientist, or donate your life savings to your alma mater.

Modern societies have a *division of labor*. The division of labor means that people—and institutions and organizations—specialize in different kinds of work, jobs, service, and goods. Different people do different things. Because they specialize, they can do those things well. As you go back in history, you don't see the division of labor disappear, but there's less of it. What you see instead is that individual people have to do a bit of everything; as a result, they do everything poorly.

One major benefit of the division of labor is that it creates opportunities for a great deal of freedom. We don't conscript all people—or businesses, nongovernmental organizations (NGOs), civil organizations, or government agencies—into the same role. Everyone should contribute in *some* way, but there's more flexibility for you—and those organizations—to decide *how* to contribute. You should play your part, but there are a million different parts for you to play.

There are a million causes out there worth contributing to. There are a million important issues to think about. There are a million jobs that need to be done. Any particular person or organization can do only a few of these things well. That doesn't mean that the person or organization fails to "do its part" or fails to care about those other things.

The Invisible Hand

At root, business is about *trade*. Trade is a fundamentally moral way for people to relate to one another. Two people (or businesses) make a trade if and only if they both value what the other has more than what they have. You value $500 more than your used guitar. The person on Craigslist values your used guitar more than $500. You meet and make an exchange, and you *both* walk away having *made a profit*. Simply by *exchanging* things, you create value for yourself and for your trading partner.

Markets as a whole bring together lots of different buyers and sellers. The main way these buyers and sellers communicate with each other—the signal that coordinates all their activities—are *prices*. Market prices are not set by any individual—they arise as a function of supply and demand, which themselves reflect both the preferences and the knowledge of the people participating in the economy. Market prices convey information about the relative scarcity of goods and services in light of the demand for those goods and services. Market prices thus tell producers and consumers how to adjust their behavior to meet other people's wants and needs.[9]

For instance, cans are now made of aluminum rather than tin. Why? Soup, beer, and soda canners noticed tin was getting more expensive and aluminum less. They didn't need to know precisely why—whether it had to do with mining problems, new manufacturing, or whatever. But they adjusted their production process. In effect, the market was telling them, "*Other* people value tin more than aluminum, so if you can use aluminum instead of tin, you'd really help out." And companies did just that. Market prices make companies preserve materials and services for their highest valued uses.

Google what soda cans looked like in the 1950s. Old Coke cans looked like plain cylinders. New Coke cans have curves on the top and bottom. Why? Coke and other aluminum users realized that this new shape allowed them to stack cans high but conserve materials. If Coke finds a way to reduce its costs by conserving scarce materials, it increases its profits.

When we think about trading, we often think of two people making an exchange. But what we don't see—unless we look a bit harder—is how markets are much bigger than that. They are systems of cooperation with millions of people working together to promote the common good.

Consider a simple object—a number 2 pencil. Now ask, how many people helped make that pencil? You might guess the factory has, say, two hundred workers. But look closer—think of the people who made the machine parts, who supply the power, who supplied the wood, who mined the graphite. Think of the people *they in turn* depended on. The lumberjack chopping the wood needed someone to make a chainsaw, a truck, a set of chains, and so on. If you keep tracing it out, what you realize is that literally millions of people worked together to produce that pencil, though perhaps only few hundred of them knew they were doing so. The person who mines the iron that will go into the ball bearings in machines that help make the graphite that will end up in the pencil might have little idea that he is helping to make pencils. Yet market prices bring these millions of people together to produce pencils.[10]

When Adam Smith said that markets get us to work together as if led by an invisible hand, what he meant was that there is something miraculous about all this. Millions of people work together, all without needing anyone to be in charge, to give orders, or to run the show.

How Business Serves Society

Thomas Robertson, former dean of the Wharton School, once said in a public speech,

> At Wharton, we believe the role of business is to advance society as a whole, creating new wealth and economic opportunity for all people, in developing nations as well as developed economies. . . . Business can and must be a *force for good* in the world.[11]

Notice how similar Robertson's message is to FedEx's. Robertson isn't saying that to be a force for good, businesses need to champion a range of social, political, and environmental causes. He was saying the main way they do good is by creating new wealth and opportunity for all people. Let's unpack what that means.

Some 10,000 years ago, everyone everywhere was poor. Until very recently, nearly every single person throughout the world lived in what we now call "extreme poverty." Economist Angus Maddison estimates the total economic output per person was about $457 (2019 US dollars) in 1 AD, rising to $712 in 1820 (see figure 2.1).[12] Keep in mind that in most of the world there were highly unequal societies, with kings, high priests, lords, and warriors getting much more than everyone else. So, we're talking about societies in which typical people lived on less than $1 a day while King Louis XIV dined in opulence. What this means is that if the average income was $712 per year in 1820, in fact, the overwhelming majority of people lived on less than that.

Then something changed. The stagnation ended. In the past two hundred years, per capita world product has increased by a factor of at least 30.[13] Here, you can see the change yourself:

We condensed figure 2.1 between 1 and 1500 because it's basically flat. Despite dark ages and renaissances, the collapse and growth of empires, bad and good harvests, global warm and cool periods, the lines hardly move until recently. And then they explode. And today Africa, Asia, and Latin America are catching up with the West.

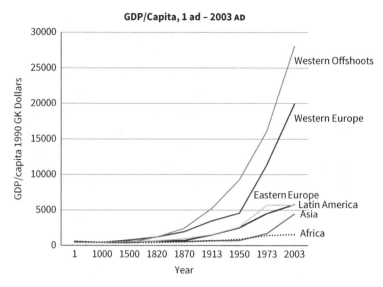

Fig. 2.1 Economic Growth Worldwide over Time.
Source: Chart uses data from Maddison 2007: 70. Taken from van der Vossen and Brennan 2018.

What does all this new wealth and money buy? A great deal:

1. *Freedom.*[14] The more money you have, the more you can do.
2. *Light.* When the sun goes down, life goes on. It didn't use to. Between the fourteenth century and today, the cost of light dropped by a factor of 12,000. A million lumen-hours of light costs you a few dollars today, but it would have cost you around $50,000 when Chaucer was alive.[15] (Keep in mind that the average person in the United Kingdom at that time made much less than $1,000 a year.) A single book back then cost far more than the average person made in a year. The ritual of reading to children before bed was for most of human history unbelievably expensive.
3. *Leisure.* In 1870, in the United States (at that time one of the richest countries in the world per capita), the average person started working full-time by age 13 and retired at . . . well, they kept working until they died. That same average person would work about 5,000 hours a year, split between home chores and work for pay. They'd spend 61 percent of their waking hours (over their lives) working. Today, that number has dropped below 28 percent. The average American starts working full-time at 20 and retires before 63. They literally have *decades* of leisure years and hundreds of thousands of leisure hours more than Americans right after the Civil War.[16]

4. *Safety.* Even though, thanks in part to climate change, the number of weather-related disasters appears to be on the rise, the number of deaths from natural disasters is far lower now than even one hundred years ago.[17] Increasing prosperity allows people to buy better housing and governments to buy better infrastructure which help insulate them from such dangers.[18] Work and transportation related accidents are down.[19]

5. *Health.* Thanks to vaccines, better nutrition, and better sanitation, people are generally healthier now than in the past. For example, in England in 1000 AD, the average life expectancy at birth was only twenty-six years.[20] In 1900 in the United States, it was only forty-three years. It is not that people used to get old and die at 26 or 43; rather, children died at such high rates that life expectancy at birth was low. But now even the poorest countries in the world have a better life expectancy than the richest countries did 120 years ago. In the West, people can expect to live into their 80s or 90s. It is hard to imagine a greater bonus to our personal freedom—to our ability to lead lives that are authentically our own—than gaining an additional few decades of healthy life.

6. *Peace.* For much of human history, including and perhaps especially pre-history, people lived in near constant states of war against others.[21] Yet as countries have gotten richer, the percentage of people dying from war has dropped dramatically, despite the massive destruction of two world wars.[22]

7. *Culture.* Think of the world's cultural centers throughout history, where the great art and music was being made. These places—Athens in ancient Greece or New York and Tokyo today—are commercial centers, where people from all over the world congregate, exchanging old ideas and synthesizing them into new ones.[23] An expanding market means the market for culture is far greater—as economist Deirdre McCloskey calculates, the possible market for culture is about *9,000 percent larger* than it was one thousand years ago.[24]

8. *Moral progress.* In chapter 1, we described the ultimatum game, which demonstrated people's tendency to be fair to others. In subsequent chapters, we will examine a host of similar economic experiments designed to measure the extent to which people are disposed to be cooperative, honest, generous, fair, trusting, and trustworthy. Economists have run such experiments around the world and discovered—contrary to what some finger-waving moralists might proclaim—that the strongest *cultural* predictor that participants will be tolerant of and play fairly with strangers is how market-oriented their society is.[25]

9. *Meaning*? Money cannot buy anyone a meaningful and fulfilling life, at least not directly. But maybe it can help purchase it, indirectly. You have probably heard of Maslow's Hierarchy of Needs. The idea here is that people tend to pursue certain goods, such as immediate physical needs, safety, shelter, and so on, before they pursue other "higher" goods, such as love, autonomy, personal fulfillment, and self-transcendence. These higher goods are more important in some sense, but the immediate physical needs are more urgent. As we get wealthier, we become liberated from having to worry about these immediate physical needs, and we acquire the opportunity to pursue higher spiritual and emotional goods.

When Dean Robertson says that business serves society by creating wealth and opportunity for all, he's not going easy on business. He's not expressing craven materialism and saying the only thing that matters is filthy lucre. Rather, he recognizes that the systematic effect of ethical, for-profit business activity is that businesses create, sustain, and improve conditions of wealth and opportunity, under which people become better able to realize their own conceptions of the good life.[26]

For-profit business activity creates wealth, opportunity, and cultural progress. Markets are an extended system of social cooperation. This cooperative system explains why each of us in contemporary liberal societies has our high standards of living and easy access to culture, education, and social opportunities. We work in networks of mutual benefit, and we benefit from other people being engaged in these networks. When we go to work in business, we help create, sustain, and improve these networks of mutual benefit. When things are going well—and overall they tend to go well—we create a series of positive externalities through our innovations, the division of labor, and the creation economies of scale.[27]

Service vs. CSR

FedEx's message is simple. It says the principal way it contributes to society and exercises social responsibility is to *do its business*. Its business connects people around the world, allowing them to trade and interact with each other. FedEx reduces what economists call the "transaction costs" of trade— that is, it makes trading with others easier and less expensive. FedEx and its competitors create a background infrastructure which liberates consumers from the confines of their hometowns and liberates producers to experiment with their vision of the good.

FedEx gives to charity, sure, and that can be a wonderful thing. (It can also be a waste, as we'll discuss shortly.) But giving to charity is not the job or the justification for business. It is not the test of business ethics or a test of whether a business serves society. It is something *extra*.

At bottom, a responsible business can claim:

1. We earned our money honestly and fairly, without coercion, fraud or deception, exploitation, and without imposing wrongful costs on innocent bystanders.
2. Our core service makes our customers and the world a better place. The world is better off with us than without us.

Remember, one of the most basic findings in economics is that trade is *mutually beneficial*. When we send a package via FedEx, we do so because we value sending the package *more* than we value the money we gave FedEx, and vice versa. They aren't *taking* from us; they're already "giving back" by completing their half of the deal. FedEx revenues are simply the aggregate of such mutually beneficial deals it makes with senders—each dollar it makes is a dollar it made by *giving back*.

After reflecting on ideas just like this, business ethicist Chris MacDonald points out how focusing on charitable CSR is unfair to businesses. He writes,

> Another way of putting the CSR idea is that, from a CSR point of view, it makes perfect sense to admit that a business:
>
> • makes a useful product or provides a useful service;
> • provides employment;
> • provides an investment opportunity for investors;
> • follows scrupulously all laws and regulations to which it is subject; and
> • pays its taxes . . .
>
> . . . and then to ask of that business, "Yes, but what do you contribute to society? How does society as a whole figure in your daily decision-making?"[28]

None of this is to say companies may not or should not engage in charitable CSR. As we discuss in the next section, in many cases they have every right to do so, and if they do it the right way, they can be acting admirably. Further, a well-designed CSR campaign can—in conjunction with a few other management strategies—help improve a company's bottom line, largely by helping to recruit more ethical employees and helping to ensure that existing employees behave more ethically.

Integrity and Standing for Something

There is not only a division of labor, but a division of *moral* labor. Not every person or business has to directly stand for or support every morally worthwhile cause. Saving the dolphins, preserving Parsi embroidery, or fighting for Nepalese freedom are all worthwhile endeavors, but that doesn't mean you or your business in particular must do much about them. Just as different charities—or clubs at your school—have different purposes, so do different businesses.

In general, businesses have a great deal of leeway about whether they want to stand for a "higher cause" or not. A small closely held corporation can decide to support a cause, or not, and can change causes on a whim. Publicly traded corporations, or firms taking money from investors, need to disclose their intentions—it's dishonest to take investment for the purpose of making a profit and then donate the profits to charity without the investors' consent. But beyond that, firms have a great deal of leeway about whether and what they'll stand for. In the same way, it's fine for Metallica to say politics isn't their job, and it's simultaneously fine for Lady Ga Ga to take a stand defending LGBTQ rights.

Once a business does stand for something, though, that changes what we should expect from it. If Lady Ga Ga says she will use her status and money to fight for LBGTQ rights, then we can rightly complain if (without some excuse) she starts ignoring those issues or gives money to political groups trying to undermine those rights—even though we don't hold other artists who have taken no stance to the same standards. The same goes for businesses.

The basic moral principle at stake here is *integrity*. Integrity is about *faithfulness* to one's convictions and values. To have integrity means that when you make commitments or say that you stand for something, you live up to those commitments and representations.

To *lack* integrity is to fail to live up to your commitments. You lack integrity if you pretend to be committed to projects or values in order to manipulate others or improve your status or reputation. You lack integrity if your commitments are shallow, or you don't stick to them when it's hard.

Back in the late 1990s and early 2000s, an email went viral, claiming that Amazon was anti-Semitic because it sold and supposedly favorably reviewed a book called *The Protocols of the Elders of Zion*.

The book is written as if Jewish elders were the authors, and they are discussing their plans for controlling the economy, media, and government. The book—which may have originally been written as far back as the late 1700s—was then "leaked," published, and spread around. But it's fake—the purpose is to convince readers that there is a Jewish conspiracy to dominate society and so they should hate Jews.

Amazon sold (and still sells) the *Protocols*, as well as other evil books, such as Hitler's *Mein Kampf* or Mao's *Little Red Book*. In the year 2000, activists and others demanded to know why Amazon would sell such books and demanded it stop doing so.

Amazon had to think carefully about how to respond. It was already on its way to being the biggest bookseller, and it correctly predicted that it would be the center of the book market within a few years. That meant, it realized, that whether Amazon chooses to sell or not to sell a book comes close to determining whether most readers have access to it.

On April 6, 2000, Amazon released the following statement:

> Should Amazon.com sell *The Protocols* and other controversial works? As a bookseller, Amazon.com strongly believes that providing open access to written speech, no matter how hateful or ugly, is one of the most important things we do. It's a service that the United States Constitution protects, and one that follows a long tradition of booksellers serving as guardians of free expression in our society.
>
> Amazon.com believes it is censorship not to sell certain books because we believe their message repugnant, and we would be rightly criticized if we did so. Therefore, we will continue to make this book and other controversial works available in the United States and everywhere else, except where they are prohibited by law.[29]

In publishing this statement, Amazon decided to take a stand and to stand for something. It decided that it will not use an ideological test to determine whether to sell something or not. It will not refuse to sell a book because the content is evil. It stated that it believed that in the long run, the best way to combat prejudice or awful ideas is to have open exchange and debate, and even to facilitate access to those prejudiced or awful ideas. It claimed that because of its special market position, refusing to sell something comes close to "censoring" that speech. It realized that while some people will be convinced by bad ideas or hoaxes, others will benefit from confronting and analyzing them.

Now, Amazon didn't *have* to say that. And other booksellers don't have to follow the same rules. The evangelical Christian bookstore in downtown Fairfax, Virginia, doesn't sell the *Protocols*, nor do they sell Mormon, Catholic, or Muslim books, or books about sex, drugs, and rock and roll. The Guitar Center down the street sells sheet music books and books about music, but it doesn't sell evangelical Christian books. The Barnes and Noble further down the street only sells the most popular titles. That's fine—it's within its prerogative to limit its selection that way. But Amazon decided it would stand for something bigger.

Now consider another case. Ten years later, Philip Greaves posted the e-book *The Pedophile's Guide to Love and Pleasure: A Child-Lover's Code of Conduct* for sale on Amazon. This book provides guidance for how to groom and sexually assault children.

In general, it is legal in the United States—protected by the First Amendment—to advocate criminal activities. You can't threaten to commit an illegal act or incite (in a narrow sense) others to do so, but you can write a book arguing we should commit illegal acts.[30] For example, you can't threaten to overthrow the government, but you can write a philosophy book arguing we should overthrow the government. You can't build car bombs, but you can write a book explaining how to do so (and you can buy such a book for $25 on Amazon right now.[31])

People threatened to boycott Amazon unless it removed the book. Amazon initially repeated its statement that it will make available any book, no matter how evil or repugnant its content, that it is legally allowed to sell. But under pressure, Amazon stopped selling the book, began selling it again in response to criticism for doing that, and then stopped selling it again.[32]

More recently, Amazon has started pulling books advocating that parents refuse to have the children vaccinated.[33] These books are indeed pseudoscience and push misinformation. We have no intention of defending antivaxxers. Nevertheless, Amazon's behavior is troubling in light of its proclamations that it would allow the sale of any book, no matter how wrong or repugnant, which it's legal to sell.

Now, it's a good question whether Amazon should have taken its "We sell everything" stand in first place. It's also a good question when and how a company should change its value commitments over time—like people, companies are allowed to have a change of heart. But in this case, what Amazon did lacked integrity. It took a stand for a certain vision of what it wanted to be, but when push came to shove, it did not live up to that vision. It wasn't even that it changed its mind about its stance so much as that it decided it was too much work to fight for that stance.

Effective Altruism

Giving profits to charity can be admirable. It can also be a waste of resources. It can waste resources in some cases because the money would be better spent reinvesting in the company—a good company is already doing good, and reinvesting in it makes the company able to expand and do more good. It can waste resources because sometimes the profits should be paid through dividends—enabling investors and shareholders to do good with their money. But—and this may be the surprising part—it can be a waste of resources because some charities shouldn't get another dime.

Various studies show that while most people give some money to charity, few put much thought into evaluating the quality of the charities they choose. They don't research how much good their money will do. They don't seem to care about bang for the buck—they don't seem to care whether a charity will save twenty lives or twenty-thousand. They tend to evaluate charities by the charity's *intentions*—or by how sexy it is to be associated with that charity—not by how well that charity achieves its goals.[34]

We advise you to take a different approach. When it comes to helping save the world, it's *not the thought that counts*. What counts is the actual helping and saving.

Let's introduce two big economic concepts:

1. *Opportunity Cost.* Any time you spend doing one thing comes at the expense of anything else you could have done with that time. Any money spent on something comes at the expense of anything else you could have spent that money on. The opportunity cost of your decision is *the next best alternative* you had to whatever you chose.
2. *Diminishing Marginal Returns.* Diminishing marginal returns means that, in general, each additional unit of an input produces less value than the unit before it. The first Oreo tastes better than the second, and the twentieth might make you ill. The first worker you hire gets your business going, but maybe you break even on the tenth, and you lose money on the eleventh.

Now, consider what that means for charity. Suppose you want to help reduce, cure, or mitigate the harm of blindness. It costs around $40,000–$60,000 to train a seeing-eye dog.[35] For about $100, one can pay for surgeries and other inventions in Africa which will prevent people from going blind from trachoma.[36] So, though it's uncomfortable to say this, helping one blind person in the United States prevents us from helping hundreds of blind people elsewhere.

Now consider giving money to, say, the Red Cross or Deworm the World Initiative. Everyone knows the Red Cross, and helping them would look slick on CSR marketing material. Deworm the World Initiative—which supports deworming programs in parts of Asia and Africa—is not so well known.

Perhaps the Red Cross has done more total good than Deworm the World Initiative. But if you're asking whether you should give to the Red Cross or Deworm the World Initiative, asking who has done more total good is the wrong question. A better question is, "If we donate $100,000 to either organization, which will do more good with that *extra $100,000*?" It may be that the Red Cross has done about as much good as it can do, while Deworm the World will get you a lot more bang for your buck—more years of life added per dollar spent—than the Red Cross.

If you want help applying these kinds of concepts, we recommend checking out GiveWell.org. Each year, GiveWell researches and recommends a small number of highly effective charities. Rather than asking crude questions about what percentage of revenue the charity spends on overhead, they research and answer more important questions: Which charities will do the most actual good with the next dollar?

Altruism that isn't effective is barely altruism at all. Some charities raise money—and accomplish whatever mission they say they support—but in doing so, make no difference. Other charities have done as much good as they possibly can, and aren't going to do much more. And still others—such as the antivaccine National Vaccine Information Center—can *hurt* rather than help; they support initiatives that harm the people they're supposed to benefit.[37]

Giving to an ineffective or harmful charity isn't just a wasted opportunity. It's a moral cost. It means taking valuable resources and transforming them into something worthless—or worse.

Summary

- The main way a responsible business serves society is by delivering its core services in an ethical way, not by donating profits to charity or by championing various causes.
- Good businesses do not just serve their customers. Collectively, they help create and sustain background conditions that promote tolerance, peace, and general prosperity. Business deserves credit for the good it has done.
- There is a division of labor—just because a cause is important doesn't mean you or your business have a duty to support that cause.
- CSR is not a substitute for ethics. A wonderful CSR campaign does not make up for unethical business behavior, nor is CSR a necessary requirement for a business to be ethical and responsible.
- If businesses do choose to donate or take a stand, they acquire duties of integrity to stand by their commitments.

Discussion Questions

1. Warren Buffet says he plans to donate all of his earnings to charity when he dies. Could he do more good keeping all/much/some that money invested in productive businesses?
2. Identify three companies you think have bad business ethics. Google their CSR campaigns. What do you see?
3. What should Amazon have done? Should Amazon sell Nazi or Stalinist literature, racist tracks, or the *Anarchist Cookbook*? Why or why not?
4. If a company changes its mind about its core values, how should it go about letting others know of its change of heart?
5. When you graduate, where do you want to work? Does that company make the world a better place simply by providing its core service? Imagine you get your dream job. Does your job make the world a better place?

Notes

1. Accessed July 23, 2018. https://about.van.fedex.com/social-responsibility/.
2. Accessed July 23, 2018. https://www.adm.com/sustainability.
3. https://www.adm.com/our-company/community-giving/strong-roots.
4. https://www.adm.com/our-company/community-giving.
5. https://www.adm.com/our-company/community-giving/strong-communities.
6. E.g., Cowen and Tabarrok 2015.
7. Adler 2000: 9.
8. Bovard 1995: 1.
9. Hayek 1945.
10. Read 2015. https://fee.org/resources/i-pencil/.
11. Caroll et al. 2012.
12. https://www.rug.nl/ggdc/historicaldevelopment/maddison/releases/maddison-project-database-2018.
13. World per capita income as of 2014 is approximately $16,100 in 2014, up from under $500 in 1800. https://www.cia.gov/the-world-factbook/field/real-gdp-per-capita/.
14. Cohen 1995: 58–59.
15. https://ourworldindata.org/light.
16. http://www.aei.org/publication/how-are-we-doing/.
17. http://www.emdat.be/disaster_trends/index.html.
18. See Richie and Roser 2019; van der Vossen and Brennan 2018: ch. 11.
19. http://www.aei.org/publication/how-are-we-doing/.
20. McCloskey 2006: 18–20.
21. Pinker 2012.
22. Roser n.d.

23. Cowen 2002.
24. McCloskey 2006: 20.
25. Al-Ubaydli et al. 2013; Brennan and Jaworski 2016: 96–102; Gintis 2012; Hoffman and Morgan 2011; Henrich et al. 2001; Zak 2008: xv; Zak and Knack 2001.
26. For more on this point, see Brennan 2012.
27. See, e.g., Krugman and Wells 2012: chs. 1, 2, 4, passim; Mankiw 2008: 8–12, Part III; Weil 2009: chs. 2, 10–12, 17.
28. MacDonald 2009.
29. https://www.amazon.com/Protocols-Zion-Trilingual-Spanish-English-ebook/dp/B004SY9H7G.
30. Note that long after the Amazon controversy was over, Greaves was eventually arrested for violating Florida's antiobscenity laws, but Florida's state laws may well violate Greaves's constitutional rights.
31. https://www.amazon.com/Anarchist-Cookbook-William-Powell/dp/0974458902/ref=sr_1_1?ie=UTF8&qid=1532442200&sr=8-1&keywords=anarchists+cookbook.
32. https://abcnews.go.com/Technology/amazon-removes-pedophilia-book-store/story?id=12119035.
33. Bever 2019.
34. Simler and Hanson 2018: 208–215.
35. https://puppyintraining.com/how-much-does-a-guide-dog-cost/.
36. https://www.givingwhatwecan.org/research/other-causes/blindness/.
37. E.g., see MacAskill 2014: 1–5.

3

Why Aren't We All Saints?

Basic Lesson: Most unethical behavior in business results not from bad people knowingly choosing to do what is wrong but from good people of goodwill falling into predictable moral traps. These traps include succumbing to perverse incentives, suffering from moral confusion, or being unable to overcome various psychological foibles which prime us toward bad behavior. To produce better ethical behavior, we need to know how people make moral decisions and why they sometimes make mistakes.

Psychologist Kiley Hamlin and her colleagues have conducted fascinating experiments examining the moral attitudes of "preverbal infants," that is, 6- to 10-month old babies who haven't yet learned to talk. Let's describe one.

The baby, sitting comfortably in its parent's arms, watches two puppet shows. In the first, a red circle with big eyes tries to climb up a hill. It can't make it. But then a blue square appears from behind and helps push it up the hill. Call the blue square the *helper*. In the second, the red circle again struggles to get up hill. Now, however, a yellow triangle appears on the top, and pushes the red circle down to the bottom. Call the yellow triangle the *hinderer*. After watching both shows, the researchers offered to let the baby hold either the helper or the hinderer. The baby almost always takes the helper.[1]

Decades ago, psychologists tended to think of human babies as moral blank slates upon which parents could write moral rules, or unmolded clay which parents could form into a moral shape. Other psychologists tended to presume children are born amoral, self-interested sociopaths who are later trained to become good.

Contemporary psychology doesn't support either picture. Instead, as early as we can measure their behavior, children divide the world up into helpers and hinderers, good and bad, fair and unfair. They prefer fairness to unfairness and helping to hindering, even when it doesn't affect them personally. They come equipped with an understanding of the difference between moral rules and mere conventions.[2] We become more moral as we grow, but we start out as moral.

As we said in chapter 1, morality is a constitutive part of human nature. We've evolved to be moral beings. Most of us have built-in moral tendencies.

Business Ethics for Better Behavior. Jason Brennan, William English, John Hasnas, and Peter Jaworski, Oxford University Press.
© Oxford University Press 2021. DOI: 10.1093/oso/9780190076559.003.0003

But we also asked, if morality is part of what makes us human, then why are we often so bad? Why don't we do the right thing all the time?

The answer is that there is no one answer. Sometimes, we don't know what the right thing to do is. Sometimes, we are confronted with bad incentives. Sometimes, we just don't notice what is going on around us.

No matter how well intentioned we may be, we are subject to all the shortcomings inherent in the human condition. In this chapter, we identify three aspects of human nature that can trip us up—three stumbling blocks—that can prevent us from doing the right thing. As human beings, we (1) have limited knowledge, (2) are susceptible to bad incentives, and (3) have limited psychological capacities. By exploring these stumbling blocks, we seek to understand why people who are wired for moral behavior nevertheless engage in wrongdoing. To produce better ethical behavior, we need to know how people make moral decisions and why they sometimes make mistakes.

Stumbling Block 1: Moral Confusion

In the novel *The Adventures of Huckleberry Finn*, title character Huck Finn faces a dilemma. Jim, a slave, has run away. Because Huck was raised in a slave-owning society and taught by all the authorities that slavery is condoned by God, Huck believes that morality requires him to turn Jim in. But Huck won't comply with what he thinks are the moral rules. Huck cannot himself explain why the rules are wrong, but he nevertheless can't bring himself to comply with them. When Jim is recaptured, Huck and Tom Sawyer work to free him. Huck believes this means he'll go to hell, but he chooses to do it anyway.

Readers know better. They realize that in reality, Huck is doing the right thing. He's confused about what right and wrong require. People in Huck's society believe slavery is just, but they're mistaken. Huck regards himself as a bad boy for violating God's will, but that's only because he isn't philosophically sophisticated enough to realize that the others are wrong.

Huck illustrates another way in which people make moral mistakes. Sometimes people are confused about right and wrong, or they lack the skill to think through what right and wrong require in a particular instance. Sometimes they are ignorant of the relevant facts or even the relevant principles. These limitations on their knowledge can cause what we will call "moral confusion." People often act wrongly because of such moral confusion.

Almost everyone has some degree of moral confusion. You probably accept a wide range of moral judgments. Some of these judgments are very general and abstract (e.g., "Equality is good"). Some are very particular (e.g., "That thing you just did was wrong"). Others are in-between (e.g., "It is right to tolerate differences in religious beliefs").

However, we aren't able to hold all of our moral beliefs in conscious thought at once. Thus, nearly everyone tends to have inconsistent moral beliefs. You probably have moral beliefs that cannot be true all at once. Usually, once we notice such an inconsistency, we might revise our beliefs or jettison the belief we are less sure of.

These inconsistencies give rise to puzzles about ethics, which philosophers and business ethicists love to dwell upon. Consider, as an illustration, the famous "Trolley Problem" devised by Philippa Foot[3]:

> Case 1: A runaway trolley is speeding down a track, where it will hit and kill five people working on the track. You can't stop the trolley or warn the people. But you can flip a switch, which will redirect the trolley to another track which has only one person working. If you flip the switch, it will kill just that one person. Should you flip the switch? (Here, most people say "yes.")

> Case 2: A runaway trolley is again speeding down a track, where it will hit and kill five people. You can't warn the people or otherwise stop the trolley, except in one special way: There is giant, muscular man standing on a bridge over the track. If you push him onto the track, the trolley will crush and kill him, but the trolley will stop and the other five will be saved. Should you push the man? (Here, most people say "no.")

The trolley problem refers to the fact that these cases seem similar—in both cases you can do something which saves five people but kills one—yet nearly everyone judges it right to flip the switch in the first case but wrong to push the giant man in the second case. This raises the question: Is there some real difference between the cases which explains why our intuitions are different, or are our intuitions simply inconsistent? Philosophers have written thousands of articles just on this one puzzle. (By the way, if you worry that the trolley problem is unrealistic, note that the people programming self-driving cars must decide cases likes these. Should a car kill its passenger to save people on the street, or vice versa?)

Now consider another type of case, which we might call a "dilemma" or a "hard case": Suppose Wilma's Widgets (WW) has been building widgets in the small factory town of Pittsfield for the past one hundred years. But times are tough and WW faces lots of competition from other manufacturers. WW realizes it can move overseas, where labor costs are lower. If it does so, the people overseas will be become much better off, as will WW's consumers, who will get equally high-quality widgets at a lower price and so have more money left to spend on other things that they value. But if WW leaves Pittsfield, the town will become destitute. What should WW do?

In this kind of case, even if you think there's a right answer, you may feel conflicted. That's because our moral intuitions tug us in different directions. You recognize that moving helps many people but hurts others; but so does not moving. You worry that the people of Pittsfield rely on WW, and think that WW may owe them some loyalty. You also worry that the future is uncertain, and if WW stays put, it might go out of business anyway. You might understand that if WW moves, it will then employ other people who need those jobs. You might not be sure how to weigh these conflicting considerations.

The existence of moral confusion suggests a strong role for moral philosophers in helping people become better. Perhaps by taking courses in ethics and moral philosophy, people will become better able to reason through hard cases, resolve inconsistent beliefs, and apply basic principles to novel situations. Many ethics courses are designed on the assumption that moral confusion explains a good deal of wrongdoing.

But there is reason to doubt that moral confusion is the source of all or even most unethical behavior. One problem is that moral philosophers—the people who work hardest on understanding how morality fits together—don't appear to be especially good people. The philosophers Eric Schwitzgebel and Joshua Rust have designed a number of studies to test, empirically, whether moral philosophers act better than others. They find, for one, that moral philosophers aren't rated by their peers as being especially good compared to other philosophers.[4] You might think that merely shows that the basic training in moral theory that all philosophers receive is good enough.

But it gets worse. Schwitzgebel finds that ethics books are more likely to be stolen than other philosophy books from the library.[5] No big deal, you might think—more people would want to read a book about the ethics of meat-eating than a book on whether chairs are real or not. But Schwitzgebel carefully controls for this by examining only obscure books that appeal to specialists—and, again, the ethics books are stolen more than others books. So, that suggests that ethics professors and grad students steal more books than philosophy professors and grad students working on other topics. Hmmm.

They further test whether ethicists are more polite or courteous than others, say, by cleaning up their messes or avoiding talking during another's presentation. Finding: No, they aren't.[6] Finally, they survey moral philosophers and find that while such philosophers are more likely to offer strong opinions about the wrongness of eating meat or the obligation to give to charity, they are not actually more likely to act on those opinions.[7]

Beyond this, dwelling on puzzles such as the trolley problem and hard cases like Wilma's Widgets can be misleading. Most of the time, when businesspeople act badly, it's not because they're dealing with a puzzle or a hard case, or because they lack the reasoning skills to resolve those cases. Usually we're in easy cases and the factors that induce us to act badly are more mundane: We work in a culture where cheating has become the norm and so we mimic our peers. We feel difficulty saying "no" to an overbearing boss. We didn't get enough sleep and have tight deadlines, so we cut corners without even noticing. We didn't think to ask whether a good idea is legal or ethical, and so didn't even notice what we were doing. We knew it was wrong but couldn't resist temptation.

So, it's not clear how often bad behavior results from moral confusion, and how often eliminating that confusion would fix the problem. Sometimes people figure out what's right, but they don't—for some other reason—bring themselves to do the right thing. And sometimes the problem is not that people do not know how to resolve an ethical dilemma but rather that they do not recognize that they are in a moral dilemma at all, a situation that we discuss in the next section.

Nevertheless, ethical confusion is *a* problem if not *the* problem. We will address the problem of moral confusion in more detail in chapters 3 through 6.

Stumbling Block 2: Bad Incentives

In 1967, B.F. Goodrich Company signed a contract with the LTV Aerospace Corporation to supply 202 brake assemblies for the new light attack aircraft it was building for the United States Air Force. To get the contract, Goodrich claimed that it could supply a four-disk brake that would be just as effective as the five-disk brake that was then in use. This represented a significant technological advance because the four-disk brake was lighter in weight, which is a crucially important consideration in aircraft design. The only problem was that the brake didn't work.

The engineer who designed the brake was an experienced, highly respected engineer who assured everyone that the design was sound. When the junior engineers tasked with assembling the prototype found that the brake could not handle the forces required to brake the aircraft and overheated, they were criticized for their failure to find the proper materials for the brake surfaces and lining. They continued to try different configurations and materials with no success. Eventually, the engineers were required to run the brake through the tests that were required by the Air Force to qualify the brake for use. When the brake failed these tests, the engineers altered the conditions of the test in an attempt to produce a successful outcome. They did this because they were not required to certify that the brake passed the test, only to run tests on the brake.

Another group of engineers were tasked with preparing the report that would certify that the brake met the Air Force's requirements. Although they were aware that the tests that had been conducted did not meet the Air Force's specifications, they did not consider themselves responsible for the conduct of the tests, only for writing up the reports of the test results. Accordingly, they prepared the report indicating that the brake met the requirements, although no member of the team was willing to sign it.

The brake was delivered the Air Force for use in test flights. It failed, causing several dangerous incidents and a near crash.

Many people working at Goodrich knew that the brake would not work. None of them wanted to cause harm to the Air Force test pilots. Nevertheless, the company allowed the brake to be delivered and tested under conditions that placed the pilots at risk.[8] Why?

The problem in this case was not (primarily) moral confusion. The people at Goodrich were not uncertain about whether sending the brake to the Air Force for testing was the right thing to do. They knew it was not. The problem was that the Goodrich employees were functioning under a set of bad incentives. The company wanted to design and deliver a well-functioning new brake. But the individual Goodrich employees were rewarded only for doing their particular tasks, and they feared punishment for delivering the bad news about the brake to upper management. In addition, no one knew who was responsible for stopping the production process. Although people were aware that something bad was happening, everyone believed that it was someone else's duty to stop it. At Goodrich, the incentives of the individual employees were not aligned with the goals and ethical obligations of the company as a collective entity. As a result, a collection of basically well-meaning people collectively engaged in unethical and extremely dangerous conduct.

We are not contending that people respond blindly to incentives. Most people do the right thing simply because it is the right thing. Nevertheless, rewarding one type of behavior tends to produce more of it and penalizing another type of behavior tends to produce less of it. Although incentives are certainly not the whole story, *all else being equal*, the right set of incentives can nudge those who might otherwise act unethically to do the right thing and the wrong set of incentives can tempt those who would ordinarily behave ethically to cross the line and act unethically. Thus, one factor that helps explain why otherwise ethical people would behave badly is that they are functioning under a set of bad incentives.

Bad *Internal* Incentives

All businesses want to motivate their employees to do their jobs well. This is usually done through a system of rewards. These are frequently financial rewards, such as bonuses or promotion and pay increases for good performance. However, nonfinancial rewards such as compliments, employee-of-the-month awards, more impressive titles, increased responsibility, and more input into decision-making are often employed as well. These are the business's internal incentive structure.

Ideally, the incentive structure aligns the interests of the individual employees with the goals of the company as a collective entity. A company that wants to build a brand for high-quality products will reward its employees by how carefully they do their jobs, not how fast, while a company that manufactures cheap plastic trinkets may do just the reverse. But problems can develop, especially ethical problems, when the interests of the individuals and the company are misaligned.

In the 1970s, H.J. Heinz Company had a corporate ethics policy that stated that no divisions should "have any form of unrecorded assets or false entries on its books or records." But it also had a management incentive plan designed to achieve a goal of consistently increasing profit margins that assigned bonuses on the basis of a division's ability to generate larger profits each year. After the plan had been in effect for several years, the company found that in good years, expenses were being falsely recorded in year before they were incurred and sales were being falsely recorded in the year after they were made. This practice produced an apparent large increase in profits from year to year, which generated large bonuses. The company's incentive structure was not aligned with its ethical obligation to engage in honest accounting.[9]

This phenomenon of "hoping for A while paying for B" is a classic example of a misalignment of individual incentives with collective ethical goals. We ourselves are intimately familiar with how such misalignment can tempt otherwise well-intentioned people into ethically questionable actions. Our institution advertises itself to the world as committed to good teaching and providing our students with a high-quality educational experience. Yet each year, we are evaluated for our merit increases on a 60/30/10 basis; 60 percent research, 30 percent teaching, and 10 percent service. Teaching is "measured" almost entirely by student evaluations, but the scientific literature on such evaluations almost univocally finds that they do not track student learning. Further, we all know that in the end, the only thing that really matters is research. Tenure and promotion, course reductions, supplementary budgets, and named professorships are all awarded almost entirely on the basis of our research output. In our school, if the best teacher in the world came up for a fourth-year review without two un-ambiguous "A" publications in hand or at least in the pipeline, he or she would be told to start looking for a new job. Would you be surprised to learn that the faculty spends almost of its time on research?

We address the problem of bad internal incentives in more detail in chapter 7.

Bad *External* Incentives

Ideally, we would like businesses to produce safe, good-quality products that people want at prices that they can afford to pay. And under ideal conditions, markets provide an incentive to do precisely this. However, real-world businesses do not function under ideal conditions in perfect markets. They function in imperfect, politically regulated markets, which often provide incentives to profit in other ways.

For example, what if a drug company could increase its profits by concealing from the public that it had not rigorously tested a drug for safety? Or an au-tomobile company could save on production costs and hence earn greater profits by failing to install a part that could make the car more resistant to gas-oline fires in rear-end collisions? Wouldn't businesses be tempted to increase profits by taking advantage of their greater knowledge of their products than the consumer?

Or what if businesses could increase their profits by altering the rules of the market to their advantage? For example, sugar can be refined and produced at much lower cost in other countries than it can in the United States. So American consumers could benefit by buying imported sugar, which would give them the product that they want at the lowest possible cost. But what if American-based sugar producers could convince the government to place import tariffs or quotas on sugar produced abroad? By thus raising the price of imported sugar, they can undermine foreign companies' cost advance over their product, which would allow them to continue selling their sugar at the higher price. By thus changing the rules, the American companies can profit despite not providing consumers with the product they desire at the best pos-sible price.

We address the problem of bad external incentives and the forces that can counteract them in more detail in chapters 8 through 10. In those chapters, we examine how the value of a good reputation, various cooperative arrangements, and self-enforcement mechanisms can counteract some of the effects of bad external incentives.

Diffusion of Responsibility

Sometimes the problem is not that a business's incentives are perverse but that they are unclear. In the B.F. Goodrich case, no one had a personal incentive to blow the whistle to stop the delivery of the brake to the Air Force, and everyone assumed that someone else would do it. This is the problem of diffusion of responsibility that is captured in the familiar saying that when everyone is responsible, no one is responsible.

This problem was illustrated in a famous experiment in 1968, conducted by psychologists John Darley and Bibb Latané. They recruited students to have a conversation about college life via intercom. The subjects were told there were a certain number of other students (one, two, or five), and that each student was in his own private room. (They were told this was to preserve anonymity.) In each version, an actor would start making noises indicating he was having seizures. The question: How does this affect the subject's behavior? When the subjects thought there were only two people—himself and the person having a seizure—nearly everyone immediately sought to help. When they thought there were six people, though (himself, the person having a seizure, and four other subjects), the overwhelming majority did not seek to help.[10]

When people see a problem and think they're the only ones who can help, they do. When they see a problem but lots of people could help, they don't—or at least they are far less likely to do so. When we know that we are the only ones who can effectively solve a problem, we see ourselves as having a high degree of responsibility over it. And responsible people pay attention and act. But when many people could solve a problem or intervene, or when solving the problem requires many people to intervene, we pay less attention to the problem and don't feel responsible. We tend not to act.

Bureaucracies—in government, nonprofits, or for-profit firms—almost by definition involve lots of people working together toward a larger goal. If no one in particular has an incentive to take charge of a problem—if responsibility is diffused among the many—then when something bad happens, employees tend to think, "Well, someone else will do something." The diffusion of responsibility is another factor that can result in well-intentioned people acting badly.

We address the problem of diffusion of responsibility in more detail in chapter 10.

Stumbling Block 3: Limited Psychological Capacities

Sometimes people act badly even though they are not confused about what the right thing to do is and they are not knowingly responding to bad incentives. Sometimes, they just do not notice that what they are doing is wrong. Sometimes, they do not have the willpower required to resist temptation. And sometimes, they are negatively influenced by the conduct of those around them. In these cases, people's unethical behavior is due to the fact that as human beings they have limited psychological capacities.

Moral Blind Spots

Jason Brennan, used to work in automobile insurance. He rarely saw cases where people knowingly violated the law or intentionally caused an accident. He rarely saw cases where a person realized she didn't know the rules determining who had the right of way but then failed to reason through them properly on the spot. Rather, most accidents occur because people are acting on autopilot. They minimize the brainpower they expend on driving and thus fail to notice when something unusual takes place. They hit another car because they didn't see it, or didn't see the stop sign, or didn't see the red light.

Consider how you make moral decisions as you walk across your college campus. You are presented with endless opportunities to murder, rob, steal, pillage, and destroy, or, alternatively, to aid and assist others. It's not as though you think about each of these opportunities one by one, reason through the moral principles, calculate the selfish risks and rewards, and then make a decision. "No, I won't murder him." "Nope, I won't mug her." Rather, you don't consider these possibilities *at all*.

You operate 99 percent of the time on moral autopilot. You pay conscious attention to (and even subconscious attention) only a small range of possibilities. Ninety-nine percent of the time autopilot works just fine. But sometimes we get into weird situations that our autopilot is not prepared to navigate, and we crash.

Consider an experiment. This one involves the Parable of the Good Samaritan. In the *New Testament*, someone asks Jesus, "Who is my neighbor?" Jesus responds by telling a story of a man who is robbed on the highway. As the victim lies injured and in need of help, a priest and other high-status people pass by, providing no assistance. Finally, a Samaritan (a person against whom the listeners had considerable prejudice) sees the man in need, saves him, and pays for his recovery. Jesus's message, at the bare minimum: Everyone is your neighbor. You should be like that Good Samaritan.

Researchers John Darley and C. Daniel Batson recruited students from Princeton Theological Seminary as experimental subjects.[11] Subjects (each of whom participated alone) were asked either to (1) prepare a speech on the moral meaning of Parable the Good Samaritan or (2) to prepare a talk on job opportunities for seminary students. Half of the subjects were given ample time to prepare their talks and then were given directions to where the talk would be directed. The other half were told, in effect, "Uh oh, you're late. You better hurry over to give the talk."

So, in short: One-quarter of the subjects have been primed to think about the Good Samaritan but are told to hurry. One-quarter have been primed to think about the Good Samaritan but are told to take their time. One-quarter have been primed to think about job opportunities and are told to hurry. One-quarter have been primed to think about job opportunities and are told to take their time.

As each subject went to give his talk, the researchers set a moral test. A man in obvious distress lay slumped against a door along the way. The question: Would the subjects stop and help? Would it make any difference whether the subjects were primed to think about the Good Samaritan or primed to think about job opportunities? How did being asked to hurry affect their behavior?

The results: Most of the subjects in a low hurry situation stopped to help. Ninety percent of the students told to hurry did not. It turned out that being immersed in the Parable of the Good Samaritan made no difference to their behavior. When asked to hurry and put in the very situation they were supposed to preach about, they either didn't notice the (apparently) sick man or otherwise ignored him. Yet, when not asked to hurry, they helped.

Some of the research subjects saw the actor and chose not to help. But many seemed not to see him at all. Being in a hurry gave them a kind of tunnel vision. They went on "gotta get there" autopilot and simply didn't intervene.

We address the problem of moral blind spots in more detail in chapters 7, 10, and 11.

Weakness of Will

Sometimes we know what the right thing is, but we just can't bring ourselves to do it. We have weakness of will, or "akrasia." We don't quite have the will-power to avoid temptation.

For instance, suppose Georgetown put a bowl of M&Ms on every faculty members' desk every morning. Suppose it was impossible to opt out of the free M&Ms policy. The four of us would end up eating far more M&Ms than we intended. As we sit around talking, writing, meeting with students, or whatever, we'd feel tempted over and over to eat a few candies, perhaps unconsciously.

Now, if we can't change the free M&Ms policy, the best solution wouldn't be to learn to develop even stronger willpower; it would be to avoid the temptation altogether. One easy way to do that: First thing in the morning, throw all the candies in the trash.

Similar remarks apply to many other situations. A good way to think of it: Once you're in the tempting situation, it's often too late. If you climb into the backseat with someone other than your significant other, you're probably going to cheat. So, don't put yourself in that situation to begin with. If you hang out in the back woods with the stoner kids, you're more likely to end up smoking pot. So, if you don't want to smoke pot, don't hang out with that crowd.

Some psychologists claim that willpower is like a muscle or a store of energy that can get used up over time. Overcoming temptation requires willpower, but various things can deplete willpower over the day and make it less likely we'll have willpower when we need it. Most of the experiments take the following form:

1. First, you have experimental subjects do some willpower-depleting task, such as avoiding crying during a sad movie, or trying to avoid the thought of white bears (it's hard; you just pictured one, didn't you?), or try to memorize strings of digits. The control group has no such task.
2. Then introduce a choice or situation where subjects can make a good or bad choice. For instance, allow them to pick a snack, and see if they pick the healthy or unhealthy one. Or have an actor drop papers in front of them, and see if the subjects volunteer to help pick them up.
3. If the control group subjects behave better than the experimental group, this suggests that the experimental group had their willpower depleted.[12]

This suggests that a promising strategy for ethical behavior is to avoid things that deplete your willpower or expose you to temptation. Some businesses require young associates to work sixty or more hours a week, which places them under high stress. This looks like a recipe for bad behavior.

Consider another famous study from law. Shai Danziger and his colleagues wanted to know the extent to which extraneous factors determine whether a prisoner receives parole. They found evidence that the cases heard right after breakfast have a strong chance of receiving it, which drops to near zero before lunch. After lunch, the chances shoot back up but continually drop down until near afternoon break. The pattern repeats after break.[13] The results don't seem to be explained by putting the easy yeas first and the easy nays last. Rather, it seems that when the judges are feeling well rested, they grant parole, and when they feel tired or hungry, they don't.

We address the problem of akrasia in more detail in chapters 3, 10, and 11.

The Tendency to Conform

Most of us tend to conform our behavior to what authorities or our peers expect of us. We find it difficult not to follow orders, even when we know they're imprudent, stupid, or unjust. We find it difficult not to go along with the group or the mob. We might not even realize we're conforming our behavior to what others do.

For instance, there's good evidence that people conform their political beliefs to whatever their in-group thinks rather than what they have evidence for.[14] People belong to one political party or another for largely noncognitive reasons, a sense that "People like me vote Democrat." People's beliefs about right and wrong can change in the face of peer pressure, and worse, they don't even realize they're changing their minds to conform to the group.

This tendency to conform—which we'll discuss in more detail later—carries some clear implications for improving ethical conduct. On a personal level, it suggests you determine what kind of person you want to be and then make sure you befriend and hang out with that kind of person. If you befriend the industrious, conscientious, kind people in the dorm, you'll become more industrious, conscientious, and kind. If you befriend the bullies and jerks, you'll become a bully and a jerk. On an organizational level, it suggests that whom you hire makes a difference. People who are on the margins slightly more ethical than average will tend to reinforce each others' ethical behaviors, leading to elevated ethical performance. People who are less ethical will tend to reinforce each others' bad behaviors and bring each other down.

We address the problem of conformity in more detail in chapters 6 and 9–12.

So What Do We Do?

Our discussion in this chapter shows that there are many reasons why people do the wrong thing. This may be because the thing we call the "mind" didn't evolve as a whole but rather our minds are made up of lots of individual modules each of which evolved for its own purpose. Our minds have the unity of a neighborhood more than the unity of a house. We have lots of things pulling us in different directions and mental processes working in parallel.

Our goal in this book is to learn how to identify when each of these stumbling blocks is most salient. If you can figure out ahead of time when you, your team, your boss, and your company are likely to fall into certain kinds of traps, you will be better equipped to avoid them. In what follows, we hope to help you learn how to preemptively plan to avoid these traps and to create mechanisms to help you escape if you do not.

Summary

- Planning for good behavior is about more than knowing the difference between right and wrong. It requires understanding why good people of goodwill nevertheless mess up.
- The social sciences can help us discover what induces good and bad behavior. We can use these findings to help manage ourselves and others for ethical performance.
- To some extent, people will do whatever produces the best expected consequences in light of their self-interest. This suggests we alter the incentives to better align self-interest with moral goals.
- But ample empirical evidence finds that people are not solely egoistic. They have some genuine moral and altruistic concerns.
- To some extent, people will make moral mistakes because they are confused about how to reason through or apply moral principles during hard case or dilemmas. This suggests we improve our ability to reason through complicated cases.
- When responsibility for a matter is diffused among the many, individuals will act less responsibly. They will be more likely to ignore the problem rather than do the right thing.
- To some extent, people will make mistakes because they operate on autopilot and are often unaware something morally significant is at stake. This suggests we take steps to identify blind spots and raise awareness of issues in those blind spots.
- To some extent, people suffer from akrasia so that even when they know and want to do the right thing, they lack the willpower to do so. This suggests we either improve our willpower or proactively avoid situations which cause temptation.

- To some extent, people tend to conform their behavior to the way others in their group behave, or to follow orders from authorities. This suggests we improve our ethical behavior by making sure we work in places with a good culture, and seek to hire people who exhibit higher than normal ethical behavior. It suggests we break up unethical groups.

Discussion Questions

1. Think back to high school or middle school. What are some things you did to conform which, in retrospect, you realize were not authentic?
2. What are ways that managers can screen for ethics? How might they assess people's ethical tendencies during hiring?
3. Studies on student cheating behavior generally find that about half of students cheat in college, but only a few habitually cheat. What do you think explains that?
4. List five or six examples where people you know did something morally wrong or questionable. Which model best explains their wrongdoing in each example? Why?

Notes

1. Hamlin, Wynn, and Bloom 2007.
2. Bloom 2010.
3. Foot 1957.
4. Schwitzgebel and Rust 2009.
5. Schwitzgebel 2009.
6. Schwitzgebel and Rust 2014.
7. Ibid.
8. This account is taken from Vandivier 2002.
9. This account is abstracted from Harvard Business School case # 382-034, "H.J. Heinz Company."
10. Latané and Darley 1968.
11. Darley and Batson 1973.
12. Now, there's considerable controversy today, as we write, about how well these experiments replicate, and whether the studies benefit from publication bias. See, e.g., https://replicationindex.com/2016/04/18/is-replicability-report-ego-depletionreplicability-report-of-165-ego-depletion-articles/; Carter et al. 2015.
13. Danzinger, Levav, and Avnaim-Pesso 2011.
14. Achen and Bartels 2016.

4

Addressing Moral Confusion

The Principles Approach

Basic Lesson: Human beings frequently disagree about matters of right and wrong. Such disagreement can generate significant moral confusion. Nevertheless, there is a set of binding ethical principles that is shared by all businesspeople. Adhering to these principles is what it means to conduct business with integrity. Further, building these principles into the business planning process is an effective way to ensure both that one is doing good and that one is building a good reputation.

One of us worked in the legal department of a large conglomerate. This company's management philosophy included developing a workforce of entrepreneurial employees. It gave its employees tremendous freedom to find ways to add value to the company and paid bonuses in proportion to their success. As a result, it was an idea factory. Its managers constantly developed new business plans and innovative strategies to enhance the company's profitability.

But managers could not implement their plans at will. Instead, the legal department reviewed plans to ensure that they were consistent with all laws and regulations. Often, what was an essential feature of a plan turned out to be a legal violation, unbeknownst to the managers. The legal department then had to kill the plan.

This made the lawyers very unpopular within the firm. Managers viewed the lawyers as killjoys and naysayers who undermined the work of the *real* businesspeople. They saw the lawyers as a drain on the bottom line.

Upper management eventually realized that things had to change. The current method of planning first, checking for legality second not only wasted time but also sowed discord. So, upper management decided to place one attorney from the legal department on every business planning team. That way they could build legal compliance directly into the business planning process, and avoid unhappy surprises at the end.

The change was a big success. The planning teams now produced new business strategies that were consistent with the law and could be implemented

Business Ethics for Better Behavior. Jason Brennan, William English, John Hasnas, and Peter Jaworski, Oxford University Press.
© Oxford University Press 2021. DOI: 10.1093/oso/9780190076559.003.0004

effectively. And the attorneys, who had previously been viewed as an impediment to innovation, were now seen as valuable partners.

In this chapter, we suggest that you take a similar approach to dealing with ethical issues in business. A bad—and dangerous—way to proceed is to first construct a business plan and then, after the fact, check to see whether it's ethical. As we'll discuss further in chapter 11, this method makes it likely you'll develop blind spots and thus miss ethical problems. It makes it likely you'll be so in love with your new plan that you'll be tempted to rationalize its moral problems away. Further, if you treat strategy and ethics as separate steps, you'll be tempted to see ethics the way the employees saw the legal department—as a nagging, scolding naysayer.

Instead, you should build ethics into the business planning process. Ethics needs to be *part* of strategic planning. This makes it more likely businesses will avoid ethical problems and be assured that their business strategies and plans are ethically ready for implementation.

An Initial Obstacle: Cultural Variation in Ethical Beliefs

Business today operates on a global scale. Trade crosses national borders, involving people from a wide array of cultures, religions, and ethical traditions. As we noted in chapter 1, people's beliefs about right and wrong can vary across cultures. People from Western cultures may value individual autonomy over group solidarity and collective welfare; those from Eastern cultures might go the other way. Favoring one's relatives is seen as improper nepotism in one culture but a moral duty in another. Catholics often have views on the morality of contraception and abortion that atheists reject. Equality for women and homosexuals is a moral requirement in some parts of the world, while other cultures see women working outside the home and homosexual relationships as moral transgressions.

Indeed, beliefs about what is right and wrong often differ significantly even within a culture or nation. Some philosophers believe men and women have different moral perspectives—that men tend to view the world through an "ethic of justice" while women tend to view it through an "ethic of care."[1] Further, people belonging to different political parties often have different views about right and wrong.[2] Some people believe morality requires increased government spending on welfare programs; others that morality requires minimizing redistributive policies. Some people think we must allow

Nazis to have free speech, no matter how deplorable their views, while others think we should punch them.

As we explained in chapter 1, moral disagreement is boring from a philosophical standpoint. The mere fact that members of different cultures or groups disagree does not imply that there are no universal ethical standards. Nor does it imply that what makes something right is that your culture believes it to be right.

However, cultural or individual moral disagreement is not boring from a managerial perspective. Moral disagreements give rise to moral confusion, which makes it difficult to reach a consensus on what constitutes ethical conduct. To work with others successfully, we need a commonly recognized standard of proper behavior. If we want to be able to trade with others with whom we frequently disagree, we have to find an ethical standard that is acceptable to all.

In this chapter, we introduce a set of basic ethical principles that constitute such a standard and are binding on all businesspeople. Further, we provide reason to believe that all those engaged in business will recognize these as binding principles regardless of their national, cultural, religious, sexual, or political backgrounds. How can that be?

The Internal Morality of Business

Despite their differences, all businesspeople share at least one common commitment. They all want to be in business. That is, they all freely agree to participate in the activity of doing business in a market environment.

This is important because agreeing to participate in an activity means accepting the obligations, norms, and rules that are built into that activity. For example, when you agree to play chess with another person, you implicitly agree to move the bishops exclusively along a diagonal and the rooks exclusively along straight lines. You also implicitly agree not to make intensely distracting noises when it's your opponent's move or to remove your opponent's pieces from the board when he or she is not looking. Similarly, when a professor gives his or her class an exam, the professor implicitly agrees to assign grades on the basis of the students' performance and not on the basis of how much he or she likes the student, what the student is wearing, or the color of the student's skin.

There is no moral obligation for one to play chess, and different cultures can disagree about whether playing chess is a good thing or a bad thing. But when individuals voluntarily agree to play chess, they also assume an obligation to play chess according to its rules. This moral obligation flows not from one's culture, religion, or national identity but from one's own voluntary agreement.

Professors have no duty to give examinations to their classes. But when a professor voluntarily decides to give his or her class an exam, the professor acquires a moral obligation to grade the students on the basis of their performance. This moral obligation flows not from the professor's culture, religion, or national identity but from his or her own voluntary decision.

Similarly, there is no moral obligation to be a businessperson. But if one voluntarily decides to pursue a career in business, then one has a moral obligation to act in accordance with any principles that are built into the activity of doing business. This moral obligation does not depend on one's culture, religion, or national identity but flows strictly from one's own voluntary decision.

It is thus possible for businesspeople across the globe to have a common understanding of what it means to be a good businessperson. They all have made a voluntary commitment to do business in a market environment, and therefore to abide by the principles built into that activity.

What are these principles?

The Principles

Principle 1: Refrain from Using Physical Coercion and the Threat of Physical Harm to Attain Your Business Objectives

The first principle instructs businesspeople to refrain from using physical coercion and the threat of physical harm to attain their business objectives.[3] This principle follows directly from what it means to function in a market environment.

The market is the realm of voluntary exchange. The Oxford English Dictionary defines market as "a place at which trade is conducted."[4] You enter a market to trade with others. Trade implies a voluntary exchange of value for value. Markets may be free or constrained, perfect or imperfect, enlightened or benighted, but for something to qualify as a market, it must involve human beings voluntarily exchanging goods or services with each other.

Since the market is the realm of voluntary exchange, then coercion—the use or threat to use physical force to attain one's ends—falls outside the bounds of market activity. Employing coercion to obtain what one cannot get through bargaining is a method of overriding another's will. This is the prime example of involuntary exchange. It's the very opposite of market action.

Principle 1 is binding on those doing business in a market because the act of voluntarily entering a market entails an agreement to refrain from using physical coercion in one's dealings with other market actors. If one understands what market activity is and voluntarily undertakes to engage in it, then one has implicitly agreed not to employ coercion in one's business dealings. The binding force of this principle is generated by one's own actions.

Principle 2: Refrain from Fraud and Improper Deception

The second principle instructs businesspeople to refrain from using fraud and improper deception to attain their business objectives. Fraud is an intentional misrepresentation of fact designed to induce someone to take a detrimental action he or she would not otherwise take. Fraud is essentially lying to take advantage of another. For instance, if a car salesperson inflates a car's horsepower to get you to buy a car, he or she is engaged in fraud.

Improper deception refers to forms of trickery that do not amount to outright lying that are similarly intended to induce someone to take a detrimental action he or she would not otherwise take. For instance, if a used car salesperson entices a customer to buy a car by truthfully stating that it had been previously driven only by a little old lady but fails to say that the little old lady was an alcoholic who had crashed the car on numerous occasions, the salesperson is employing improper deception.

Not all forms of deception are ethically objectionable. "Little white lies" designed to spare people's feelings are usually not problematic. You don't have to tell your grandmother you didn't like the birthday present she sent, and during a business dinner, you don't have to say you hate the food.

In addition, deceptive practices to which the parties have consented are not improper. Thus, bluffing in poker or making false promises in the board game *Diplomacy* is acceptable because all parties understand that it will occur and have agreed to permit it. Similarly, in business negotiations in which all parties know that they must exercise "due diligence," it is not an improper deceptive practice to fail to reveal information that the other parties can discover for themselves. But, aside from special cases like these, deceptive practices that are designed to trick others into doing things that they would not otherwise do are ethically unacceptable.

Like Principle 1, this follows directly from what it means to participate in a market. In fact, Principle 2 is an extension of Principle 1. Fraud and improper deception serve as substitutes for coercion. Coercion employs force or the threat of force to cause people to act against their wills. Fraud and improper deception accomplish the same end through trickery—they trick rather than force people into acting against their wills. Like coercion, such fraudulent and deceptive practices are intentional acts designed to override the free will of a trading partner. Hence, like coercion, they undermine voluntary exchange, and are inconsistent with market activity. And, hence, one who understands what market activity is and voluntarily undertakes to engage in it has implicitly agreed to refrain from employing such practices.

Principle 3: Honor All the Terms of Your Contracts

The third principle instructs businesspeople to honor all the terms of their contracts. A contract is a binding agreement with another party or parties that one enters into voluntarily. The duty to honor the terms of such an agreement follows from both the nature of markets and from what it means to "do business."

The market is the realm of voluntary exchange. But in the modern world, it is not the realm of simultaneous voluntary exchange. When contracts are formed, one party usually performs his or her part of the bargain before the other. Payment may precede delivery or vice versa. Parties enter into such contracts only because they expect the other party to perform if they do. Since the act of entering into a contract manifests one's belief that one's trading partner is bound to honor it, he or she implicitly accepts the principle that parties are bound to honor their contracts.

Markets can function well only if people adhere to this principle. In a world in which people did not recognize a moral commitment to honor their contracts, trade would require people to either engage in simultaneous performance or incur large enforcement costs. Simultaneous performance may work for limited types of retail transactions. When you buy a burrito, you hand over money at the same time they hand you your food. But most deals aren't like that. You get an apartment without paying the full cost up front. You get a car by taking out a loan. Oxford University Press pays us an advance before we even write this book, and then we give them the completed book before they pay us the royalties. If all such transactions had to be enforced with lawsuits, markets would collapse because the cost of enforcing contracts would exceed any gains that could be realized from their execution.

A commitment to honor the terms of your contracts is also built into what it means to "do business." Other than sole proprietorships, most businesses involve arrangements in which the owners of capital and other resources hire others to use these resources to realize specified ends. In doing so, the owners are entering into an agency contract in which they advance their resources to others in return for a commitment to use the resources only for the purposes and in the ways the owners designate. No one would enter into such a contract as a principal unless he or she believed that the agents were bound to act in accordance with its provisions. There would be no point in hiring an agent if one had to spend all of one's time monitoring his or her conduct. By the same token, no one would accept employment as an agent unless he or she believed that the principal was contractually bound to pay for his or her performance. Thus, the act of forming a business by hiring employees entails a commitment to the principle that individuals have an obligation to abide by the terms of their contracts.

Principle 4: Treat All Parties with Equal Respect for Their Autonomy

The fourth principle instructs businesspeople to recognize that all those with whom they have business dealings are entitled to equal respect as autonomous agents—as people who have goals, desires, and life plans of their own and the ability to pursue them. This principle is essentially an antidiscrimination principle instructing that there can be no "second class citizens" in the business world—there are no parties whose interests do not matter or may be discounted due to social prejudices.[5]

Like Principle 3, this principle is inherent in both the nature of markets and what it means to do business. The market is where people go to realize their goals, satisfy their desires, or advance their life plans through voluntary exchange with others. Trades occur only when both parties believe their goals, desires, and plans will be advanced by the transaction. By engaging in trade, each person expects his or her trading partners to recognize him or her as an autonomous agent acting to achieve personally important objectives, and to treat him or her accordingly. Hence, by engaging in trade, each person also implicitly agrees to treat his or her trading partners in a similarly respectful manner. Thus, entering the market carries with it a commitment to treat all trading partners as full human beings whose personal goals, desires, and plans are as important to them as one's own goals, desires, and plans are to oneself.

The obligation to treat business partners with equal respect for their autonomy is also implicitly assumed by entering into the contractual relationships necessary to do business. Owners and investors advance their resources to employees who act as their agents in order to better realize their personal goals, desires, and plans. In accepting employment, employees agree to use these resources to advance their employers' goals, desires, and plans in preference to their own or anyone else's. Regardless of your personal beliefs or desires, accepting employment in a business requires you to recognize the goals, desires, and plans of the employer as equally worthy of respect. Hence, the obligation to treat the goals, desires, and plans of others as on a par with one's own is inherent in the agreement that creates the employment relationship itself.

Principle 5: Personal Ethical Responsibility Is Inalienable

The fifth principle instructs businesspeople to act with the awareness that they always bear ethical responsibility for their actions. There is nothing about entering a market that relieves individuals of ethical responsibility for their actions. Electing to engage in voluntary exchange not only does not relieve individuals of any of their ethical obligations, it adds the implicit ethical obligations identified in Principles 1–4.

There is also nothing about doing business that can relieve either an employer or employee of such personal responsibility. The act of forming a contractual relationship can create new obligations for the employee, such as the obligation to use the employer's resources in accordance with the employer's instructions. But it does not relieve either the employer or employee of any of their preexisting personal ethical obligations.

For instance, if your boss instructs you to create a deceptive advertisement, you are not permitted to do so. When you agreed to work for the company, you may have agreed to create advertising to help the company outperform its competitors, but your obligation to avoid deception didn't vanish. How could one argue the contrary? "I used to have a duty not to lie to others, but then I agreed to follow someone's orders in exchange for salary and benefits, so now I don't." That's not how promises work.

Similarly, employers can delegate to their employees only those tasks that they are ethically authorized to perform. Those who do not have the ethical authority to engage in deceptive practices themselves cannot authorize their employees to employ such practices on their behalf.

Principle 5 implies that employees must always question whether the actions they take in pursuit of their employer's interests are consistent with their ordinary ethical obligations and are those that they have been ethically authorized to take.

The Principles' Significance

In chapter 2, we defined integrity as faithfulness to one's convictions and values. To have integrity, you must live up to the commitments you voluntarily undertake. When you voluntarily decide to pursue a career doing business in a market environment, you are simultaneously committing yourself to adhere to Principles 1–5. So to do business with integrity requires you to conduct your business affairs in conformity with the principles.

Now, at first glance, these principles may seem platitudinous, but, in fact, they do a lot of work. As uncontroversial as a principle banning the use of physical coercion may appear, there are many places in the world in which the direct use of physical force and slave labor remain live issues.[6] Physical coercion is often an issue in cases involving captive domestic workers or "sweatshop" labor in developing economies. Businesses often try to rig markets to their own advantage by lobbying for legislatures to impose predatory and harmful regulations, zoning rules, subsidies, or tariffs. Similarly, the temptation to gain an advantage through deception is ever-present in business dealings, and hence, a principle banning the use of fraud and improper deception is virtually always relevant to business decision-making.

The principle requiring one to honor the terms of one's contracts, which may also seem obvious, is far from trivial. This principle does a great deal of work specifying a business's obligations to the consumers of its products or services. In forming contracts with their customers, businesses make many representations about their product's performance or the nature of their service—what the law calls express warranties.[7] They describe the product's reliability, the extent of its expected service life, the costs of maintenance and upkeep, and, especially important, the safety risks associated with its use.[8] Service providers make analogous representations. In addition, the mere act of offering products or services for sale as a merchant carries with it certain implicit representations as to the product's nature, quality, and purposes for which they may be used—what the law calls implied warranties of merchantability, fitness for particular use, and those arising from "course of dealing or usage of trade."[9] The principle requiring one to honor all terms of one's contracts obligates businesses to live up to all such express and implied warranties. This can be a powerful tool for analyzing businesses' duty to protect their customers from both physical harm and psychological disappointment.

For instance, imagine you hire a taxi to take you from the airport to a hotel. It's understood—an implicit warranty—that the taxi driver will take a short and fast route, won't pick up other people, won't try to sell you hair care products, and won't try to convert you to his religion. When you order food at restaurants, it's understood that you agree to pay for what you eat, even though you never explicitly say, "I'll pay for this food." When you buy a book from Amazon, it's understood that the book's paper isn't coated in cyanide, even though Amazon makes no explicit claims one way or another.

Similarly, the principle requiring one to treat all market actors with equal respect for their autonomy can play an especially powerful role in the analysis of businesses' obligation to their employees. This principle bears directly on questions of employment discrimination, diversity and affirmative action, and sexual and other forms of workplace harassment.

Finally, the principle reminding us that we are always ethically responsible for our actions acts as a warning that you can never rely entirely on the ethical judgment of another—that the fact that you were following another's orders is never an adequate ethical justification for your conduct.

Principle 5 is often forgotten. This is especially true in the business environment in which subordinates are required to rely on the judgment of their superiors with regard to matters of strategy. Our bosses often know more than we do or have greater authority in deciding strategic matters. It's tempting—but a mistake—to let this spill over into ethical matters. If your boss orders you do dump toxins in the pond, he or she is blameworthy for issuing the order, but you're nevertheless blameworthy for following it.

What makes these five principles unique and uniquely valuable is that all businesspeople have implicitly agreed to abide by them merely by the act of doing business in a market. This means that despite the existence of cultural relativism, there can exist a common understanding of what it means to be a good businessperson that holds everywhere that business is conducted. And this, in turn, means that regardless of where one does business, it is possible to reap the benefits of having a good reputation by actually being good.

Their Limitations

These five principles do not capture all of a businessperson's ethical obligations. It is better to think of them as a minimal "starter set" of obligations—the basic set of implicit commitments a businessperson makes by doing business in a market. Businesspeople may, of course, be subject to other ethical obligations, and there is room for debate over how extensive these additional obligations are. For example, in chapter 5, we will examine what it means for a business to avoid pursuing one's business objectives by exploitative means.

Further, these principles are not absolute. They do not impose duties that are binding in all circumstances. Instead, they should be understood as what philosophers call *prima facie* principles—principles that are binding but which may be overridden when doing so is necessary to realize a more important moral value.

To illustrate this with a famous example, suppose that during World War II, you are hiding a Jewish family from the Nazis. You would not be morally obligated to tell the truth to the Gestapo when they ask where the family is. Similarly, a limousine driver who happens upon the scene of serious traffic accident does not act unethically if he violates his contractual agreement to pick up a client in order to rush a seriously injured accident victim to the hospital.

Nevertheless, the principles we identify in this chapter are powerful ones in the business context. Although they may sometimes be overridden to protect a more important moral value, increasing a company's bottom line is almost never such a value. In extreme circumstances, breaching one's contract or employing coercion or deception may be justified by the need to save someone's life, prevent a catastrophe, or avoid a great injustice, but they are almost never justified to avoid a financial loss or achieve an economic business objective. In the normal business context, these principles are almost never overridden.

How Not to Use the Principles

In 2001, Enron Corporation collapsed when it was revealed that the company was employing fraudulent accounting practices. In 2007, Countrywide Home Loans began a program of creating high-risk mortgage loans which were sold to Fannie Mae and Freddie Mac and helped trigger the financial crisis of 2008. In 2016, it was revealed that Wells Fargo bank had created more than a million fake customer accounts.

We could research and examine the facts of these and similar business scandals to identify the ways in which the companies involved failed to live up to their ethical obligations. With careful analysis, we may be able to identify the specific points at which individuals within the companies violated an ethical principle. We could then recommend measures that would make it less likely that such violations would occur in the future.

There is nothing wrong with such an investigation. In fact, this is precisely what most business ethics courses do.

Nevertheless, this is decidedly *not* the best use of the principles that we identify in this chapter. If build your business plan first and only *then* check for ethics, you're likely to miss your mistakes. A better approach would be to use the principles when constructing business plans to avoid ethical problems rather than to resolve such problems after the fact.

We opened this chapter by saying that you need to make ethical compliance part of strategic planning. If you first develop, say, a franchising plan, and only after it's completed ask whether you're doing anything wrong, you're likely to make ethical mistakes. You're more likely simply to overlook the mistakes in the first place, and even if you notice them, you're more likely to feel tempted to ignore them. After all, the plan is there, ready to go, and you worked so hard on it. (In chapter 11, we'll explain the psychology behind this in greater detail.) But if you constantly ask yourself about ethical issues as you develop each step of your plan, you're more likely to catch the mistakes and you won't feel the urge to rationalize your mistakes away. After all, it takes less motivation to edit an unfinished plan than to scrap a finished, polished plan.

We have our own in-class experimental illustration of this very point. Many years ago, Peter Jaworski developed an experiential learning method called the "Business Project." This project, which lasts an entire semester, requires students to form a number of groups. Each group has to develop a mock business and then make a series of presentations in which they outline various strategic decisions the business would make. For instance, a group might first present its basic business plan, then later a social responsibility campaign, a marketing plan, an employee compensation plan, or a capital generation campaign. Students get to role-play running a business of their own design. At the end of the semester, though, Peter gives his students a custom-made ethical dilemma, one tailored to the various decisions and commitments the students have made over the semester. Students then have to decide how their business will react to that dilemma.

We liked Peter's teaching methods so much that the rest of us adopted this project in our own classes. Now, at Georgetown University, all sophomore students taking one of our business ethics classes complete the Business Project.

Ideally, these dilemmas do not result from sheer bad luck but instead demonstrate or are based on flaws in students' own business designs. For instance, in one of Jason Brennan's classes, students created an SAT prep tutoring business. But, unfortunately for the students, when it came time to create a dilemma, Jason realized that they had implement a highly racially discriminatory hiring policy. Without getting into all the details, they had created hiring rules which all but ensured they would have no Latino or black tutors. The students had no racist intentions, but they had inadvertently violated Title VII of the 1964 Civil Rights Act, which forbids hiring policies that have a "disparate impact" on members of protected classes. Jason constructed a dilemma for the students based on this unintentional mistake.

For a few years, though, Peter and Jason did the Business Project in parallel classes, but with a slight difference between the two sets of courses. Jason required his students to build ethics into every step of their strategic decision. When they presented their initial business plan or created their marketing campaigns, the students had to spend time examining whether their plans were ethically sound, and whether their plans could potentially lead to ethical problems down the line. Peter, in contrast, didn't *require* his students to explicitly think through ethical problems *until* they received their custom dilemma at the end of the semester. (The students were free to build ethics into every step of strategic planning, but they were not directed to do so.)

Peter and Jason would get together each semester to brainstorm possible dilemmas to give their students. They quickly noticed a pattern. In Peter's classes, where students were *not* required to build ethics into each strategic decision, it was *easy* to construct dilemmas. Nearly every group had made serious—but usually unintentional—ethical mistakes. In Jason's classes, where students were required to build ethics into each decision, it was difficult to construct dilemmas. Many times, when Peter or Jason thought of a potential problem, they would review the students' prior work and realize that the students had already taken measures to prevent such a problem from arising.

Peter and Jason had inadvertently conducted an experiment. Their students were the same quality, at the same institution, in the same academic year. The only difference was requiring or not requiring them to build ethics into every step. Yet Jason's students ended up creating businesses with far fewer vulnerabilities, simply because his students took time to ask "Is this ethical?" at the same time they asked "Will this work?"

The students learned the lesson. The good news for them is that the Business Project is a simulation. If their businesses inadvertently do something wrong or break the law, they suffer no consequences other than a lower grade. In the real world, though, such mistakes could mar their consciences for life, kill their businesses, and land them in jail.

Living by These Principles

These principles may seem easy to understand, but living by them is easier said than done. In the abstract—in the cool and pressure-free moment when you read this book—you'll think to yourself, "Of course, I won't coerce people, deceive them, commit fraud, or discriminate against them. Of course, if my boss tells me to do such things, I'll say no."

But—here's the problem—most of the people who act unethically in business already *agree* to these principles, and they fully intend to follow them. The people who break them often fail to recognize they've broken them, sometimes because they just don't notice, or sometimes because they've convinced themselves that what they're doing is an exception to or somehow doesn't break the rules. Since normal people want to be ethical, when they do something unethical, they also want to believe the unethical act is in fact ethical.

Accordingly, it's not enough to know what right and wrong is and to know how to apply these principles. You need to know how ordinary, good but imperfect people like yourself fall into traps where they act unethically. In chapter 6, we'll explain how you can find yourself in legal trouble even when you think that you are acting ethically. In chapter 11, we'll uncover how people deceive themselves about their own ethical behavior, and how ethical blind spots can cause them to act unethically without even noticing. In chapter 2, we discussed how people sometimes use charitable behavior as an excuse for acting unethically. In chapters 8, 9, and 11, we'll show how in dysfunctional cultures, our tendency to conform to others' behavior, and other factors can induce good people to act unethically.

Conclusion

There is little that we can do to directly affect another person's basic moral character. The most eloquent textbooks cannot create goodwill in others when none is present. No philosophical argument will actually turn a sociopath into a virtuous person. None of us has the power to reach into another person's heart and turn a dial setting from bad to good.

What this book—and what a business ethics course—can do is to make it less likely that people of good character will inadvertently engage in unethical behavior. Some ethical scandals in business result from the intentional wrongdoing of ill-motivated individuals. But many arise because otherwise well-meaning people do not notice the ethical implications of their actions until they are in an ethically compromised position—until they are in a situation from which they cannot extricate themselves without engaging in unethical conduct. Countless instances of insider trading result from businesspeople not realizing that they are sharing confidential information until it is too late. Countless instances of fraud or illegal backdating result from attempts to cover up indiscretions or oversights that occur because one was too focused on his or her objective to notice that he or she was crossing an ethical line. And countless business scandals result from people of goodwill assuming that if their superiors signed off on an action, it must be okay without questioning the ethics of the action for themselves.

The best way to reduce the likelihood of such ethical lapses is to build explicit consideration of ethical principles into the business planning process. Thus, when gathering data on labor costs and other economic conditions in developing countries to determine whether to locate there, one should also be asking whether the potential contracting partners in the area employ coercive measures to get or retain workers. When developing a marketing initiative, one should continually monitor the representations one is considering making to ensure that they will not mislead customers as to what is being offered—something that is especially important when the target audience consists of cultural minorities or those with limited education or English proficiency. When creating a negotiating strategy for the purchase or sale of a property or business, one should simultaneously be checking to see whether there is any material nonpublic information that he or she has a duty to disclose. When preparing a bid on a contract or a collective bargaining agreement with one's employees, one should be making careful calculations to ensure that one has the financial capacity to meet the contractual obligations one is assuming. When compiling financial data and doing market research on the desirability of doing business with organizations based in Latin America or the Middle East, one should also be asking whether doing business with those organizations was likely to result in the mistreatment or unfairly reduced career prospects of one's women, African American, or Jewish employees. And perhaps most importantly, no matter how focused you may be on your job, you must constantly be on guard against blindly assuming that whatever your superiors order is ethically acceptable. One must always be paying attention to whether the actions he or she is taking are right or wrong.

Sophisticated businesspeople call upon their knowledge of finance, marketing, accounting, information technology, statistics, and management in creating their business strategies. In this chapter, we have argued that they must call upon their knowledge of the ethical principles that are inherent in the activity of doing business in a market as well.

Summary

- There is a set of principles built into the activity of doing business in market that is binding on all those who voluntarily engage business.
- Regardless of where or with whom one does business, it is possible to earn a good reputation by abiding by these principles.

- Building these principles into the business planning process is an effective means of avoiding ethical problems.

Discussion Questions

1. Would you continue to do business with someone who violated one of these principles?
2. Have you ever personally been in a situation in which an authority figured instructed you to do something that you thought was wrong? What did you do?
3. Academic dishonesty is a serious problem at many universities. Have you personally been in a situation in which you have been tempted to violate one of the principles? Did you? If not, why not? Have you been aware of others who did violate a principle? If so, what did you do? What should you have done?

Notes

1. See Gilligan 1983.
2. See Iyengar and Westwood 2014.
3. Note that this principle bans the use of *physical* coercion. It does not address the issue of *psychological* coercion in which a party feels forced to act in a certain way by circumstances or must choose among a severely constrained set of options. This issue will be considered in our discussion of exploitation in chapter 5.
4. "Market" 2000. Accessed August 3, 2018. http://www.oed.com/view/Entry/114178?rskey=I v7RKy&result=1#eid.
5. The French philosopher Voltaire (1961: 26) captured the essence of this principle well in 1734 when he declared,

   > Go into the London Stock Exchange—a more respectable place than many a court— and you will see representatives from all nations gathered together for the utility of men. Here Jew, Mohammedan and Christian deal with each other as though they were all of the same faith, and only apply the word infidel to people who go bankrupt.

6. E.g., in 2002, Unocal Corporation was sued for partnering with the Myanmar government on a pipeline project in which the government employed forced labor in the construction of the pipeline. See Doe I v. Unocal Corp., 395 F.3d 932 (2002).
7. See Uniform Commercial Code §§ 3–313.
8. See Velasquez 2012.
9. See Uniform Commercial Code §§ 3–314, 315.

5

Addressing Moral Confusion

The Right and Wrong of Exploitation

Basic Lesson: Sometimes voluntary agreements that are beneficial to all parties can still be unethical. This occurs when the benefits of the agreement are unfairly divided among the parties. The benefits of a mutually beneficial transaction are unfairly divided when one party unconscionably takes advantage of the vulnerability of another party. World poverty presents a special challenge. Here, we must be especially careful to judge decisions by their good results, not by our good intentions. You don't make the poor better off by removing their best option unless you can replace it with an even better option.

Imagine that you are part of the strategic planning team at I&N Fashion, a "fast fashion" company. Fast fashion—sometimes called disposable fashion—is devoted to delivering a designer product to a mass market at low enough prices for consumers to frequently update their wardrobe. To succeed, such a business must keep production costs low.

I&N's competitors reduced their production costs by having their clothing manufactured in China, India, and other Southeast Asian countries where labor costs are lower than in the United States and Europe. Your planning team is exploring the possibility of outsourcing the manufacturing of I&N's line to Faristan. Faristan, a developing country in Southeast Asia, is one of the poorest countries in the world, with high levels of unemployment and few social services. The average wage for garment workers in Faristan is 97 cents an hour, and workers typically work ten hours a day, six days a week without overtime pay. In addition, there are no benefits such as health, life, or disability insurance associated with employment. Further, due to the lack of public schools and day-care facilities, garment workers often have their children employed at the same plant at which they work.

I&N's advance planning team has identified several contractors in Faristan who can produce I&N's clothing in a timely manner. Aware of I&N's ethical responsibilities, the team has investigated these potential partners to ensure that (1) none of them employ any coercive or deceptive measures to force or trick people into working for them, (2) all of them honor their contractual

Business Ethics for Better Behavior. Jason Brennan, William English, John Hasnas, and Peter Jaworski, Oxford University Press.
© Oxford University Press 2021. DOI: 10.1093/oso/9780190076559.003.0005

obligations to their employees by paying the correct amount of their salaries on time, (3) none of them discriminate in their hiring and promotion practices on the basis of race, religion, or sex, (4) all of them operate safe plants that do not pose an unreasonable risk of injury to their employees, and (5) all of their employees voluntarily accept employment with full understanding of their compensation and the working conditions.

Your group is thinking of signing contracts with those contractors who agree to (1) pay their employees at least $1 per hour; (2) not employ workers for more than ten hours per day, six days a week; (3) limit child labor to the children of their employees who request to have their children employed; and (4) provide an in-plant infirmary staffed by a nurse who can dispense nonprescription medicines to employees at no cost. (No other Faristan manufacturing plants provide such an infirmary.) The contractors would provide no other benefits to their employees. Entering into contracts under these terms would greatly reduce I&N's labor costs, which could provide the company with a competitive advantage over its main competitors.

As part of I&N's strategic planning team, would you recommend that the company enter into these contracts? Why or why not?

What Is the Problem?

In chapter 4, we identified five ethical principles built into the activity of doing business in a market to which all businesspeople are committed. The contracts that I&N is considering entering into with garment manufacturers in Faristan do not run afoul of any of these. I&N has been careful to make sure that its contracting partners do not employ coercion or improper deception; do not engage in invidious racial, religious, or sexual discrimination; and honor the terms of their contracts in the operation of their businesses. Does this mean that entering into the proposed contracts is ethically acceptable? If the answer to this question is not a clear yes, then something else must be relevant to the ethics of the situation. But what?

What the Problem Is Not

The problem is not coercion. In our hypothetical case, neither I&N nor any of its potential contracting partners are forcing their employees to work for them. None of the contractors lock employees into their workplaces or threaten them or their families with physical harm if they do not come to work. None of them conspire with local government authorities to conscript labor.

If any of the potential contractors employed any of these practices, the case would be uncontroversial. Doing business with such contractors is clearly unethical. It would violate Principle 1, which requires businesspeople to refrain from using physical coercion and the threat of physical harm to attain their business objectives.

Something else is at work in this case. In choosing to work for the contractors in Faristan, the employees are making a severely constrained choice from a poor set of options. They agree to work long hours under arduous conditions not because they really want to but to escape from desperate poverty. People often describe situations like this by saying that the workers are being "coerced by their circumstances" into accepting such employment. But being "coerced by circumstances" is not the same as being coerced by another human being.

Treating them as though they are the same is a source of significant moral confusion. It is generally clear when one party is using force or the threat of physical harm to override the will of another. It is considerably less clear how constrained a choice must be, or how few and how bad the options must be, for the choice to be "coerced by circumstances." Is a single mother who lost her job when the local coal plant closed coerced to take a job at Walmart? If so, is it unethical for Walmart to hire her? How about an ad executive who loses his job in the middle of a custody fight with his ex-wife and desperately needs a job to retain custody of his children. Is he coerced into accepting employment as a low-level account representative if that is the only position open to him at the time? How about recent graduates with PhDs in English who cannot obtain a tenure-track teaching position at a college or university. Are they coerced into accepting low-paid adjunct teaching positions in order to pursue their chosen careers?

Much moral confusion can be avoided if we restrict the use of the term "coercion" to cases in which some human beings threaten harm to induce others to comply with their will. This means that a party who is required to make a constrained choice when the constraint does not come from the direct threat of harm by another human being is not being coerced.[1] Limiting the use of the term "coercion" in this way allows us to focus on what ethical obligations we have when dealing with individuals facing constrained choices without getting them confused with those that flow from Principle 1.

A Paradoxical Situation

Let's call the problem we are examining in this chapter the problem of "sweatshops." We will use the term "sweatshop" to refer to employment situations in which employers *offer* jobs that involve unpleasant work for low pay that are nevertheless *voluntarily accepted* by the employees. (We mean "voluntarily accepted" in a minimal sense: The employers do not literally threaten workers to get them to work but instead offer their workers a new option without removing their other options. The workers choose this option over their other options, however few and bad those might be.) Such jobs may require long hours, impose harsh working conditions, offer few or no benefits or overtime pay, and pay less than a "living wage"—the wage necessary for a worker to sustain a basic but decent life for his or her family given the local cost of food, housing, clothing, and other essential needs. The problem of sweatshops is usually associated with the efforts of multinational enterprises to reduce production costs by outsourcing labor to the developing world. The question we want to answer is what, if anything, is wrong with such employment practices.

Opponents of sweatshop labor advance what may be called the *antisweatshop thesis*. This thesis holds that it is unethical for corporations based in the developed world to outsource labor to the developing world without guaranteeing workers some specified minimum level of compensation and/or working conditions. For example, antisweatshop advocates could argue that in order to employ workers in the developing world, foreign corporations are ethically required to pay at least a living wage, and/or require no more than forty-eight hours of work per week, and/or provide overtime pay and some form of heath benefit. Corporations whose employment practices fall below these specified minima act unethically.

Note that an employment package that fails to meet any set of specified minimum conditions can nevertheless be beneficial to the workers if it is better than any of their alternatives. A worker employed by a foreign corporation who is paid less than a living wage is still better off if all other jobs open to him or her pay even less. Or a worker required to work fifty-four hours per week without overtime pay or health benefits is still better off than he or she would be if the only alternative were arduous agricultural labor. In fact, an employment package that fails to meet specified minima must appear relatively advantageous to the worker or else he or she would not have voluntarily accepted the employment. We'll return to this point in Section 12 below.

Note further that—at least according to the proponents of the antisweatshop thesis—it is not unethical for corporations based in the developed world to refrain from outsourcing labor to workers in the developing world at all. There is nothing ethically objectionable about a corporation hiring its workforce exclusively from its local community or home country.

But now note that combining these two observations with the antisweatshop thesis leads to an apparently paradoxical conclusion. For if it is ethical for corporations to refrain from outsourcing their labor, then it is ethical for corporations not to benefit workers in the developing world at all. Yet the antisweatshop thesis states that it is unethical for corporations to outsource labor to workers in the developing world in ways that provide some benefit, if the benefit is not great enough. This appears to paradoxically imply that it is ethically acceptable to not benefit workers in the developing world at all but not ethically acceptable to benefit them a little.[2] The anti-sweatshop thesis implies it can be better not to offer someone a job at all rather than offer him or her a "bad" job, even if that person would prefer the bad job to no job.

How can we account for this counter-intuitive result? Shouldn't be OK to provide even a small benefit? In the sweatshop context, corporations are offering workers in the developing world an employment situation that is better than any of the workers' alternatives that the workers are voluntarily accepting. What can be wrong with that?

What Is Exploitation?

A corporation offers employment to workers in the developing world that the workers voluntarily accept. No coercion is used to conscript the workers into the corporation's labor force. Both the corporation and the workers benefit; both prefer to enter into the contract than not. The corporation receives the benefit of low-cost labor, which increases its profitability. The workers receive the benefit of a *better* employment situation than is otherwise available to them, which improves their standard of living. After the transaction, both parties are better off. The transaction creates a social surplus–a greater amount of wealth than existed before the transaction. In this situation, how can the corporation be wronging the workers?

One possible answer is that corporation might take an unfairly large proportion of the social surplus. Even though the transaction between corporation and worker is voluntary, it would be wrong for the corporation to appropriate more than its fair share of the wealth that is created by it. When a stronger party takes advantage of a weaker party to absorb an unfair amount of their mutually created product, the stronger party unethically *exploits* the weaker party. Exploitation refers to the unethical division of the proceeds of a mutually beneficial transaction.

What Makes a Division Unethical?

Understanding the nature of exploitation allows us to resolve the apparent paradox discussed above. The problem with corporation's employment practices is not that it is unethically coercive. The workers freely accepted the employment. The problem is also not that the employment practices are harmful. The workers benefit from the employment. But the practices may nevertheless be unethical if they are exploitative–if the corporation absorbs an unfairly large proportion of the proceeds of the mutually beneficial employment relationship.

Understanding what exploitation is in the abstract is fairly easy. But determining what practices are exploitative in the real world is not. To do so, we need a standard for determining what constitutes an unfairly large proportion of the proceeds of a transaction. What makes a division unethically exploitative?

It can't be merely that one party gets a much better deal than the other or that one has more bargaining power than the other. A person who spends time and energy researching the market and understanding the potential value of a purchase may get a much better deal than a lazy seller who fails to exercise due diligence. In such a case, we might say the industrious person "exploited" the other's laziness. But that does not make the trade unethical. Students attend business school to attain the knowledge and skills that will allow them to take advantage of–to exploit–market opportunities and to profit at the expense of their less knowledgeable or less skilled competitors. Similarly, a homeowner in a tight housing market in no rush to sell has a great advantage in bargaining power over a buyer who needs a home fast. That does not make it unethical for the owner to "exploit" this advantage to obtain an above average purchase price. Recently, Jason purchased a new Gibson SG standard at about 1/3rd the normal market price from Guitar Center, taking advantage of a slump in the market and some miscalculations by Gibson about which options most buyers would want. But even if Jason "exploited" the market, few would regard this as unethical.

Many market transactions result in an uneven division of the social surplus the transaction creates. But that alone cannot make the transactions unethically exploitative. If it did, then virtually all market activity would be unethical. Exploitation requires that the division be *unfairly* uneven. What we need to know is what makes an uneven division an unfairly uneven division.

The best answer to this question is that a division is unfairly uneven when one party takes advantage of a vulnerability of the other party to reap a disproportionately large percentage of the value of the transaction. Thus, exploitation occurs when one party takes unconscionable advantage of the vulnerability of another party.

A Test for Exploitation

This understanding of exploitation yields a test for distinguishing unethical exploitation from the ethically acceptable exploitation of competitive advantages that are normal in market transactions. Unethical exploitation occurs when two conditions are met: 1) one party must suffer from a significant vulnerability, and 2) the other party must unconscionably target that vulnerability to gain disproportionate rewards. It is important to understand what each of these conditions requires.

The first condition defines vulnerable parties as those who are unable to adequately protect their interests *for reasons that are no fault of their own*. People who are physically or mentally disabled are vulnerable in contests that require physical or mental prowess. Members of socially disfavored or subordinated minority groups are vulnerable to invidious discrimination in the employment market. People living in extreme poverty in societies in which there are few employment opportunities are vulnerable to having to accept harsh working conditions. In each case, the individuals' vulnerability is not due to any personal choice of their part or any factor over which they exercise control.

In contrast, businesspeople who fail to exercise due diligence or cut corners on their research may suffer in the market, but do not constitute the type of vulnerable party subject to unethical exploitation, because their vulnerability is due to their own negligence. Similarly, those who do not devote sufficient time and effort to developing their skills or pursuing their educational opportunities or otherwise cultivating their human capital may end up having to make constrained choices, but do not constitute vulnerable parties subject to exploitation. Even industrious individuals who elect pursue highly competitive positions, as, for example, professional athletes, actors, or university professors, may find themselves having to accept what they regard as extremely undesirable forms of employment. But their vulnerability in this regard was a result of their own decisions, and thus not the type that can make them victims of exploitation.

The second condition requires that the stronger party specifically target the other's vulnerability in order to reap excessively large rewards that would not otherwise be obtainable. This requirement is important because we do not want a definition of exploitation that would exclude vulnerable parties from the market. We don't want to say that to avoid exploitation, Walmart must refuse to hire single moms who need a job and instead only hire retirees who are working not for money but for something to do. Parties who are disabled, the victims of discrimination, or suffer from extreme poverty often desperately need the employment and other economic opportunities that come from the ability to participate in the market. Remember that the transactions we are considering are mutually beneficial ones and the vulnerable parties need the benefits they provide. Hence, a proper definition of exploitation must exclude only a limited set of these transactions–those in which one party targets the other's vulnerability to get more than its fair share of the proceeds of the transaction.

Adding a Principle

In chapter 4, we introduced five fundamental ethical principles that apply to all those doing business in a market. Here, we introduce a sixth.

Principle 6: Avoid exploitation

Unlike the original five principles, Principle 6 is not derived from one's own voluntary commitments. The obligation to avoid exploitation is not inherent in one's decision to do business in a market. However, we believe that the argument for Principle 6 that we present in this chapter is a strong one. Hence, we contend that Principle 6 should be added to the set of starter principles identifying the minimal requirements of ethical business practice.

How to Apply Principle 6

You should build consideration of Principle 6 into every step of the business planning process. When constructing your business plans, you should first check to make sure that they fully comply with Principles 1–5. You can then apply Principle 6 in a two-step process. First, ask whether any parties that you are dealing with are vulnerable parties–parties who are unable to protect their interests for reasons that are no fault of their own. If no parties have this characteristic, then exploitation is not an issue, and you may proceed with your plans. However, if you find that you are dealing a vulnerable party, then you must apply the second part of the test. You must ask whether your plans are unconscionably targeting the vulnerability to reap disproportionately large rewards. If the answer to this is yes, then your plans must be altered. This doesn't necessarily mean you shouldn't deal with those parties, but instead you should offer them a fairer split.

Unfortunately, we cannot supply an unambiguous standard for determining when one is unconscionably targeting another's vulnerability to reap disproportionately large rewards. But we can offer some factors to consider that should be helpful in doing so. One we call "the shadow of the future." If an employer is offering a package of wages and working conditions that are so burdensome that it is unlikely that the employees who accept them can ever escape from poverty, that makes it more likely that the compensation package is unconscionably targeting their poverty, and thus is exploitative. In contrast, if the package is one that, although arduous, allows the employees to save enough to improve their standard of living over time, that makes it less likely that the package is exploitative.

Another relevant factor is the risk of irreparable harm. If an employer requires work that poses the risk of serious harm without compensation for the danger, that increases the likelihood that employer is unfairly target the employees' vulnerability. If, in contrast, the employer maintains a safe work environment or provides additional compensation for dangerous work, that decreases the likelihood that the employer is engaging in exploitation. In general, the more likely the compensation package is to damage the employee's long term interests, the more likely it is to be unethically exploitative; and the more likely it is to help the employee realize long term life goals, the less likely it is to be exploitative.

We are aware that we have not provided a bright-line test for distinguishing unethical exploitation from unobjectionable conduct. Nevertheless, we believe that by separating Principle 6 from Principle 1 and providing a two step test for applying Principle 6, we can greatly reduce the amount of moral confusion associated with the problem of exploitation. Exploitation is a difficult ethical issue that requires us to be careful not to damage the very parties that we are trying to protect by excluding them from the market and the benefits the market provides. In contrast, coercion is an easy issue. You should not employ coercion in your business dealings, period. Separating the analysis of exploitation from that of coercion can help ensure that we don't hurt the people we want to help in our zeal to do the right thing. And although our two step test for exploitation may have not always yield a perfectly clear result, it provides a structured way of thinking about the issue that can move people with differing moral intuitions opinions closer to agreement in many cases.

Application to the I&N Hypothetical Case

In the hypothetical that began this chapter, I&N made sure that its plans to contract with manufacturers in Faristan did not run afoul of the five basic ethical principles to which all those who do business in markets are committed. And yet, that alone did not appear to settle the issue. It seemed that something else remained to be considered. We now know that it was whether the proposed contracts violated Principle 6 that instructs us to avoid exploitation in our business dealings. Was I&N's proposed course of action one that would produce an unethical division of the proceeds of mutually beneficial transactions?

We know that Principle 6 is in play because I&N is dealing with vulnerable parties. Its potential workforce will be drawn from people living in extreme poverty with few alternative sources of employment. Their desperate situation does not result from any choice or negligence on their part. Hence, they constitute a vulnerable group. Because this is case, I&N must exercise care to ensure that it is not targeting their employees' vulnerability in order to absorb a disproportionately large share of the benefits of its contractual relationship with them.

I&N is considering contracting with those who employ children in their plants. This would be unethically exploitative if it was doing so in order to pay the children less than adults for jobs that would be dangerous to children in order to reap significantly above market returns. However, this does not appear to be the case. If I&N is sure that its contractors employ the children of their employees because the parent or parents have no access to child care and would not be able to work in the plant unless they could bring their children with them, do not require work that would be dangerous or harmful to children, and employ the children at the request of and as a benefit to their employees, then I&N is not targeting the childrens' vulnerability to reap disproportionate rewards. This suggests that I&N's contractors are not exploiting the children by hiring them, and may ethically do so.

Beyond the question of child labor, there is also the matter of the wages and working conditions that I&N's contractors are offering their employees. These contractors are drawing their workforces from a highly impoverished, and hence, vulnerable population. I&N's reason for dealing with contractors in Faristan is to reduce its labor costs, which suggests that it is targeting this vulnerability. But this alone does not mean that it is engaging in exploitation. If I&N were locating in Faristan to obtain labor costs greatly below those of its competitors by offering compensation packages that would keep the employees trapped in poverty in order to realize above market profits, then it would be likely that it was unethically exploiting its workforce. However, in the hypothetical, I&N is locating in Faristan not to reap inordinate rewards, but in an effort to meet competitive pressures and maintain an ordinary level of profits in a market in which many firms outsource labor to the developing world. Especially because I&N insists that its contractors pay slightly more than the market rate for labor in a competitive labor market, the proposed contracting arrangements do not appear to be unethically exploitative.

Hard Problems Are Hard

Many people have the intuition that making employment deals with desperately poor people always involves something morally questionable. Sometimes the problem is that some businesses genuinely do exploit or coerce their workers. But sometimes, even when there is no coercion or exploitation, people still think *something* is going wrong. The thought may be that we should be doing even *more* for the worst-off workers. Maybe avoiding exploitation isn't enough. Maybe, they think, there's a moral duty to provide significantly above-market pay. If that isn't possible, they think, then maybe it's better not to employ such people at all.

Above, we discussed how to apply the ethical principle that instructs us to avoid exploitation. Here, we want to explain why "Should we do *even* more?" is harder than you think.

Workers Are Not Idiots and Parents Love Their Kids

In 1996, talk show host Kathy Lee Gifford became an overnight moral pariah after union activist Charles Kernaghan testified before congress that her Walmart clothing line was "being made by 13-year and 14-year-olds working 20-hour days in factories in Honduras."[3] Americans reacted with horror, blamed her for endorsing child labor, and didn't accept her ignorance as an excuse. It took years for her to recover her good name.

Kernaghan's motives were questionable. Domestic unions feel threatened by international competition just as Honda feels threatened by Toyota. They have a selfish incentive to making Americans averse to buying foreign products. It means more money in their pockets.

But most Americans meant well and had a genuine concern for social justice. They were horrified at the idea of child labor. In their minds, that was something the United States overcame long ago. They believed that it is unjust to profit from a practice elsewhere that we've eradicated here. This reasoning sounds compelling.

However, things are more complicated than that. You see, implicit in these moral judgments are certain rather offensive assumptions about the workers themselves; assumptions that Americans would probably not endorse if they were stated out loud. They are:

Assumption 1:Sweatshop workers are imprudent and make bad choices.
Assumption 2: Parents in the developing world don't love their children.

If somebody actually asserted either claim, you'd probably think they're classist and maybe even racist. But many people who claim to be concerned about social justice and poverty implicitly make these two assumptions. Let's explain why:

Regarding assumption 1: Workers in developing countries often have few options. Sometimes, all of their options are bad. Because their options are bad, we might not want to dignify their decision to work in sweatshops as "free" in some deep philosophical sense. Nevertheless, other than the exceptional cases in which managers actually chain workers in, sweatshops do not literally enslave workers. They do not yank them from farming villages at gunpoint and force them to make sneakers. Rather, workers choose to work in sweatshops because these offers what they themselves consider their best option. If the workers had even better job options, they would take them instead.

We in the rich West sometimes talk as if workers were duped into taking bad jobs—as if things were wonderful until the Nike sweatshop came along and the workers fell into a trap. But that's not how things work.

Poor workers in the developing world may be poor, but they aren't stupid. They have an even stronger incentive than you (a rich person living in relative comfort) do to take whatever job gives them the best overall deal. Whatever job they take, no matter how bad it is by our standards, we should presume that it's their best available option unless we have strong evidence otherwise.

Regarding assumption 2: We, the authors, don't make our kids work in sweatshops. Why not? It's not that we're unusually loving and good parents. Rather, we're *rich*; we don't need our kids to work to support our families.[4] Indeed, the reason Americans stopped making their kids work on farms and factories wasn't because the law forbade it. It was mostly because Americans became rich enough to allow their kids to have a childhood as we know it.

Now think about the developing world. If you see parents sending their teenagers (or even younger children) to work on farms or factories, it *could* mean the parents just don't love their kids enough to send them to school or let them play and be kids. But it probably means instead that the parents view this is their best option, out of the limited set available to them.

Workers in the developing world are generally industrious, smart, and prudent. They are not poor because they are vicious or dumb; they are poor because they were born in the wrong place, in places with low levels of capital development and with dysfunctional political institutions.[5] Nevertheless, they generally do the best they can given the lousy options they have. If we see parents sending their kids to work rather than school, this is extremely strong evidence that going to work is the kids' best option, given the background constraints and conditions. If we see workers in sweatshops, then no matter how awful those sweatshops are, that's strong evidence those sweatshops are the workers' best option.

In fact, we can verify this. Economist Benjamin Powell did a major study examining sweatshops in developing countries that were the targets of protests in the developed countries. What he found was that, in general, sweatshops pay their low-skilled workers significantly more than the national average— and keep in mind these are countries with great economic inequality where low-skill workers typically earn far less than the national average. He also found that even the sweatshops that are the targets of protest pay their workers near the national average, and far more than the other kinds of jobs available to those workers.[6] Sweatshop workers in Bangladesh average more than $2/day, in a country where 77 percent of workers make less than that.[7]

The Most Important Principle When Dealing with the Vulnerable

In the previous section we discussed a principle of business ethics which said we should avoid exploiting others. To exploit someone is to consciously target their vulnerabilities in order to reap disproportionate rewards.

It's easy to imagine that all sweatshop workers are exploited. They get low pay and bad conditions in part because they have no better options. After all, *you* would never work in a sweatshop because you have better options. Even if sweatshop managers offer workers a much better deal than the workers' other options, it's still not what you'd consider a good deal.

So, would it be better to just not offer the deal at all? Is it better to boycott countries with child labor? To boycott sweatshop-produced goods? Not so fast.

Imagine an unjust regime falsely convicts Innocent Ivan on bogus charges. They sentence him to death. But they offer him the choice of how to die: (1) death by boiling, (2) death by a thousand cuts, and (3) death by the guillotine. Ivan chooses the guillotine, as this is the least painful of his options. However, right before Ivan is executed, you intervene. You recognize that it's unjust and unethical for Ivan to be decapitated, so you destroy the guillotine. The executioner shrugs and tosses Ivan into boiling water, his number 2 choice.

In this thought experiment, you stop an injustice from occurring. But you don't do Ivan any favors. Indeed, what this thought experiment shows is that sometimes stopping an injustice can itself be unjust.

Going back to sweatshops and child labor, here's what it all means:

> **The Best Option Principle**: If you are trying to help someone, you should not take away a person's *best* option—no matter how awful and unjust it is—unless you can replace it with an *even better* option.

If you refuse to buy products made in sweatshops or do business with companies that use child labor, you aren't necessarily doing the workers any favors. What happens to them afterward?

Consider, for example, the following from economist Paul Krugman:

> In 1993, child workers in Bangladesh were found to be producing clothing for Wal-Mart, and Senator Tom Harkin proposed legislation banning imports from countries employing underage workers. The direct result was that Bangladeshi textile factories stopped employing children. But did the children go back to school? Did they return to happy homes? Not according to Oxfam, which found that the displaced child workers ended up in even worse jobs, or on the streets—and that a significant number were forced into prostitution.[8]

A later UNICEF study agreed with Krugman and Oxfam.[9] The bill against child labor was well-intentioned. Yet even though it was never passed, companies pre-emptively moved their factories out of Bangladesh or fired the children. This didn't help the children, though:

> A series of follow-up visits by UNICEF, local non-governmental organizations (NGOs) and the International Labour Organization (ILO) discovered that children went looking for new sources of income, and found them in work such as stone-crushing, street hustling and prostitution – all of them more hazardous and exploitative than garment production. In several cases, the mothers of dismissed children had to leave their jobs in order to look after their children.[10]

Again, parents love their kids. If lots of kids are working in a factory, that's strong evidence that's their best option. If you take that option away, you force the kids and their families to do something even worse than working long hours in a factory. You're no hero.

No Easy Fixes

You might think the Best Option Principle is easy to implement. We should just demand all the current workers get paid more and get better treatment, and that parents get enough money to ensure their kids don't have to work. Wonderful goals, but realistically, how can we achieve them?

Let's tell a story. Alta Gracia is a clothing brand famously dedicated to paying its workers a living wage, providing them with higher levels of job security, and ensuring that they enjoy heightened levels of autonomy and input into work methods. There's a good chance your college or university bookstore sells Alta Gracia clothing, since many college students are willing to pay a small premium to make a difference to workers' lives. Even then, as our colleagues John Kline and Ed Soule report, labor costs represent only a small portion (between 2% and 6%) of the cost of retail apparel, so increasing laboring costs, even if passed entirely onto consumers, won't have a giant effect on the final price of the product.[11] (One researcher says that Alta Gracia workers get paid about 90 cents more per sweatshirt compared to workers making comparable garments.[12])

So far, so good. But there's a missing bit. Alta Gracia purchased and renovated a preexisting clothing factory. The previous owner, BJ&B, paid its workers far less and treated them worse than Alta Gracia does. Still, at one point BJ&B had over 3,500 employees at the plant, and still had about 600 when it closed in 2007. When Alta Gracia took over in 2010, they employed—and apparently still employ—only about 130 workers, mostly former BJ&B workers.[13]

So, here's a hard question, which company had the more ethical business model, BJ&B or Alta Gracia? Which is better, A or B?

A: Employ a large number of workers with low pay.

B: Substitute capital for labor, and then employ a low number of workers with high pay.

It's not obvious to us which is the more just or caring behavior. Choice B is great for the workers who get a job, and bad for the workers who would have been employed but now are stuck with something even worse than the low-paying job they would have had under Choice A.

To give you some numbers, Alta Gracia workers appear to get about $497/month. We don't know what BJ&B paid its workers, but let's pessimistically assume it paid them the minimum wage legally allowed and that no workers worked overtime. In that case, BJ&B would have paid its workers about $148/month.[14] So, what was better, A or B?

A: Pay 600 workers $148/month. ($88,000/month total.)
B: Pay 130 workers $497/month. ($64,610/month total.)

We're not arguing for either option here. Even giving you the total salaries paid per month isn't meant to induce you to pick A over B. But we hope you recognize that moral platitudes about living wages often ignore deeper ethical trade-offs.

Imagine a company has sufficiently high demand and enough of a profit margin that it can afford choice C:

C: Pay 600 workers $497/month. ($298,200/month total.)

C seems obviously better than A or B; it employs as many workers as A but pays them as much as B. Let's stipulate there's no option D, which employs more workers or pays them even more. So, is C the best option for workers?

Again, there are unseen trade-offs, trade-offs professional ethicists might miss but professional economists learn to spot. The thing is, when you're paying workers three times as much, you're generally using more capital-intensive types of production, which require workers to be more skilled. The actual workers you hire under choice A might be different people from those you hire under Choice C.

But for the sake of argument, let's say that somehow under choice C you don't need more skilled workers than under choice A. You nevertheless will still end up with more skilled workers, even though that's not your intention.

Consider a domestic analogy. Suppose Walmart—the largest private employer in the United States—decides to double the base hourly wages of floor workers from $10–$12/hour to $20–$24/hour.[15] This will be wonderful for the people who end up working at Walmart. But it might not be so wonderful for the kinds of people who currently work at Walmart.

According to the Bureau of Labor Statistics, here are some other median hourly wages in the United States as of July 2018:[16]

1. Chemical technicians $22.73
2. Carpenters: $21.71
3. Carpet Installers: $18.67
4. Pipelayers: $18.46
5. Agricultural and food science technician: $19.19
6. Dental assistant: $18.09
7. Tax preparers: $18.62
8. Motorcycle mechanics: $17.15
9. Mechanical door repairers: $19.00
10. Solar panel installers: $18.98

The kinds of people doing these jobs have to have significantly more skill, experience, education, and other kinds of human capital than most of the people who now work at Walmart as cashiers or floor associates. They might be more conscientious on average too, as shown by the fact they were able to develop the skills necessary to work wood, prepare taxes, repair motorcycles, or assist in medicine.

Here's the bummer: As Walmart raises its wages, more and more of skilled workers like these will decide to apply for and accept jobs as Walmart floor associates instead of their current, skilled jobs. Sure, their employers will have to compete by raising wages too, and so some will stay. Still, overall, as Walmart raises wages, the kinds of people who choose to compete for Walmart jobs changes. Further, since Walmart is now paying so much in labor costs and needs to make a profit from its workers, we can expect the higher skilled, more productive, more reliable, or lower risk workers to beat out the kinds of workers currently getting Walmart jobs.

This phenomenon is called *job gentrification*. Just as hipsters, trust-fund artists, and yuppies can squeeze poor people out of their traditional neighborhoods—see Washington, DC, or Brooklyn, NYC, for examples—so better skilled workers can squeeze low skilled people out of their traditional jobs.

In short, if a company decides to pay significantly above-market wages for a low-skilled job, this can benefit the people who get those jobs. But it doesn't necessarily mean that the worst off, lowest-skilled workers with the worst options will benefit. Rather, paying higher wages can induce higher skilled workers with better options to compete for—and win—those jobs, leaving the worst off workers even worse off.

How to Make Poor Workers Rich Workers

Development economist Jeffrey Sachs famously said, "My concern is not that there are too many sweatshops, but that there are too few."[17] Economist Paul Krugman agrees. It could be that these economists are heartless, soulless, and callous. Or it could be that they know something most people don't: "that low-wage plants making clothing and shoes for foreign markets are an essential first step toward modern prosperity in developing countries."[18]

Most academic economists now acknowledge that there is a strong economic, consequence-based case for employing sweatshop labor. Economists say that sweatshops pay better, often significantly better, than the alternatives and so dramatically improve the lives of workers, despite having what we in the first world would consider miserable working conditions.

Further, sweatshops are typically a temporary phenomenon. Businesses set up sweatshops where labor is abundant and opportunities are scarce. But the normal course of development is that sweatshops start the process of industrialization and development. These kinds of factories take the risk of investing capital in poor places with relatively dysfunctional institutions. If the risk pays off, the workers get richer over time, and other, more capital-intensive factories that pay better wages tend to move in. Over time, worker productivity rises, and more and better kinds of jobs become available. That has been the case with pretty much all of the industrialized countries of the world, and it appears to be the case also with the currently developing countries.

Nearly every rich country went through a development period with sweatshops. For the United States and the United Kingdom—countries that industrialized early—the sweatshop period lasted more than fifty years. For more recent countries, such as South Korea, Japan, and Taiwan, the transition was far faster. As China industrializes, it's replacing its sweatshops with better factories, service work, and the kinds of jobs we in the developed world enjoy. The same phenomenon is happening elsewhere.

In chapter 2, we told you how in 1800 AD, about 95 percent of the world lived in what we would now consider extreme poverty. Even as late as 1960, 65 percent of the world lived on less than $2/day (in 2015 USD) and 45 percent on less than $1/day (in 2015 USD). But today the percentage of people living in extreme poverty is well under 10 percent.[19] World population is the highest it has ever been, but 6.5 billion people today have escaped extreme poverty, and the median per-capita income worldwide today is higher than the average income in the United States in 1900.[20] As the world opens up to markets, trade, business, and industrialization, poverty disappears before our eyes.

There is great deal to dislike about sweatshops. We'd prefer to live in a world in which everyone had access to better jobs than that. But if we care about the global poor, we must not simply boycott sweatshops or products made by sweatshop labor. Instead, we must grapple with complex economic realities. We must not remove what represents workers' best option—however bad it may be compared to our luxurious options in the developed world—unless we can substitute an even better option. As we've shown you, that's harder to do than it sounds. Even something as simple as offering a living wage or raising wages well above prevailing market conditions might mean that you help better off workers rather than the poor workers you wanted to help.

Summary

- Mutually beneficial transactions that are voluntarily accepted by both parties may still be unethical if one party unconscionably targets a vulnerability of the other to obtain a disproportionate share of the benefits of the transaction. Such conduct is unethical exploitation.
- The test for exploitation has two prongs: (1) there must be a vulnerable party, and (2) the stronger party must be targeting the weaker party's vulnerability for the purpose of obtaining disproportionately large gains.
- A party is vulnerable if it is unable to adequately protect its own interests through no fault of its own.
- Unethical exploitation requires both targeting a vulnerability and disproportionate gain by the party doing the targeting.
- Avoid exploitation, which is Principle 6, should be added to the list of basic ethical principles that are binding on all those doing business in a market.
- Workers in the developing world do the best they can given their limited options. If workers are working in sweatshops and sending their kids to work, that means that's their best available option.
- We should never remove someone's best option unless we can replace it with an even better option.

Discussion Questions

1. Imagine Walmart announces it will pay cashiers $50/hour henceforth. Would you be willing to work at Walmart for that much after you

     graduate from college? How about for $75 or $100/hour? What does that tell you about the effects of raising wages?

2. In 1979, Chinese leader Deng Xiaoping started allowing increased liberalization of the Chinese economy. Liberalization further picked up in the 1990s. What has happened to the standard of living in China since then? If China had never had sweatshops, or if the developed countries had refused to buy Chinese products, would the Chinese be better off today?

3. Is it better to employ a small number of people at a high wage, or a large number of people at a low wage? What would the potential workers themselves say?

4. Economics tell us that employers don't care about salaries per se. What matters to employers is the total cost (wages, benefits, working conditions and amenities) of employing a worker versus the total revenue that worker generates. What does that tell us about the trade-off between raising workers' wages vs. giving them better working conditions?

Notes

1. See Holcombe 1994.
2. This argument is introduced and discussed by Matt Zwolinski. See Zwolinski 2007: 699–700.
3. Strom 1996.
4. For at least one of us, part of the reason he is rich is that his grandfather, uncles, and father did engage in sweatshop labor.
5. See Acemoglu and Robinson 2013; de Soto 2000; Milanovic 2007; van der Vossen, and Brennan 2018.
6. Powell 2014.
7. Powell 2013.
8. Krugman 2001.
9. UNICEF, "State of the World's Children, 1997," p. 60, https://www.unicef.org/mexico/spanish/EMI1997.pdf.
10. Ibid.
11. Kline and Soule 2014: ii.
12. White 2017.
13. https://georgetown.app.box.com/s/wntf7bah8ls1vbbg6ar3.
14. Ibid., 16.
15. Isidore 2015.
16. http://www.bls.gov/oes/current/oes_nat.htm#00-0000.
17. Meyerson 1997.
18. Ibid.
19. https://ourworldindata.org/extreme-poverty.
20. Phelps and Crabtree 2013.

6

Addressing Moral Confusion

Ethics Isn't Law

Basic Lesson: Ethical principles and laws are not the same thing. Ethical princi-
ples embody obligations we owe our fellow human beings because they are au-
tonomous beings whose lives, projects, and goals are as valuable to them as ours
are to us. They are not the creation of any human act of will. Laws are rules of be-
havior created by state legislatures and the federal Congress in the United States,
and by the analogous governmental bodies in other nations. Businesspeople are
ethically obligated to act in accordance with law when the law has been justly
enacted and does not require unethical behavior. But the law has no independent
moral authority. When the law prescribes oppressive or unjust conduct, business-
people, like all people, may have an ethical duty not to obey the law. Principle 5
applies to the law as much as it does to the orders of a business superior.

Between 1996 and 2003, the accounting firm KPMG marketed several tax
shelters designed to allow wealthy investors to avoid federal taxes. In July
2001, the Internal Revenue Service "listed" two of these tax shelters, putting taxpayers on notice that the IRS considers them suspect and subject
to challenge in tax court. The IRS did not, in fact, challenge any of KPMG's
shelters in court. Hence, whether the shelters were legal or not has never been
determined.

In 2003, Congress began an investigation of potentially abusive tax shelters
including those marketed by KPMG. KPMG maintained that its shelters were
legal. It asked Jeffery Eischeid, one of its tax partners, to appear before a Senate
Subcommittee to testify to their legality. Eischeid had not created the shelters
and was not an attorney. His belief that the tax shelters were legal was based on
the representations of KPMG's attorneys and upper management. According
to Eischeid, everything he said and did with regard to the tax shelters "was
scripted by KPMG and approved by KPMG's professional-responsibility
committee."

After Eischeid's testimony before Congress, the US Department of Justice
opened a criminal investigation into KPMG's marketing of the tax shelters.

Business Ethics for Better Behavior. Jason Brennan, William English, John Hasnas, and Peter Jaworski, Oxford University Press.
© Oxford University Press 2021. DOI: 10.1093/oso/9780190076559.003.0006

When that happened, KPMG radically altered its position. It no longer claimed that its tax shelters were legal. It officially stated that a number of its tax partners, including Eischeid, had engaged in unlawful fraudulent conduct. It agreed not to make any statement, in litigation or otherwise, that was inconsistent with that assertion, and not to retain any employee who makes such a statement. It demanded the resignation of many of its tax partners, including Eischeid. It refused to honor its contractual obligation to advance the attorney's fees of any partner or employee who asserted his or her constitutional rights and refused to cooperate with federal investigators, which in Eischeid's case required pleading guilty to at least three felonies. It waived its attorney-client privilege and disclosed all information regarding the actions of its present and former partners and employees that the government requested. It agreed to inform the government which documents its partners and employees were requesting to prepare their defenses. It refused to inform its former partners and employees of the documents it was supplying to the government to aid in their prosecution. These actions left Eischeid unemployed, facing hundreds of thousands of dollars in legal fees, with the legal deck stacked against him.[1]

Why would KPMG behave in such a way? The illegality of the shelters has never been authoritatively established. Under the circumstances, wouldn't the ethical course of action be to support loyal employees like Eischeid who relied on the firm's representations and wound up in legal jeopardy for doing so?

The answer is that KPMG was confronted with an extremely powerful legal incentive to behave as it did. Under the law, KPMG is guilty of tax fraud as a company if any of its partners or employees participated in the sale of the shelters with the belief that they were illegal—the firm is vicariously liable for the actions of any and all of its employees. KPMG's management was keenly aware that a federal indictment could amount to a corporate death sentence. Just two years earlier, the Arthur Andersen accounting firm had collapsed after it was indicted for obstruction of justice. Under US Department of Justice policy, the only way for KPMG to avoid indictment was to fully cooperate with the government's investigation of its employees. As defined at the time, such cooperation required KPMG to affirmatively accept responsibility for criminal conduct, waive attorney-client privilege and disclose all potentially incriminating information to the government, refuse to help suspected employees mount a legal defense, and otherwise do everything in its power to ensure that its employees cooperated with the prosecution, including sanctioning any who refused to cooperate. Hence, KPMG's behavior can be seen as an effort to protect the firm's employees, clients, and investors from the fate suffered by Arthur Andersen's stakeholders.

KPMG's management faced a difficult choice in which ethics and the law were pulling in opposite directions. On the one hand, KPMG had ethical obligations to treat its employees fairly and honor the terms of their employment contracts. In Eischeid's case, this would mean (1) not accusing him of fraud, (2) not aiding in his prosecution unless it had a good faith belief that he was guilty, and (3) honoring its contractual obligation to pay his attorney's fees for legal jeopardy arising from the performance of his job. On the other hand, KPMG had a duty to protect its employees, clients, and investors against the disastrous effects of a corporate indictment, which appeared to require it to do precisely the opposite.

Did KPMG do the right thing?

Two Types of Law: Part I

The law that governs the marketplace within which business is conducted can be divided into two types: private law and public law. Private law is the law designed to settle disputes between the individual members of society. Contract law is the law that governs disputes arising between parties in a contractual relationship. Property law governs disputes arising over the ownership and use of private property. Tort law governs disputes that result when one party intentionally or inadvertently causes personal injury or property damage to another. Commercial law governs disputes arising out the creation and use of commercial and financial instruments. The purpose of private law is to facilitate the nonviolent resolution of interpersonal disputes, thereby enhancing peaceful cooperation among the members of society.

Public law is the law designed to govern the relationship between the government and individuals. Criminal law is the law that authorizes the government to impose punishment on individuals. Constitutional law is the law that establishes the powers of government and imposes limitations on their use. Administrative law governs the functioning of government agencies and offices. The purpose of public law is to establish and regulate how the government interacts with citizens.

Two Types of Law: Part II

The law of the British Commonwealth of countries that includes the United Kingdom, the United States, Canada, and Australia can also be divided into two types along other lines: legislation and common law. Legislation consists of rules of law that are consciously created by those who exercise political power—in liberal democracies, by the political representatives of the community. Thus, in the United States, legislation is the output of the state legislatures and the federal Congress. Legislation is law that is intentionally designed by a guiding human intelligence.

Common law is case-generated law or law that arises from the settlement of actual disputes. Originally, the common law consisted of rules of law that were abstracted from a series of cases thought to represent just resolutions of past disputes. Over the past century and a half, the common law came to be understood as rules that are derived from the examination of specific cases that constitute relevant precedents. Common law is law that evolves over time on the basis of past legal experience. Unlike intentionally created legislation, common law is "the result of human action, but not the execution of any human design."

Legislation is the type of law that is most familiar to the ordinary citizen. Given that the legal education of most Americans began in elementary school with a video of a bill singing and dancing its way through the House of Representatives and the Senate to be signed by the President,[2] it is not surprising that most of them assume that all law is legislation. Nevertheless, legislation represents only a small proportion of the law upon which our commercial society rests. Almost all of the private law that allows citizens to cooperate, trade, and prosper—contract law, property law, commercial law, tort law—arose from the common law, not legislation.

Legislation and common law are equally law, but they are law produced by distinctly different processes. Legislation is produced by a political process. Common law is produced by a trial and error, evolutionary process. Legislation originates in the actions of those invested with political authority and is imposed on the citizenry to regulate their interaction—law that proceeds from the top down. Common law is law that originates in the uncoordinated actions of the individual members of society and grows to govern human interaction—law that proceeds from the bottom up.

The Relationship between Law and Ethics

Human beings come into the world clothed with ethical obligations. Some are negative. We are ethically obligated not to murder and assault others; not to steal from them, burn, or otherwise destroy their property; not to defame them or subject them to unwarranted humiliation or ridicule; not to engage in invidious racial, religious, or sexual discrimination against them. Some are positive. We are ethically obligated to deal with others in good faith, to keep our promises, to render aid to those in danger or desperate need when we can do so safely. We have these ethical obligations simply because we are human beings living in society with other human beings.

Most human beings—all those living under nation states that have legal systems—also have legal obligations. These obligations are determined by the law—whether legislation or common law—of the country within which one lives. These too may be negative or positive. Most legal systems prohibit murder, assault, arson, rape, robbery, and fraud. Many impose legal duties to serve in the nation's armed forces, to serve on juries, and to care for one's children. Some impose legal duties to render aid to those in danger. We have these legal obligations because we reside in the jurisdiction of the state that issues the law.

Our ethical and legal obligations frequently overlap. The law of most liberal democracies translates many of our ethical obligations into legal obligations as well. Thus, we are legally obligated to live up to our ethical obligations to refrain from murder, assault, arson, theft, fraud, extortion, and invidious discrimination. The addition of the legal obligation to the underlying ethical obligation means that violation of the obligation can now be punished by the state.

However, we have many ethical obligations that are not legal obligations. We have ethical obligations not to lie to others, not to unfairly exploit their vulnerabilities, not to engage in bullying and other forms of disrespectful treatment, and perhaps, not to tease our younger siblings. But we have no legal obligation to refrain from such actions and are not subject to punishment by the state if we violate these obligations. Only a totalitarian government would try to embody all of our ethical obligations in law.

We also have many legal obligations that are not ethical obligations. Americans have no ethical duty to drive on the right rather than the left, but the law that requires them to do so has great value in facilitating safe travel. Indeed, much of private law has no moral content. Its purpose is to help individuals coordinate their behavior so that they can cooperate more effectively. The contract law "mailbox rule" states that an offer is accepted when the notification of acceptance is sent rather than when it is received. This is not because such a rule is ethically required but because having a definite rule facilitates commercial transactions. Similarly, public law often creates legal obligations that have no underlying ethical obligations. There is nothing morally objectionable about hiring someone to wait tables in your restaurant for $10 an hour, but if the minimum wage in your jurisdiction is $12 an hour, then you have a legal obligation not to do so.

A problem arises when our ethical and legal obligations conflict. This occurs when the law prescribes unethical conduct or ethics prescribes illegal conduct. For example, a state statute could require railroads to racially segregate its cars or restrict women's working hours more than men's.[3] In such cases, businesspeople would have both an ethical obligation not to engage in invidious discrimination on the basis of race or sex and a legal obligation to engage in such discrimination. Similarly, a doctor may have an ethical obligation to give a patient a drug that the doctor believes can save the patient's life, but if the drug is still experimental and has not been approved for use by the proper government agency, he or she has a legal obligation not to do so.

These problematic situations often beset multinational enterprises. For example, an international corporation could have an ethical obligation not to use coercion to obtain its labor force but be legally obligated by the host country to employ local contractors who do.[4] It might have an ethical obligation to treat men and women equally but a legal obligation to discriminate against women. A company might have an ethical obligation to protect its work force against harm but be legally prohibited from paying ransom to terrorists who have kidnaped some of its employees.[5] An Internet service provider or search engine could have an ethical obligation to provide access to information on a nondiscriminatory basis but have a legal obligation to censor the internet imposed by the government of the country in which it is doing business.[6] What ethics requires can conflict with what the law requires.

Implications

This understanding of the relationship between law and ethics gives rise to several implications.

Compliance with the Law Is Never Enough

Some of our ethical obligations are embodied in the law and are legal obligations as well as ethical ones. But many are not. This means that you can never fulfill all of your ethical obligations merely by obeying the law.

As discussed in chapter 4, nothing about accepting employment or entering into a business relationship relieves you of your preexisting ethical obligations as a human being. Nothing magical happens when you go to work for another that implies that as long as you obey the law, you may engage in otherwise unethical conduct to advance your principal's interests. You are bound by your ethical obligations whether they are enacted into law or not. Hence, "I didn't do anything illegal" is never an adequate justification for engaging in unethical wrongdoing. You might as well say, "I followed the rules of tennis!"

You Should Obey the Law When It Coincides with Your Ethical Obligations

As noted above, in liberal democratic societies, there is some overlap between your ethical and legal obligations. The law frequently requires you to refrain from intentionally harming others, keep your promises, respect other's property rights, avoid fraudulent misrepresentation, and deal with others in good faith. In such cases, the law embodies your preexisting ethical obligations, and, in some cases, helps refine our understanding of their scope and how best to meet them. In this class of cases, ethical business behavior requires you to act in accordance with the law.

When Your Legal Obligations Do Not Coincide with Your Ethical Obligations, Whether You Should Obey the Law Is an Open Question

There are two possibilities when our legal obligations do not coincide with our ethical obligations. The first is that the law has imposed additional obligations on us that are completely compatible with our ethical obligations. The second is that the law has imposed additional obligations on us that are not compatible with our ethical obligations.

The first is likely to be the case when the law is serving its function of helping members of society coordinate their actions so that they can cooperate more effectively. Most of the common law rules of private law have this characteristic. Thus, rules of law that determine when an offer has been accepted, what constitutes adequate consideration to turn a promise into a binding contract, what formalities are necessary to create a secured transaction, what actions are required to transfer title to real property, and how careful we must be not to endanger others by our activities are all compatible with our preexisting ethical obligations.

Many rules of public law similarly fall into the first class of cases. Regulatory legislation frequently prohibits conduct that is not wrong in itself as a means to advancing overall social welfare. Such *malum prohibitum* offenses may require compliance with specified price or wage restrictions, workplace hour and safety requirements, methods of handling and shipping designated drugs or items that pose environmental hazards, or prohibitions on engaging in certain activities without a specified amount of training or a license. Compliance with such measures rarely conflicts with our ethical obligations.

Nevertheless, there are cases in which the law requires unethical action. The Jim Crow laws that mandated racial segregation in public transportation, restaurants, and public schools are archetypical examples of such laws. These laws *required* businesses to engage in the type of invidious discrimination that would violate Principle 4. As noted in Section 3, multinational enterprises often run into such conflicts where laws or law enforcement agents of the host country require unethical actions such as paying bribes, violating contract terms, engaging in discriminatory hiring, or making fraudulent representations.

But such situations can and do arise even in liberal democracies. In some cases, professionals, such as attorneys, physicians, and clergy, are legally obligated to disclose information that they obtained under a promise of confidentiality in violation of their ethical obligation to keep the information secret. Similarly, businesses, banks, and other financial institutions may be legally obligated to violate their ethically binding promise of confidentiality to provide law enforcement agents with the ability to examine or decrypt their clients' confidential communications and records. Sometimes, the law requires business people to breach their fiduciary obligations, as was apparently the case after the recession of 2008.[7] And there are also situations that pit the requirements of the law against ethical obligations derived from one's conscience or religious commitments, whether it be the requirement that employers aid governmental efforts to identify and deport undocumented workers or that Catholic organizations include contraceptive coverage in their health insurance packages.

When the law imposes obligations on us to that do not coincide with our ethical obligations, we must always ask ourselves whether we should obey the law before acting. This follows directly from Principle 5.

Principle 5 states that personal ethical responsibility is inalienable. That means that we can never blindly rely on an authority to make our ethical decisions for us. This, in turn, means that the claim that one was just following the orders of a superior can never justify unethical conduct. And this is true whether one's superior is an individual, such as one's corporate supervisor or a United States Attorney, or a collective, such as the corporation's board of directors or the majority of a state's legislators.

Legislators are not invested with magical powers that enable them to transform unjust actions into just actions by enacting them into law. This holds true even if they are accurately representing the will of the majority of their constituents. At least since Plato's *Republic*, we have had good reason to doubt the claim that justice is the interest of the stronger.[8] This observation applies just as forcefully to the claim that justice is the interest of the more numerous. Might doesn't make right. And ethics is not just whatever most people say.

The fact that an action was legally required cannot relieve us of personal responsibility if we act unjustly in taking it. This proposition was firmly established by the Nuremberg trials following World War II.[9] And the fact that we are subject to legal punishment for acting in accordance with our ethical obligations does not free us from these obligations. This proposition was eloquently expressed by Martin Luther King in his *Letter from a Birmingham Jail*.[10]

Of course, these observations do not imply that one is ethically justified in violating the law whenever one believes that his or her legal and ethical obligations are in conflict. They imply only that whether to obey the law when there is such a conflict is always an open question. One is always required to ethically evaluate whether he or she should obey the law before deciding how to act.

General Applications

Compatible Obligations

Almost always, when your legal and ethical obligations do not coincide, they will nevertheless be compatible. Most of these cases will involve the rules of private law generated by the common law process that, although not ethically obligatory in themselves, evolved to facilitate interpersonal cooperation and help human beings coordinate their actions. In such cases, one should almost always obey the law.

Some of these cases will involve rules of public law created by legislatures to regulate the way business is conducted. When you have no objection to such laws, there is no problem. However, in some cases, you may disapprove of the law. You may think that it is unlikely to accomplish its objective, that it is inefficient, or that it is just plain stupid. You may decide to undertake political action to try to change or repeal it. You may decide to write op-eds denouncing it. Nevertheless, in most cases, if you live in a relatively just society and the law was properly enacted, and if complying with the law does not impose some serious burden upon you, you should probably obey the law until you succeed in getting it changed.

Despite this, there may still be cases in which even though the law does not directly conflict with any of your ethical obligations, you nevertheless decide that the right thing to do is to violate the law. For example, assume that you live in a jurisdiction that requires a cosmetology license to be allowed to charge money for hair braiding. This law does not require you to act unethically and is compatible with all of your preexisting ethical obligations. However, you believe that this law has no legitimate purpose but was enacted to protect established hair and beauty salons against competition from small, independent entrepreneurs. Your evidence for this is that obtaining a cosmetology license requires 1,500 hours of classroom instruction, none of which concerns hair braiding, and costs over $3,000.[11] In other words, you believe that the law is a result of the process known as "rent-seeking," in which businesses or industries try to gain a competitive advantage by securing rules of law that favor their interests. (Rent-seeking will be discussed in greater detail in chapter 9.) In such a case, you may decide to open a hair braiding business without a cosmetology license as a means of challenging the legitimacy of the law. This would be an example of an ethically justified violation of law.[12]

Incompatible Obligations

In a small number of cases, your legal obligations will be incompatible with your ethical obligations. In such cases, careful thought must be given as to how to act. In many cases, the only way to meet your ethical obligations will be to sacrifice what would otherwise be profit-enhancing business opportunities.

For example, assume that a multinational enterprise has an opportunity to increase its profits by opening a plant in a developing country. But to do business in that country, the company is required by the host country's law, law enforcement agents, or local political authorities to contract with local firms that conscript labor or exploit their workers; or engage in discriminatory hiring practices that favor one group, family, or caste; or pay extortionate fees or bribes to officials who promise to "protect" the plant and its employees. In such cases, the company's ethical obligations require it to forgo the opportunity to profit from complying with such legal requirements.

And in some cases, one may have an ethical obligation, not merely to avoid the law but to violate it. The most obvious example would be laws that require invidious racial discrimination. Laws that mandate racial segregation, deny members of minority groups equal access to employment or education, or are otherwise oppressive toward minorities clearly require unethical conduct.

You should not obey such laws *even if refusing to do so means going out of business.*

Few contemporary situations are as clear-cut as this, and many place individuals in difficult and often poignant positions. Consider an employer who learns that one of his or her loyal employees is an undocumented immigrant. The employer may know this worker to be an honest and reliable individual who is responsibly supporting a family. Yet if the employer retains the worker he or she is violating federal law and is liable to criminal penalties.[13] In cases such as this, there is at least a reasonable argument that the employer has an ethical obligation to violate the law and retain the worker.

Or consider being called before a congressional committee and being asked to "name names" of those who work for you that are sympathetic to communism so that they may be subject to harassment and shunned;[14] or being subpoenaed by the state of Alabama to identify the members of the NAACP among your workforce so that they may be attacked by racists;[15] or ordered by a court to identify the LGBTQ members of your workforce or those who have received financial support from the Open Society Foundation or the Koch Foundation or contributed to political campaigns against same-sex marriage or conservative social welfare organizations so that they may be subjected to public opprobrium. In all such situations, one may have an ethical obligation to refuse to obey the law.

One recent example of this type of case arose when Apple was ordered by a court to create special software to thwart security measures on the cell phone of a suspect in a mass shooting case.[16] Apple refused on the ground that creating such software would violate its obligation to protect the privacy and security of all those who use its products and could be abused by oppressive governments to crack down on dissent. In this case, it is entirely reasonable to argue that Apple is ethically obligated not to comply with the court order.

Application to KPMG Case

Let's apply these observations to the KPMG case which began this chapter. KPMG appears to have several ethical obligations to its employees, including Eischeid. One is to honor the terms of its contract with them, which in Eischeid's case requires it to advance the attorney's fees he needs to defend himself against job-related legal jeopardy.[17] Another is to treat its employees fairly, which includes affording them "due process" before taking actions that can harm their interests. In Eischeid's case, this would require that it not take action that could result in his conviction of a criminal offense unless it had a good faith belief that he is guilty of the offense. An argument could be made that this obligation also includes a duty not to punish its employees for exercising their constitutional rights. Finally, KPMG has an ethical obligation to refrain from fraud and improper deception, which means that it should not make false statements that others rely upon to their detriment. In Eischeid's case, this means either that KPMG should not have told him that its tax shelters were legal when it sent him to testify before Congress if it believed they were illegal, or that it should not have issued a statement declaring them to be illegal and agreed not to make any statement, in litigation or otherwise, that was inconsistent with that assertion if it believed that they were legal.

But as described at the beginning of the chapter, KPMG faced an extremely powerful legal incentive not to meet these obligations. Under federal law enforcement policy, honoring its ethical obligations to Eischeid and its other employees would amount to failing to cooperate with the government's investigation, which could subject the firm to corporate indictment with potentially disastrous consequences for the firm's business.

KPMG faced a situation in which ethics and the law were pulling in opposite directions. We ended the first section of this chapter by asking: Did KPMG do the right thing? We did so not because we expect you to answer the question definitively but because we want you to see that it is an open and difficult question. KPMG cannot escape moral responsibility for its action merely by claiming that it was complying with the law and federal law enforcement policy. Corporate policymakers are as bound by Principle 5, which states that personal ethical responsibility is *inalienable*, as anyone else. They must carefully weigh whether sacrificing the interests of and violating their obligations to individual employees can be justified by the need to protect the interests of the firm's other stakeholders. There are reasonable arguments on both sides, but it may well be that KPMG was ethically obligated to resist the legal incentives.

In fact, if KPMG's upper management truly believed that its tax shelters were legal, we believe this to be the case. To be meaningful, ethical principles must have some bite; adherence to them must carry some cost. If they can be overridden whenever they interfere with one's business objectives, they would be vacuous. The essence of ethical principles is that they require us to act in certain ways even when doing so retards our efforts to achieve our goals. Hence, it will very rarely be the case that a threat to one's business success can justify the violation of an ethical principle. And this is the case even if the threat comes from a government and even if it is packaged in the form of a legal penalty.

In the case of Escheid, unless the management of KPMG had a good faith belief that he was engaged in criminal conduct, we believe that KPMG was ethically obligated to risk federal indictment by (1) refraining from asserting that he was engaged in such conduct, (2) refusing to pressure him to waive his constitutional rights, and (3) honoring its contractual commitment to advance his attorney's fees. The fact that doing so may have had a significant deleterious effect on KPMG's bottom line cannot justify violating the company's ethical obligations to Mr. Eischeid and similarly situated employees.

Sometimes doing the right thing means taking a hit. Ethical people and ethical companies are willing to take such a hit. The fact that the hit comes in the form of a legal sanction changes nothing. Ethics is not law, and when ethics and law conflict, it is ethics that should prevail.

Some Useful Advice for Dealing with the Law

The title of this chapter is "Ethics Isn't Law." By this point, we hope it's clear that law isn't ethics either. The present law of the United States and most other industrialized nations prohibits a wide array of conduct that is not morally wrong in itself. It's possible to violate the law even though you are not doing anything unethical. This means that your moral intuitions—your feeling and judgments about whether what you are doing is right or wrong–are not a good guide to whether your actions are legal. Don't assume that as long as you do the right thing, you're not breaking any laws; you could end up in big legal trouble.

If you have not been to law school, you may not know much about the law. However, if there is one legal doctrine that you have heard of, it is probably the one that states that ignorance of the law is no excuse. You cannot defend yourself against a criminal charge by claiming that you did not know that your conduct was against the law. That should be frightening. Back in 1998, the American Bar Association, declared that "[s]o large is the present body of federal criminal law that there is no conveniently accessible, complete list of federal crimes."[18] The *Federal Register* contains well over 60,000 pages of rules. There's no way you could ever learn all the laws which apply to you or which carry criminal penalties, but they nevertheless apply to you.

For this reason, you would be smart to acquaint yourself with the legal regulations that apply to your business activities to the greatest extent possible. If you work for a company that is large and highly capitalized enough to have its own corporate counsel, he or she would be a good source for such information.

Several years ago, we had a guest speaker addressing the course in Leadership and Business Ethics that all Georgetown MBA students were required to take. The speaker was a professionally dressed, attractive man in his mid-40s. His talk was an account of his experience working in a corporation where other middle managers were taking illegal kickbacks on their sales contracts. He described the way in which his colleagues set up the illegal deals, indicated his repugnance of the practice and his refusal to participate in it, and his struggle over whether to blow the whistle on his colleagues. (His father-in-law was the president of the company, and the speaker did not know whether he was aware of the practice.)

The students were intrigued by the speaker's account, and followed along with it, often visibly nodding their heads. It was as if they were listening to his story and thinking, "That's what I would have done, too." This probably accounted for their shocked reaction when, at the end of his talk, the speaker revealed he was giving it as a condition of his parole from federal prison. Not having been trained in law, he did not know the legal definition of conspiracy, which consists in the knowing mutual cooperation with those engaged in criminal activity. By engaging in business with those he knew to be committing fraud, he opened himself to the charge of conspiracy, which federal prosecutors used to get him to testify against his coworkers and father-in-law in return for a reduced sentence. We have never found a more effective method for showing the students that their ethical intuitions are not an accurate reflection of their legal obligations.

But this leads to another piece of important practical advice. We advised you to consult your corporate counsel, if your company has such counsel. But you must understand that your company's attorneys represent the company's interests, not yours. As the example of the KPMG case illustrates, when a business comes under investigation for a criminal offense, the interests of the business and its employees often diverge.

To see why, you must understand the nature of corporate criminal liability. For the past 110 years, businesses have been subject to the criminal law as collective entities.[19] But how can a business commit a crime? The answer is supplied by the legal doctrine of *respondeat superior* (Latin for "Let the Master Answer"), which holds that a business is guilty of any crime committed by any of its employees acting within the scope of their employment. This is the case no matter how conscientious the business has been in trying to prevent improper action by its employees. Hence, businesses are vicariously liable for the crimes of their employees.

Current US Department of Justice policy exploits this fact to drive a wedge between businesses and their employees. Given that whenever an employee commits a crime, the business is guilty as well, the only way a business can protect itself against criminal liability is to convince prosecutors not to indict it in the first place. But under Department of Justice (DOJ) policy, the only way for a business to avoid indictment is to cooperate with the DOJ's investigation of its employees. And because the DOJ defines cooperation as helping it make its case against the business's employees, to protect itself a business must help the government obtain convictions of its employees. This may not sound so bad when the company knows for sure the employees have broken the law, but it should be alarming when there is doubt about this. In the vernacular of corporate counsel, Department of Justice policy creates an incentive for businesses to "throw their employees under the bus."

When a business becomes a subject of a federal criminal investigation, it typically instructs corporate counsel to conduct an internal investigation into the conduct of its employees. In doing so, corporate counsel will issue what is called the "Upjohn warning"[20] to any employee it interviews, in which it informs the employee that his or her communications with counsel is protected by attorney-client privilege but that the privilege belongs to the business, and the business may waive the privilege at its discretion. Understood correctly, the *Upjohn* warning is informing you that your communications are *not* protected by attorney-client privilege, and that the business *will* inform the government of anything you say that will help it avoid corporate indictment.

So our last piece of practical advice to you is that should you ever receive the *Upjohn* warning, you should hear it for what it is—an instruction to get your own attorney.

Conclusion

In the overwhelming majority of cases, the law and ethics pull in the same direction. This means that in the overwhelming majority of cases, you should conduct your business affairs in conformity with the law. Nevertheless, there are cases in which the law and ethics pull in opposite directions. In such cases, to conduct your business ethically, you may have to resist legal incentives and sometimes even directly violate the law. We focus on such cases of conflict in this chapter, not to be alarmist or to suggest that they are common, but because they call several ethical stumbling blocks—moral confusion, moral blind spots, and conformity—into play.

Most people do not draw a sharp distinction between law and ethics, running the two together in their minds. This can lead to significant moral confusion in the cases in which law and ethics pull in opposite directions. Without a clear understanding of the relationship between them, it is difficult for people to figure what proper behavior is when they conflict. Perhaps, more significantly, most people intuitively believe that there is a duty to obey the law. Relying on this intuition can cause people to overlook the cases in which the law is incentivizing or commanding unethical conduct, producing moral blind spots. If you believe that there is an ethical duty to obey the law, you are much less likely to notice that the law may be commanding you to do something wrong. And the danger that people will blindly go along with whatever the law commands is reinforced by our psychological tendency to conform our behavior to others'.

In this chapter, we have attempted to clarify the relationship between law and ethics and reminded you that Principle 5 is always in play. In doing so, we hope to help you see through the moral blind spot the law sometimes creates, and, in cases in which the law and ethics conflict, to resist your impulse to conform, and carefully consider what your ethical duties truly are.

Summary

- Law consists of both private law—the law designed to settle disputes between the individual members of society, and public law—the law designed to establish and govern the relationship between the government and individuals.
- Law also consists of the rules of legislation—rules of law that are consciously created by those who exercise political authority, and common law—case-generated law that arises from the settlement of actual disputes.
- Ethics is not law. Our ethical obligations derive from the fact that we are human beings living in society with other human beings. Our legal obligations derive from those with political authority in the state within which we reside.
- Our ethical and legal obligations frequently overlap, but there are ethical obligations that are not legal obligations and legal obligations that are not ethical obligations.
- Our ethical and legal obligations are usually compatible, but in some case are incompatible.
- When our legal and ethical obligations do not overlap, whether to obey the law is always an open question.
- Although rare (at least in liberal democracies), there will be some cases in which one is ethically obligated not to obey the law.

Discussion Questions

1. Do you believe that there is a duty to obey a democratically enacted law? If so, why?
2. How can you tell whether a law is in fact democratically enacted? Were the Jim Crow laws in the Southern states of the United States democratically enacted? If not, why not?
3. In the past, 18-year-olds could be drafted even though they did not have the right to vote. Did they have a duty to obey the law and report for the draft?
4. How many examples can you think of in which businesses that should be subject to criminal punishment are not also liable for compensatory (and potentially punitive) damage under tort law?
5. Any employee of a business who commits a crime while working for the business is liable to criminal punishment as an individual for his or her criminal action. Under tort law, businesses are liable to pay compensatory and sometimes punitive damages to anyone harmed by the negligent or intentional wrongdoing of their employees acting within the scope of their employment. Businesses are also subject to criminal fines for any crimes committed by their employees within the scope of their employment. But if the individuals who commit the crimes are subject to criminal punishment and the business must compensate any party that its employees have harmed, what purpose is served by imposing criminal fines on the business as a collective entity?

Notes

1. The facts of this account of the KPMG case are taken from Cohen 2004; Post 2006: 4; "KPMG in Wonderland" 2005: A14; and Deferred Prosecution Agreement (Re: KPMG) from David N. Kelley, US Attorney for the Southern District of New York (Aug. 26, 2005).
2. See, e.g., the School House Rock video "I'm Just a Bill." Frishberg 1973.
3. E.g., the Separate Car Act, 1890 La. Acts No. 111, p. 152, was upheld in the case of Plessy v. Ferguson, 163 U.S. 537 (1896); the Oregon labor statute, 1903 Or. Laws p.148, upheld by the Supreme Court in Muller v. Oregon, 208 U.S. 412 (1908).
4. See, e.g., Doe v. Unocal, 395 F.3d 932 (9th Cir. 2002).
5. Between 1997 and 2004, Chiquita Brands International made extortion payments to both left-wing and right-wing paramilitary groups in Columbia's banana-growing region "to protect the well-being and lives of its employees." Because these groups were on the US State Department's list of terrorist organizations, it is a violation of US federal law to do business with any organization on this list. Chiquita pled guilty to the violation and paid a $25 million fine for the violation. See Yager 2007.

6. Waddell 2016.

7. See, e.g., Story and Becker 2009.

8. Plato, *The Republic*, Book 1 (T. E. Page et al. eds., Paul Shorey trans., G.P. Putnam and Sons, 1930).

9. Principles of International Law Recognized in the Charter of the Nuremberg Tribunal and in the Judgment of the Tribunal, princ. IV, [1950] 2 Y.B. Int'l L. Comm'n 375.

10. King, Jr. 1963.

11. See Erickson 2016.

12. The most famous historical example of this type of legal violation is the case of *Plessy v. Ferguson*, in which the plaintiff, who was one eighth African American, intentionally violated Louisiana's Separate Car Act by riding in the whites only car of the East Louisiana Railway, for the purposes of challenging the legitimacy of the Act.

13. See 8 U.S.C. §1324a(a)(2) ("It is unlawful for a person or other entity, after hiring an alien for employment . . ., to continue to employ the alien in the United States knowing the alien is (or has become) an unauthorized alien with respect to such employment.").

14. See Navasky 1980.

15. See National Association for the Advancement of Colored People v. Alabama, 357 U.S. 449 (1958).

16. See *In re* Matter of the Search of an Apple iPhone Seized during the Execution of a Search Warrant on a Black Lexus IS300, California License Plate 35KGD203, No. ED 15-0451M, 2016 WL 618401 (C.D. Cal., Feb. 16, 2016); Lichtblau and Benner 2016.

17. The contract required employees to reimburse the firm if they were convicted of criminal activity.

18. See Strazzella 1998.

19. See New York Central and Hudson R.R. Co. v. United States, 212 U.S. 481 (1909).

20. So-called because it is derived from the Supreme Court decision in Upjohn Co. v. United States, 449 U.S. 383 (1981).

7

The Effect of Incentives

The Value of Reputation

Basic Lesson: It's in your self-interest to be seen as a good person. The easiest way to be seen as a good person is to actually be a good person. But the desire to be seen as a good person creates its own ethical traps.

In 2002, right after graduating college, Jason Brennan took a job at GEICO. The first day of the job, the regional vice president addressed all of that month's new hires. After welcoming everyone, he turned to the new salespeople. He said, "We can make somewhat higher profits by selling customers slightly more insurance than they need. But your job is not to make us a profit. Your job is to sell the customer exactly the right amount of insurance that's best for them, given their assets." He turned to the new adjusters—the people who would decide how much to pay when someone files a claim. He said, "We can make somewhat higher profits by paying claimants slightly less than what they are entitled to. But your job is not to make us a profit. Your job is to *keep our word*. That means we pay every penny we owe, not a cent less."

This speech had quite an impact. Years later, when Jason had left insurance for academia, people would joke that he must have felt slimy working at GEICO every day. On the contrary, Jason said, he got to spend all day every day doing the right thing, surrounded by people who did the same. He went home with a clean conscience every night. Academia, in contrast, is far worse.[1]

The VP wasn't running a charity. GEICO exists to serve customers *and* to make a profit. Its market share has been growing over the past few decades. The VP explained to us that we do the right thing because it's the right thing. We *also* do it because ethics is strategic. Insurance, he said, is a commodity. It's not like GEICO claim money tastes better than Allstate money. The main things insurance companies can do to differentiate themselves—to help win new customers and keep old ones—are (1) offer better customer service, and (2) be as honest and trustworthy as possible.

The VP understood the central lesson of this chapter. People are regularly presented with opportunities to lie, cheat, and steal, a little here and a little

Business Ethics for Better Behavior. Jason Brennan, William English, John Hasnas, and Peter Jaworski, Oxford University Press. © Oxford University Press 2021. DOI: 10.1093/oso/9780190076559.003.0007

there. We are all aware that self-interest can influence people to behave un-ethically. This makes us worry that if we act ethically, others will take advantage of us—that by being moral, we're being *suckers*. But in general, you can't have a good life or be happy without the service, help, and companionship of others. Other people aren't going to serve, help, or befriend you unless they think you're a decent person. Customers aren't going to buy your business's service unless they believe your business and its people do the right thing and keep its word. In the long run, *being ethical* and *doing well* tend to come together.

You can probably think of many ethical scandals in business. For instance, the energy firm Enron started investing in myriad unrelated businesses and ventures. It acquired huge amounts of debt. For a while, it concealed its debt through dishonest accounting practices and creative business partnerships. Eventually, it got caught. Sure, that was a disaster, but think of what happened next—when it got caught, its stock price collapsed and the business failed. We don't mean to celebrate this as a total victory of good over evil. Lots of innocent people worked for Enron and lost their jobs, having done nothing wrong. Only about 300 out of 28,000 employees at Andersen (Enron's accounting firm) knew anything about or helped contribute to the accounting malfeasance, but they lost their jobs too.[2]

Still, you can see the lesson: When customers know you're dishonest, you lose business.

Thus, it makes sense that most us desire to be seen as good people. But this desire can itself lead people astray.

For instance, what if you have to impress people who indeed have the wrong values, or (more commonly) people who apply the right values in the wrong way? For instance, in the 1980s, McDonald's packaged many of its foods in foam containers. Customers worried that these containers were not biodegradable and so were bad for environment. They weren't wrong. But what they didn't know is that McDonald's had consciously chosen foam *over* paper packaging. To serve burgers in paper without the paper getting soaked through, they needed to coat the paper with materials that made the paper even worse for the environment than the foam. Nevertheless, customers didn't know that, and in the face of consumer pressure, McDonald's caved and switched to a packaging material that *seemed* better but was in fact worse. Here, the desire for a good reputation induced them to do the wrong thing.[3]

If you want to see another problem, open up Facebook or Twitter and read for ten minutes. You'll notice lots of people one-upping each other, trying to prove they are more moral and more concerned about justice than their friends and neighbors. You might suspect they are not quite so concerned with ethics as they are with *self-promotion*. They engage in what Justin Tosi and Brandon Warmke call "moral grandstanding," that is, abusing moral language for the sake of increasing one's own status and promoting one's image.[4]

In chapters 3–6, we examined the ways in which moral confusion can led to unethical behavior. In this and the following three chapters, we explore the effect of incentives on people's behavior, both the incentives within the firm and those of the politically regulated market environment within which firms operate. In this chapter, we focus on how the value of reputation creates incentives for both good and bad behavior. Our goal is simple. We want to show you that although self-interest is often an impediment to ethical behavior, thanks to the power of reputation, it can also be a spur to such behavior—that morality and self-interest generally go together. Nevertheless, the self-interested desire for a good reputation itself contains traps that can ensnare us and cause us to act *badly*. An ethics book—and an ethics course—needs to teach students how to avoid these traps–how not to abuse ethics for unethical purposes.

Why Be Moral?

Over 2,300 years ago, the philosopher Plato wrote a book called *The Republic*. Despite its title, the goal of *The Republic* is not so much to identify a perfectly just society but instead to ask, "If I could get away with being unethical, is there any reason to be ethical?"

In the book, Glaucon asks Socrates to imagine that a poor shepherd finds a magic ring. This magic ring enables the shepherd to do evil things with impunity. The shepherd uses the ring to seduce the queen; together they assassinate the king and he becomes the new king. He's never caught and dies rich and happy. Glaucon asks why anyone should bother to resist that kind of temptation if they had that power. He pushes further: If you had the choice between being a good person whom everyone hated, or a bad person whom everyone loved, why choose the former over the latter?

Over a few hundred pages, Socrates tries but ultimately fails to answer Glaucon's question. Socrates suggests that evil people have disordered psyches and can never be truly happy, but that's just speculation.

Plato's question—why be moral?—stays with us even if his answer does not. We all worry that some people cut corners on ethics and get away with it, and are perfectly happy doing so. We read history and see so many predatory kings and queens who seem untroubled by all the bloodshed they've caused. We look at some of our coworkers who seem to take more than they give and yet get paid the same and wonder: By doing the right thing, do we just open ourselves up for exploitation?

It's clear that ethics is *useful*. There is a nail for which morality is the hammer. In general, moral norms create conditions under which people can and will cooperate with one another. They ensure that the benefits of cooperation flow to everyone involved rather than just a few; they make sure cooperation doesn't come at anyone's expense.

Some people think asking "Why be moral?" is a kind of mistake.[5] The idea is that a good person does the right thing *because it's the right thing*. And most people do care about morality for its own sake. But they might still wonder if it's in their self-interest to be moral. Businesspeople in particular run their firms for profit. Some people—for example, your Marxist history professors—treat "profit" as a dirty word, as if by definition profit is evil and profit-seeking and ethics don't mix. That's extreme, but you might still wonder just how seeking profit-seeking and ethics do and don't go together.

Glaucon wants to know, if you could avoid all punishment for wrongdoing, would it still be in your self-interest to be a good person? But that question is probably irrelevant. There's almost always a risk of getting caught. That changes things.

So, let's revise Glaucon's example and his question: Take the lead character from the recent Showtime series *Dexter*. Dexter, you see, is a psychopath—he has no capacity or tendency to empathize with others. He only cares about himself. He values other people merely as *instruments*—they are useful tools that can help him get what he wants. This doesn't mean Dexter acts badly all the time—he brings doughnuts for coworkers, smiles, does favors, and the like.[6] But Dexter does so only because he wants a good reputation.

So, here's our first question: Imagine we invented a pill that would rewire Dexter's brain—it would turn him from a psychopath into a normal person, the kind of person who, though imperfect, genuinely cares for other people and ethics for their own sakes. Would Dexter have any reason to take the pill?

And here's our second question: Imagine we invented a second pill that would make you just like Dexter. It would turn you into a psychopath. Do you have good reasons not to take that pill?

The answer to both questions is yes.

The Prisoner's Dilemma and Other Games

Back in 1950, mathematicians, economists, and game theorists wanted to turn decision-making into a science. Two of them—Merrill Flood and Melvin

Table 7.1 The Prisoner's Dilemma.

	Player 2 Cooperates	*Player 2 Defects*
Player 1 Cooperates	*2 gets a small gain.* 1 gets a small gain.	*2 gets a large gain.* 1 suffers a major loss.
Player 1 Defects	*2 suffers a major loss.* 1 gets a large gain.	*2 suffers a small loss.* 1 suffers a small loss.

Dresher—produced what's perhaps the most famous decision-making dilemma of all time, now called the "Prisoner's Dilemma." The game gets its name from a hypothetical story in which two captured criminal suspects are given the opportunity to rat on one another or stay silent. The district attorney offers each of them "deals" about how much time they'll serve if they rat or keep quiet, but at the same time, how much time they serve depends on whether their accomplice—now locked in another room so the two criminals can't talk—talks or keeps quiet.

Let's give you the game in its most common form. There are two players, player 1 and player 2. They can't communicate with each other ahead of time. Each player has to make a move at the same time as the other. They each have only two moves, which we'll call "cooperate" and "defect." "Cooperate" means cooperating with the other prisoner, not with the police, by keeping quiet, while "defect" means ratting on your fellow prisoner. Table 7.1 shows what happens when the players make their moves. Imagine both players have access to this table and so know the payoffs:

Notice something weird about the game. Both players know ahead of time that they would rather be in the Cooperate-Cooperate box on the upper left than the Defect-Defect box on the lower right. Mutual defection is worse than mutual cooperation.

However, at the same time, both players have a strong incentive to defect. No matter what player 2 does, player 1 does better by defecting. If player 2 cooperates, player 1 gets a larger gain by defecting than by cooperating. If player 2 defects, player 1 suffers a smaller loss by defecting than by cooperating.

But the exact same thing goes for player 2. No matter what player 1 does, player 2 does better by defecting than by cooperating.

Consider how the game looks from either player's perspective.

As Table 7.2 shows, both players have a strong temptation to defect even though mutual cooperation is beneficial. So, the worry here is that even though mutual cooperation beats mutual defection, both players will defect.

Table 7.2 The Prisoner's Dilemma from a player's perspective.

	The Other Player Cooperates	*The Other Player Defects*
I cooperate	Mutually beneficial cooperation	Player 2 takes advantage of me. I'm a sucker. Temptation to cheat.
I defect	I take advantage of player 2. Temptation to cheat.	Mutually harmful defection.

This seems paradoxical because everyone knows mutual defection is a bad result.

Economists have played the Prisoner's Dilemma game with experimental subjects around the world. The game fundamentally measures whether players have a propensity to cheat or cooperate with each other. They've tried hundreds of variations on the game—for example, by having players meet ahead of time, having players play while stressed or happy, using players from different countries—to see how different factors affect how players play.

Consider also a few other experimental games. In each of these games, players are taught the rules ahead of time. Subjects play only after they show they understand the game.

A. *The Dictator Game.* Two subjects are randomly placed in two roles, the Dictator and the Recipient. The Dictator is given, say, $10. He may share as much money as he wants with the recipient or keep it all for himself. Whatever he says, goes. This game tests whether people placed in the "Dictator" role will be *unconditionally generous.*

B. *The Ultimatum Game.* We mentioned this game in chapter 1. Two subjects are randomly placed in two roles, the Proposer and the Responder. The Proposer is given, say, $10. He may propose to split the money however he likes (e.g., $6 for him and $4 for the Responder). The Responder then either accepts or rejects the split. If she accepts, they both get what the proposer proposed. If she rejects, they both get *nothing*—the money disappears. This game tests whether Proposers will be fair and whether Responders will punish unfairness at their own expense.

C. *The Trust Game.* Two subjects are randomly assigned to two roles, player 1 and player 2. Player 1 is given, say, $10. Player 1 may keep as much of that as he wants. Or he may send as much as he wants to player 2. Whatever amount player 1 chooses to send gets multiplied by 3. So, if player 1 chooses to send $1, then player 2 gets $3; if player 1 chooses to send all $10, player 2 gets $30. When player 2 receives the money, he may then decide to keep as much as he wants for himself, or send as much as he wants back to player 1. This game tests whether player 1 is disposed to trust player 2, and also whether player 2 turns out to be trustworthy. It also tests how player 2 reacts if player 1 doesn't trust him.

These games all have a few things in common: People play for real money (sometimes for very large amounts). Each game creates uncertainty about what other people will do. Each game creates a selfish incentive to violate or ignore some basic moral norm.

Now consider these two questions:

1. How would perfectly selfish people play these games?
2. How do *real* people play the games?

The first question you can figure out on paper. The Dictator keeps the money for herself, the Proposer proposes the minimum amount and the Responder accepts that, and player 1 in the Trust game keeps all the money for herself and sends nothing.

But real people don't play like that very often, even when large amounts of money are at stake, and the game is anonymous. Real people are generally disposed to share, be fair, trust, and be trustworthy, even when they won't be punished for acting otherwise. In the real world, people tend to cooperate rather than defect. In the real world, they share some money when they are the dictator. In the real world, they trust others and reward others for trusting them. Why? We don't play these games the way self-interested psychopaths would. Why not?

How Reputation and Sorting Change Everything

These games are supposed to illustrate the temptations and trade-offs we face in real life. Many real-life interactions are kind of like the Prisoner's Dilemma because we can benefit from taking advantage of others' cooperativeness, and we worry that others can do the same to us. We constantly face opportunities to be generous toward others or act selfishly. We can be fair or unfair, and we can decide whether to punish wrongdoing or not. We have to decide when and how much to trust others, knowing they might take advantage of our trust. And finally when people trust us, we sometimes have the power to betray their trust without any consequences.

But the basic versions of these games are also unrealistic in important ways. Players are strangers, chosen at random. They don't learn who the other player is. The experimenter anonymously records their moves, but no one ever learns how people play. Real life isn't quite like that.

Imagine we change how we play these games, to make them a little more realistic. Suppose you and one hundred other experimental subjects walk into a big auditorium. The experiment's administrator announces:

> Welcome, everyone! Please put on your name tags—you're going to need them. Today we're going to play a game called the Prisoner's Dilemma. Take a moment to study the rules. [If you need to review them, please do!] Now, here's the twist. I'm going to assign you a partner for the first round of the game. However, we're going to play many rounds, though I'm not going to tell you how many. Could be 3, could be 10, could be 100. After the first round, you will get to choose, by mutual agreement, your partner for the next round. To help you with that, I'm going to post how each of you played in previous games on this giant bulletin board over here. Oh, and if no one wants to play with you—if you can't find a willing partner—then come the next round, I'll once again assign you a partner at random.

This version of the game introduces two big twists. First, every move you make is public record. People know whether and how often you cooperate or cheat. Second, players get to choose their partner for each new round—or they get stuck with someone because no one wants to play with them.

So, how do you think this game would go? Notice how the incentives change. Come round 2 and beyond that, the cooperators find it easy to find partners. But no one wants to play with the defectors. Now, the connection between defection and self-interest looks very different. Sure, in any individual round, if you defect, you do better by defecting than by cooperating. But—and this is crucial—you then lose the chance to play with a cooperator in the next round, and get stuck playing with the other defectors. Having a public reputation changes the incentives. Taking advantage of others by defecting helps you in the short term but hurts you in the long term. In the long term, it's important to be seen as the kind of person who cooperates. So, over time, as this game continues, nearly everyone switches from defecting to cooperating.

These changes make the Prisoner's Dilemma more realistic, if not perfectly realistic. In real-life, people *choose* whether to do business, to make deals, to trade, to trust one another. In real life, people and companies have reputations. You buy Starbucks coffee in a strange place because you know what you're getting. Before you hire a plumber, you read reviews on Yelp, or ask people on your neighborhood Facebook page whom they recommend. When you apply for a job, potential employers might ask for recommendations from your previous bosses or your professors, or they might use your college's reputation as a proxy for *you*.

Now you might understand why we all seem to love gossip so much. Gossip is a mechanism our ancestors evolved to help keep everyone in line. We're constantly assessing whom we can and cannot trust. For almost anything our ancestors wanted or we today want to do, success requires collaborating with the right people.

Glaucon's magic ring thought experiment suggests that it's in your self-interest to be *seen* as good, not necessarily to actually *be* good. However, Glaucon imagines away an important real-life constraint: In the real world, it's difficult for most people to be seen as good unless they actually *are* good. Consider:

1. *Lying takes extra effort.* It's easier to recall memories than to fabricate something. When you lie to someone, you have to invent new details and then simultaneously push them into memory, so you can use those same details again if that person asks you.

2. *People aren't great lie detectors, but we get better over time, the longer we know someone.* It's easy to get away with a quick lie in a quick interaction: "Oh, sure, I love that band, too," you say to impress some person you just met. But as the conversation progresses, it gets harder to keep up the façade: "Really, what's your favorite album?" "Um, well . . ."[7]

3. *Cheating, defrauding, and taking advantage of others is much harder.* Lying is difficult enough. But if you send the customer the wrong item, cut corners on quality, overcharge for repairs, and so on, it's easier for the customer to detect your bad behavior, and you're far more likely to be caught.

4. *Once exposed, it's difficult to fix your reputation.* In any interaction, your chances of getting caught might be low. But once you do get caught, the harm can be long-lasting. When we learn, for example, that Kevin Spacey made sexual advances on a 14-year-old and may have sexually abused others, he loses his job and his movies get cut from theaters. We don't know yet whether he'll make a comeback.

So, think back to Dexter's Dilemma. Dexter is a psychopath. We offer him a pill that will turn him into a normal, decent, but morally imperfect person, like you. Would he take the pill? The answer: Yes, of course! Indeed, Dexter admits as much for most of the show. Dexter knows that if others learn his real feelings, it'll be a disaster for him. He has to "fake" it, to pretend to care about others and to care about right and wrong, but he finds that *exhausting*. He's constantly on the verge of getting caught. Dexter knows he'd be happier if he could just take a pill that made him *actually care*.

In short: It's in your interest to be seen as a good person. The easiest way to be seen as a good person is to actually be a good person.

What Games Reveal about the Structure of Morality

Games like this don't simply help us answer the question "Why Be Moral?," they also tell us something about the structure of ethics itself.

Back in the 1980s, the political scientist Robert Axelrod wanted to investigate the best general way to play the Prisoner's Dilemma game in the long run.[8] To do so, he created artificial "players." Each player was a mathematical algorithm with a built-in strategy. (Eventually he turned these into computer codes.) Strategies included behaviors such as (A) "Always cooperate," (B) "Always defect," (C) "Alternate between cooperating and defecting," (D) "Do the opposite of what the other player did," and a number of other both simple and complicated strategies. He had the players play hundreds of games against other players. He then examined which types of strategies ended up generating the best outcomes for the players.

He found that the best strategies were variations on "TIT FOR TAT," a move proposed by mathematical psychologist Anatol Rapoport. In TIT FOR TAT, the player cooperates the first round. In every subsequent round, it copies whatever the other player did the last round.

In general, Axelrod found that successful strategies—the ways of playing repeated prisoners dilemmas which generate good results for the player—tend to have the following features.

1. *Nice:* They begin by cooperating. Successful strategies cooperate by default and are never the first to defect.
2. *Punishing:* If the *other* player defects at some point, successful strategies at some point *punish* that player's defection by defecting in response.
3. *Forgiving:* If the other player stops defecting and starts cooperating again, successful strategies give that player another chance and begin cooperating again too.
4. *Nonenvious:* Successful strategies aim to maximize personal returns, but do not try to *beat* the other player. Successful players do not try to get *more* than the other players.

Now think about commonsense, day-to-day ethical codes. Think about various cultures around the world, especially those where people seem to be happy and flourishing. Think about the various moral codes and ideas those people espouse, or more importantly, *actually practice*. You'll probably notice that their moral codes also seem to be nice, punishing but forgiving, and nonenvious. In the West, for instance, we play fair with others by default. We think wrongdoers at some point should be punished for wrongdoing, but we also create various ways for them to demonstrate contrition, to pay their "debts," and to be accepted back into the moral community. We have prohibitions against envy.[9]

The Limitations of Reputation: Avoiding Traps

Although the value of a good reputation goes a long way toward overcoming the pernicious effect of self-interest, it is no panacea. In real life, we don't have an impartial, perfect experimental administrator who broadcasts our every move. Reputation is imperfect. Some people are scoundrels, but "get away" with lying, cheating, and stealing. Other people acquire bad reputations despite doing nothing wrong. People often confuse things like how charismatic or friendly a person is with how trustworthy and fair a person is. They even confuse how *physically attractive* a person is with how trustworthy and fair a person is.[10] Our "morality monitoring" systems can be tricked or hacked. Sometimes they track the wrong thing.

Reputation is a valuable but imperfect proxy for ethical behavior. We can rely on it for guidance, but we cannot rely on it blindly We must be on guard against the situations in which the desire for a good reputation can lead us astray.

Looking Good vs. Doing Good

The desire for a good reputation is the glue that binds self-interest and morality together. But there's a downside. Sometimes the desire for good reputation can cause us to act badly or focus on the wrong things.

In the middle of 2018, there was suddenly a frown campaign against using plastic straws. Using a plastic straw certainly isn't environmentally friendly, but activists have somehow seized on the idea that we should cut them out entirely. They often claim that Americans use 500 million straws a day (one and a half straws per person), though the source of this widely cited figure comes from questionable, non-peer-reviewed "research" conducted by a 9-year-old boy.[11]

Unfortunately, this gesture is largely symbolic. It feels good to skip the straw, but straws aren't much of a problem. The great garbage patch in the Pacific Ocean wasn't created by American straws. Even if somehow all the straws thrown out on the coasts ended up in the ocean, that would account for less than three-hundredths of a percent of plastic pollution entering the oceans each year.[12]

As we write this, Starbucks plans to eliminate straws from its stores in response to consumer pressure. However, as of our writing this, it turns out the proposed replacement lids use even more plastic then the old lids and straws together.[13] If everyone recycles the lids, that might be better for the environment, but most people will probably throw them out.

Glaucon's question—Is it better to be bad but seen as good or to be good but seen as bad—turns out not merely to be hypothetical. Businesses face this kind of problem every day.

One reason businesses face this problem is that they operate in a global business environment. As we'll explain further in the coming chapters, to evaluate the moral status of various business decisions, it won't be enough to consult our untutored moral intuitions. We also need to trace cause and effect, which requires having some solid understanding of economics.

But, alas, the average consumer—and even the average business ethicist—has no background in economic theory, and turns out to be systematically mistaken about basic economics.[14] The same goes for other issues. Tracing environmental impact requires a sophisticated understanding of ecology. Tracing a social impact requires a sophisticated understanding of sociology.

Consumers usually lack this kind of knowledge. This means they'll tend to evaluate business activities based on *what sounds good* rather than what *is good*. They'll sometimes reward you for doing the wrong thing and punish you for doing the right thing.

For instance, you'll notice every year Major League Baseball and the National Football League will partner with the Susan B. Komen Foundation, a charity which aims to reduce the incidence of and help cure breast cancer. MLB and NFL players will wear pink on various days to signal their leagues' support.[15] But despite rising donations and revenues for the Komen Foundation, only about a third of its funding goes to cancer research, screening, or treatment.[16] Much of it goes to "education," which means "raising awareness." "We're raising awareness!" is the first excuse people make when they're not doing much good. Charity Watch—a charity watchdog organization—gives Komen only a C+ rating.[17] Consumer Reports, Charity Navigator, and Charity Watch give many *other* breast cancer organizations far higher ratings. Nevertheless, MLB and the NFL partner with the Komen Foundation not because it's the most effective charity but because it has the most effective *branding*. Before you go blaming MLB and the NFL, remember that they do this because consumers reward them for doing so. They take the bait but we set it.

In some cases, businesses make business decisions which in fact do a great deal of good but sound awful. For instance, consider the following scenario:

> A hurricane has destroyed power lines. Using backup generators, Home Depot is able to remain open. The manager anticipates a large number of people will come to the store, hoping to buy generators, batteries, and plywood. A thought occurs to him—there's not enough supplies for all the customers. What should he do?

Now consider a possible answer: He could raise prices dramatically in light of the dramatic increase in demand. To most people, untrained in economics, this sounds downright *evil*. They'll call it "price gouging" and say that it exploits desperate customers.

In this case, though, their hearts are in the right place, but their heads are not. On the contrary, once you understand economics, you understand that after a disaster, raising the prices has a far higher chance of getting the goods to the people who most need them than keeping prices the same.[18] Keeping prices the same guarantees that items will fly off the shelf. There will be a massive shortage of goods. The goods will go not to the people who need them the most but the people who get there first. In contrast, raising prices forces customers to economize on scarce resources—and there is no time where that is *more important* than after a disaster. It will eliminate a shortage and help ensure the goods are widely distributed. Higher prices may prevent the poorest customers from getting what they need, but they still do a far *better* job distributing according to need than keeping prices the same.

All that is basically uncontroversial among economists, but it sounds monstrous to most people, and, if you haven't taken ECON yet, it probably sounds monstrous to you. The issue here is that our moral intuitions often fail to track the underlying reality of what causes what.

We'll return to this point a few times over the next few chapters. In chapter 9, we'll explain more about basic economics and how making socially responsible decisions requires business leaders to know some social science. In chapter 6, we discussed at greater length the issues of dealing with poverty.

Moral Grandstanding

In 2017, Anheuser-Busch (AB) donated about two million cans of water to places hit by hurricanes and other disasters. That's wonderful, and AB is to be commended. It's fine for AB to advertise that it helped people. But Anheuser-Busch spent on the order of $5 million during the Super Bowl LII bragging about giving the water away.[19] It may have spent more money advertising its good deeds than it did doing good deeds. Many people felt there was something unsavory about that. (Still, even if the critics are right, AB still did more good for needy people than its critics did.)

Reputation is the glue that binds self-interest and ethics. Because of that, there's constant temptation to try to inflate your reputation, to make people think you're more ethical than you are. As the philosopher David Schmidtz likes to say, "If you're main goal is to show your heart's in the right place, it isn't."

Moral grandstanding is the act of using moral language for the purpose of self-promotion. We may live in the Golden Age of Moral Grandstanding. Social media means we're all monitoring each other's behavior all the time, and so people compete to display how good and virtuous they are. The current trends of (1) linking everything to politics and (2) pushing for socially conscious capitalism have the unfortunate by-products of inducing pop stars, TV celebrities, firms, and your friends to frequently use moral language for self-aggrandizement. Just like Anheuser-Busch, many of us are spending more time and effort trying to convince others we're good than we are actually doing good.

Justin Tosi and Brandon Warmke identify a few different forms of grandstanding:[20]

1. *Piling on*: This a self-serving form of "me too!" Someone else makes a moral claim, and then everyone has to show they agree, not because they want to reinforce the moral norm but because they want to display their good character.
2. *Ramping up*: This is a tendency to compete to assert the most extreme version of a moral claim. The more extreme you are, the better you must be. For instance, imagine someone says, "That was unkind." Another responds, "It was not merely unkind, but sexist." A third says, "It was unkind, sexist, and classist." A fourth adds, "This is literally worse than Hitler." Here, people exaggerate their moral claims not because they want to get ethics right, but because they want to display they have heightened ethical sensitivity.

3. *Trumping up*. A closely related way to display heightened ethical sensitivity—and therefore heightened virtue—is to try to find moral problems in innocent activities. Imagine you start eating General Tso's chicken. Your friend says, "Oh, that's inauthentic and disrespectful of Chinese culture." You buy a pair of sneakers. Your friend says, "Do you know that that brand is owned by another brand whose CEO gives money to [insert evil cause]." Maybe your friend says this because he's an especially moral person. Or, maybe your friend is trying to signal to everyone that he's *better* than everyone else, because he sees all the injustices others overlook. Maybe you need a new friend.

4. *Dismissiveness*. Moral grandstanders characteristically dismiss disagreement with their judgments. They also characteristically refuse to answer questions about why their judgments are correct. If you disagree or ask them to explain themselves, they say, "I'm obviously right. It's not my job to explain things to you. Shape up." If a person says a hard math problem is easy, he's probably trying to show off how smart he is. Similarly, when a person says a complicated moral issue is obvious, he's probably trying to show off how moral he is.

Tosi and Warmke say that of course not all cases of piling on, ramping up, trumping up, and dismissiveness are instances of grandstanding. Sometimes it's important to signal agreement. Sometimes it's important to identify additional wrongs or rights. Sometimes people do notice injustices that others overlook. And some opinions aren't worth arguing for or against. But, they add, that's all partly why moral grandstanding is a dangerous activity. Grandstanders not only use moral language to promote their status, they also pervert what in other cases would be appropriate uses of moral language.

Reputation matters. But one danger of chasing reputation is that it may cause us to engage in moral grandstanding.

Charitable CSR, Reputation, and the Bottom Line: Trap, Benefit, or Both?

In chapter 2, we explained that to serve society, a business does not need to engage in charitable corporate social responsibility (CSR) or support various civic and political causes. A business should and can serve society through producing its core product or service. We also explained that CSR is not a substitute for business ethics. Donating 5 percent of your profits to charity doesn't make up for unethical business practices, nor does failure to donate to charity suffice to show your business is unethical.

Here, let's pause to ask how CSR activities can affect a firm's reputation. When companies engage in various CSR endeavors—especially when these endeavors are effectively marketed—this can change public perception of the firm. In some cases, CSR can improve their reputation. (In certain cases— such as with Enron or ADM—the firm might not deserve that.) How does that affect the firm's bottom line?

One hypothetical mechanism is that if your firm donates 1 percent in profits, perhaps this will enhance your firm's reputation sufficiently to attract a high enough number of new or repeat customers that you'll end up making all that money back and more. For every dollar you donate, you earn a dollar and fifteen cents in revenue. Unfortunately, while there are a few businesses that benefit from this strategy, there's little evidence it systematically succeeds.

Instead, a more plausible mechanism has to do with how CSR affects recruiting. Imagine a firm has taken some strong moral stances, with CSR as a guiding vision of the firm. Imagine the firm has done things which demonstrate it actually sticks to its word when push comes to shove—so it's clear the CSR message is not just empty moral gesturing. Now think of how this affects employee recruitment. Although most employees will mostly be motivated by the intrinsic enjoyment of the job, salary, work-life balance, and the like, all things equal, more ethically minded applicants would prefer to work at more ethically minded companies. People hate the cognitive dissonance that comes with working for a company they think is immoral or whose leaders they cannot admire.

So, all things equal, having a company with a strong reputation for ethics, including to some degree having a reputation for engaging in worthwhile CSR endeavors, can help attract a slightly more ethical workplace. As a result, such firms have slightly more ethical internal cultures, and are filled with employees who are somewhat less likely to break the law, engage in fraud, or make bad choices. In turn, this means companies are less likely to do things that lead to major scandals, lawsuits, or costly fines from regulatory boards.

At least, that's what the research generally shows. For instance, Marc Orlitzky and John Benjamin analyzed more than fifty studies examining the relationship between CSR and corporate financial performance. They find that, combined, these studies show slight positive relationship—more CSR causes (and is not simply correlated) with better financial performance. The reason is that such firms have a significant decrease in serious financial risk for lawsuits and fines.[21]

However, there is also evidence of some danger from focusing too much on CSR. Economists John List and Fatemah Momeni have conducted a series of experiments with 3,000 workers. They find that introducing CSR components into their jobs tends to induce the employees to lie and shirk a bit more.[22] The problem seems to be related to a general phenomenon psychologists call "moral licensing" or "moral accounting." When people feel like they are doing *extra* good on one dimension, they give themselves permission to do a little extra bad on another. Good deeds count as merit slips and bad deeds as demerits, so they "cancel out" in their minds. A badly implemented CSR program can thus do more harm than good.

What this means for managers is that in principle, a CSR campaign can help attract somewhat more ethical employees and help reduce the financial risks of bad behavior. But this works only if you help employees understand our main advice, that CSR is no substitute for ethics. That your firm donates 5 percent to a good cause doesn't "balance" employee malfeasance.

As we write, Elizabeth Holmes of Theranos has been indicted for fraud. Theranos promised to disrupt the blood testing industry by providing a means of testing smaller amounts of blood, more cheaply, for a wider range of medical purposes. Theranos raised hundreds of millions in venture capital and at one point was valued in the billions as a firm. But the problem— as you may know—is that the technology didn't work. It's possible that the Elizabeth Holmes, the founder of the company, was simply selling snake oil and thought she could get away with it. However, at least one major documentary argues she was a true believer in her technology, who thought lying/exaggerating today was necessary to raise the capital and do the research to make the product eventually work as advertised.[23] We don't know which theory is true. But we do know that people find it relatively easy to lie for a good cause.

Beyond Reputation: Aligning Incentives

We have seen that reputation is a useful but imperfect tool for combating the effects of unchecked self-interest. The most important thing we can do to supplement the value of a good reputation is to create incentive structures in which individuals are rewarded for ethical behavior. In the story that opened this chapter, GEICO's regional VP set the tone for the entire office. He told salespeople their job is to try to sell the right amount of insurance for the customer and told adjusters that they should pay claimants every penny they're owed. He explained why this was a good business plan. The research backs him up. GEICO could benefit in the short run by underpaying claims but would lose in the long run when people switch to other insurance carriers.

But of course a nice speech isn't enough. GEICO (at least when Jason worked there) spends a great deal of time training salespeople and adjusters. After initial training, coaches help them with their first few days of cases and calls. They spend weeks under higher levels of supervision with a mentor, who will monitor at least a few calls from each employee every day. Even once they're independent, they know that at random, their calls will be monitored and their work audited.

None of this is done in an aggressive or punitive way. Employees don't fear being monitored. Rather, the company makes it clear that they're trying to help ensure employees do their best. They're also trying to ensure the employee helps the company keep its word. To illustrate, if an employee pays $3,000 on a claim, but should have paid $5,000, the company will quickly tell the employee his mistake and pay the rest. Employees who excel at keeping the company's word—at paying every cent the company should pay—get promoted faster. When GEICO evaluates employees for raises and promotion, they are rewarded for doing the right thing.

Imagine if, instead, when doing evaluations, GEICO rated adjusters by how *little* they paid. Imagine they kept a bulletin board up scoring each employee by how little in claims they'd paid out that month, and the employees with the lowest numbers had the best chance of moving up. If GEICO did that—rest assured, it does not!—it wouldn't have mattered what the big boss said. It would mean that GEICO in fact valued cutting corners, and that adjusters' job was to make the company money.

This means that you always must be careful that the thing that you are measuring and rewarding is a good proxy for the type of behavior you want to encourage. Further, individual employees have their own incentives. What's in an employee's self-interest can go against the group interest. In addition, even though GEICO benefits in the long run from its reputation as an honest, service-oriented company, individual employees remain largely anonymous. You remember that GEICO was fair and honest, not that Kara at GEICO was fair and honest. So, how do we keep Kara fair and honest? We take up these question in chapter 8 where we explore how a company can align what it values with what it rewards.

Note that while it's important to align incentives with a company's goals, too much focus on incentives can backfire. Consider why a high-level creative employee might do high-quality work. For one, the employee has "intrinsic motivation": She might enjoy her work, value excellence for its own sake, and so on. Two, she has "external motivation": She wants to be paid, be promoted, receive prestige and acclaim, and so on. What psychologist Edward Deci and others have found is that when management schemes make incentives too strong and too prominent, employees often lose their internal motivation and instead focus on external motivations.[24] For instance, if a university pays faculty a piecemeal bonus for each paper they publish, the faculty might stop caring about doing good work for the sake of good work and instead simply try to publish as much as possible.

Summary

- For almost everyone, long-term success requires cooperating with, getting assistance from, making deals with, and partnering with others.
- Your ability to do these things depends upon whether people regard you as fair, honest, deserving, respectful, and trustworthy.
- In the short run, lying, cheating, and stealing can benefit you, but only if you don't get caught.
- In the long run, the chances of getting caught are sufficiently high that the best policy is to simply be honest and fair.
- The easiest way to have a good reputation is to actually be good.
- The desire for a good reputation presents its own moral traps.
- In a complex economy, sometimes actions that do the most good sometimes *sound bad* to consumers and journalists, while actions that are harmful, wasteful, or do little good sometimes *sound good* to consumers and journalists.
- People, and businesses, often abuse moral language for self-aggrandizement. Sometimes, when people take a moral stand in public, their main goal is to convince you they are morally better than others.
- We'll cover how to deal with these last two problems in more depth in later chapters.

Discussion Questions

1. In the real world, customers, activists, journalists, and others might punish your company for doing the right thing. Sometimes actions that do the most good *sound bad*, while actions that hurt people or do little good *sound good*. How many examples of this can you think of?
2. Go through your social media accounts for ten minutes. How many of your friends' posts seem to be about increasing their status and

reputation? How often do they seem to engage in moral grandstanding? What about you and your posts?

3. What kind of reputation do you think you have? What kind of reputation do you want?

4. Pick five companies. What is their reputation? Do they deserve it? Do some of them have a worse reputation than they deserve? Do others have a better reputation? How might someone—a marketer, a journalist— change that?

Notes

1. Indeed, see Brennan and Magness 2019 for an account of just how bad academia is.
2. Ainslie 2006.
3. Holusha 1990; Hart and Svobada 2008.
4. Tosi and Warmke 2018.
5. Prichard 1912.
6. He's also a serial killer of serial killers, but we'll leave that part out here, since it doesn't bear on the question we're about to ask.
7. Bond and DePaulo 2011.
8. Axelrod 1984.
9. Envy is distinct from jealously. Jealousy takes the form of: "My friend has a cool car and I don't; I wish I also had that cool car." Envy takes the form of: "My friend has a cool car and I don't; I wish my friend didn't have that car."
10. Hollier 2021.
11. Minter 2018.
12. Jambeck et al. 2015; Minter 2018.
13. Britschgi 2018.
14. Caplan 2007.
15. Footer 2017.
16. Begley and Roberts 2012.
17. Carrig 2017.
18. Dorfman 2016; Zwolinski 2008.
19. Orlov 2018.
20. Tosi and Warmke 2018: ch. 3.
21. Orlitzky and Benjamin 2001. See also Verschoor and Murphy 2002.
22. List and Momeni 2017.
23. *The Inventor*, HBO.
24. Deci and Ryan 2010.

8

The Effect of Incentives

Managing for Ethics

Basic Lesson: Every business has to determine how to motivate its employees to cooperate in a productive manner, while also limiting temptations for employees to exploit the business for private gain. Normative commitments can help address this problem, but designing good incentives is essential. If inputs are easy to measure, employees can be compensated based on how much work they do, but if inputs are hard to measure, it may be more effective to tie compensation to a firm's output in the form of stock options and profit-sharing. However, care must be taken to ensure that executives do not misrepresent the value of the company or engage in fraud in order to inflate stock prices. Compensation packages that lengthen the vesting period of stock options and allow ill-gotten gains to be clawed back, as well as whistleblower programs that reward those who expose fraud, can help prevent bad behavior and ensure that business leaders focus on genuine productivity.

What Was the Mayor's Office Thinking?

The Boston Fire Department is one of the oldest institutions in America. It traces its origins to the mid-1600s, when the Massachusetts Bay Colony hired its first fire chief and organized a paid department to assist him. As the city of Boston grew, so did the size and budget of the Fire Department, which now stands at around $187 million per year. Like many old institutions, the Department has been formally reorganized on a number of occasions, but it also has traditions that go back generations.

Through accidents of history, the Boston Fire Department arrived at the year 2000 without having any formal limits on the number of paid sick days firefighters could take. Within the Department, there was an informal norm that someone should only take sick leave if he or she really needed it. However, the Mayor's Office became concerned with the unlimited sick leave policy as it reviewed the Department's budget and saw that firefighters took 6,432

Business Ethics for Better Behavior. Jason Brennan, William English, John Hasnas, and Peter Jaworski, Oxford University Press. © Oxford University Press 2021. DOI: 10.1093/oso/9780190076559.003.0008

sick days the previous year. That's a lot of days to be paying firefighters for not working! Or was it? People get sick and you don't want them bringing germs into the workplace or to be a weak link in an emergency situation. In any case, the Mayor's Office thought that the number looked high.

The position of the Mayor's Office was straightforward. If there's no limit on sick days, then firefighters would have no incentive to conserve them. The Mayor's Office presumed that people were likely abusing the unlimited paid sick leave policy. The office wanted to prevent any such abuse and ideally save money. Besides, they thought, every other modern organization places limits on paid sick leave, why should the Fire Department be different? Any consultant brought in to control costs would think that this is a no-brainer—simply place a limit on sick days. So, that's what the Mayor's Office did. On December 1, 2001, the old policy was terminated and a new policy put in place that limited each firefighter's sick days to fifteen per year. Firefighters taking more than fifteen days per year of sick leave would have their pay docked.

Was this policy change a good idea? Think about the possible benefits and downsides. One way to approach this is to ask yourself how a firefighter might feel about this change, and how he or she might respond.

The new policy was declared shortly before the holiday season, which is a busy time for the Boston Fire Department. It's cold around Christmas and New Year's, and many people build fires at home. More than a few people consume libations around the holidays as well, which can lead to reckless or forgetful behavior. It's no surprise that medical and fire emergencies increase during this season. It's one of the most important times to have firefighters on the job.

However, firefighters are people too. They have families and friends with whom they'd like to spend the holidays, drinking eggnog around a cozy fire. For the first time, firefighters also know that they are entitled to fifteen days of sick leave. So, what did they do?

Ten times as many firefighters took sick leave during the holiday season compared to earlier years. Thus, fire stations ended up being understaffed at the busiest time of the year. Why did this happen?

In previous years, firefighters knew that the holidays were a busy time. If someone called in sick, he or she would be burdening their colleagues, and there was also a strong norm against using sick days if you weren't really sick. So, firefighters policed themselves, raising eyebrows and asking questions if someone seemed to be taking a lot of sick days at an inconvenient time. For the most part, people didn't abuse the system of unlimited sick days.

However, when the Mayor's Office identified a specific number as a limit, all of a sudden, sick days turned into something different—they became something that firefighters felt entitled to. It was as if the policy said, "You can take up to 15 days, and it's no problem." The norm against using sick days only when sick vanished. If you have ten sick days left when Christmas rolls around, why not call in sick to spend some time with your family? The policy says that you're allowed to.

A second dynamic was also at play. Do you think the firefighters liked being told that the Department needed a new policy because people were abusing the old one? That's quite an accusation. Firefighters felt that they had been responsible in how they took sick days, and here was the Mayor's Office telling them that they couldn't be trusted. To firefighters, the new policy sent a message, and many of them resented what they saw as an attempt to micromanage their behavior. As a result, firefighters likely felt less of a duty of loyalty to the Mayor's Office as well.

As you might imagine, the Mayor's Office was not pleased. In response to the increase in sick leave over the holiday, the Fire Commissioner cancelled holiday bonuses for all firefighters. How do you think firefighters liked that? By this point, whatever goodwill existed between the rank-and-file firefighters and the people who called the shots in City Hall was severely compromised. The following year, firefighters used a total of 13,431 sick days. This was more than double the amount of sick leave that was claimed the year before the new policy went into effect (6,432).

The entire point of the new policy was to save money by conserving the amount of sick days that firefighters took. It was a colossal failure. The policy not only doubled the number of sick days claimed; it also lead to distrust and resentment and decreased the number of firefighters on the job when they were most needed.

Managing human beings is hard. We saw in the last chapter that the value of reputation alone was not sufficient to ensure ethical behavior by employees. Success also requires an alignment of the incentives of individuals with the values of the firm. This requires attention not only to financial rewards but also to the effect of norms and convictions that can lead people to act well, even when they can personally benefit from unethical action.

In the case of the Boston Fire Department, firefighters had developed informal mechanisms for limiting the abuse of sick days. Despite the apparent incentives to take advantage of an unlimited number of sick days, in practice the Fire Department had, over the course of decades and even centuries, developed norms that led firefighters to use sick days only when they were really needed and to police each other if someone started to abuse the system. The Mayor's Office was right to be concerned about the incentives at play with an unlimited policy, but officials didn't understand the role that norms and informal self-governance were already playing.

When it comes to being an effective manager and devising effective corporate policies, there isn't a one-size-fits-all approach. Managers have to understand the existing norms at play in their organization and to take into account the unique features of any given industry, an organization's history, and local context. On top of that, they have to take into account human psychology, which may be the most difficult task of all. When we impose rules upon others, they may resent or react negatively to our imposition. They may try to game those rules. There's no guarantee new policies will work as intended, or even make things better, despite our good intentions. Ultimately, managing human beings is hard because it requires judgment regarding how these pieces all fit together.

There are, however, general principles and mechanisms that managers can draw on to help people do their best and to incline organizations to be successful.

In this chapter we'll examine ways to encourage people to do their best, as well as ways to prevent people from doing their worst. The two are related, and you'll see common themes that overlap. The overarching question that we want to answer throughout is: How can we provide people with the motivation and knowledge needed to act well?

Measuring and Rewarding Performance

One of the most difficult problems besetting corporate management is how to assign rewards to employees that align everyone's incentives with the success of the corporate venture. One of the reasons for this is that it's often hard to know exactly how much work someone is really doing. The principal (manager) will not possess the information needed to accurately assess and reward the agent (employee). There are two potential ways to solve this.

One approach is to develop techniques for better measuring the input of employees and then rewarding them according to those inputs. Another approach is to make it in employees' interest to work hard by giving them a share of the output.

Rewarding Inputs: Hours, Metrics, and Employee Reviews

You are probably familiar with one the most basic methods of measuring input, which is counting hours worked. Some companies require workers to check in when they arrive at work and check out when they leave. Others allow employees to self-report, while keeping an eye out for any discrepancies. Some law firms require reporting in intervals as short as five minutes, which makes sense if you're charging a client $1,000 an hour. However, how do you know that an employee is actually working after he or she clocks in? What's to stop employees from just playing games on their phones?

Many companies institute review processes through which employees receive feedback from peers and managers regarding how well they are perceived to be doing their job. These reviews also generally involve setting goals or milestones for the future, which will later be used to judge an employee's performance. These sorts of performance reviews aim to measure and reward inputs at a general level, but it may be possible to measure inputs more directly.

The management scholar Peter Drucker famously argued, "If you can't measure it, you can't improve it."[1] Identifying and measuring all the factors that contribute to a firm's productivity are common goals for any executive team. If metrics can be developed to track these factors, then it may make sense to reward employees according to those metrics. For example, an insurance agent could be rewarded for the number of policies she sells each month. A customer service representative could be rewarded for the number of inquiries he resolves per week. And a coffee shop barista could be rewarded for the number of customers she serves per hour during busy periods. These metrics provide some indication of how much work an employee is doing, and rewarding employees for high metrics should incentivize them to be productive.

There are, however, two potential drawbacks to using metric-based compensation. First, a metric may not capture everything that is important, which can create perverse incentives. If workers try to maximize their performance on a partial metric, that may lead them to neglect other important aspects of their job.

For example, if a customer service agent is paid based on the number of inquiries that she answers on a helpdesk platform, she may race through responses in order to answer as many as possible. However, the quality of these rushed responses will likely be low and thus not address a customer's question, leading to additional inquiries or to losing a customer altogether. So, the raw number of responses is a poor metric on its own. Perhaps it could be combined with customer satisfaction ratings to produce a better metric— one that tracked both the quantity and quality of a customer service agent's responses.

In sum, managers need to be careful that what they are measuring and rewarding is, in fact, what they want to be improving.

A second problem with metric-based compensation is that it can provide strong incentives for wrongdoing. Recall that the principal-agent problem is fundamentally about the limits of information. Managers often find it difficult to monitor the positive contributions of employees in real time. However, it's also the case that managers find it difficult to monitor the negative actions of employees as well. If a significant portion of an employee's compensation is tied to hitting some performance metric, you can be sure that an employee is going to care about performing well on that metric. Employees might care so much, however, that they resort to unethical or illegal conduct to ensure that the metric looks good. This conduct could avoid detection by management for a long time, doing a great deal of damage to the firm before it is discovered. Put another way, if management provides large incentives to perform well on certain metrics and employees can raise their numbers through unethical actions that are hard to monitor, then management is effectively incentivizing employees to act badly.

For example, after the financial crisis of 2008, banks struggled to put themselves on solid financial ground. One of the most profitable strategies for a consumer bank to pursue was a practice known as "cross-selling." This involves selling new products and accounts to existing customers. If a customer has a checking account, a bank can increase its revenues by getting that customer to open up credit card accounts, a mortgage or home equity line of credit, or even an insurance policy. Not only do these additional accounts bring in more fees, but a customer who has multiple accounts with a bank is less likely to leave.

Executives at Wells Fargo heavily encouraged cross-selling. In 2008, bankers at Wells Fargo were told that they were each expected to cross-sell eight products per day, and in 2010 the quota was raised to eight and a half per day.[2] During some months, the quota was set as high as twenty products per day.[3] At some branches, employees were told that anyone falling short of their quotas for two months would be fired. The pressure to meet sales quotas was intense.[4] So, what do you think happened?

From 2011 to 2016 some 5,300 Wells Fargo employees fraudulently opened accounts in customers' names without their consent. How many accounts? Estimates range from 2 million to 3.5 million.[5]

Who was to blame? Wells Fargo executives blamed these employees and fired most of them once the pattern of fraud was exposed. However, the problem was clearly systematic. 5,300 bankers didn't all come up with the idea to commit fraud on their own. They were responding to management's quotas—quotas that were often impossible to meet without committing fraud.

Who benefited from these inflated sales numbers? Primarily, it was executives and stockholders. From 2010 to 2015, Wells Fargo's stock more than doubled because of the impressive sales numbers the bank reported. So, while low-level employees were pressured to fraudulently open accounts and then fired when they did, top executives who set the quotas and applied the pressure received tens of millions of dollars as the value of their stock options rose. At least, that's what happened until the scandal became public and the lawsuits started. Wells Fargo was ultimately forced to pay over $2 billion in penalties.[6]

This kind of thing has happened before. In 1992, Sears faced a major scandal when it became clear that employees around the country were selling customers unnecessary parts and charging for unnecessary labor. When this is happening everywhere, it can't be a problem of a few bad apples. It has to be a bad barrel spoiling otherwise good apples. It turns out that in the face of declining revenues, Sears management had introduced specific quotas to their outlets—sell this many brake pads, this many shock absorbers, and the like. Since the quotas were arbitrarily determined, there was no way for most employees to comply with them other than by ripping off unwitting customers. This doesn't excuse the employee's behavior—they are still responsible for making bad choices. But Sears management was responsible for setting up the bad incentives.[7]

Economists have long pointed out that "You get what you incentivize." However, when using metrics to reward performance, managers need to understand exactly what they are incentivizing. Metrics that are too narrow may lead people to neglect important aspects of a job that aren't captured by those metrics. And placing a lot of weight on metrics that are difficult to satisfy may lead people to take shortcuts that are unethical and illegal in order to hit their targets.

Employee review procedures can have the same effects, even if they go beyond simple metrics. In the years leading up to its catastrophic bankruptcy, Enron employed an extremely competitive employee review system. A twenty-person "performance review committee" would evaluate each employee twice a year based on whether the employee brought in more money than his or her colleagues as well as on feedback from peers, customers, and supervisors. Employees in the bottom 20 percent could be fired, while top-performing employees would receive large bonuses.[8] Many believe that this process helped create a cutthroat culture that incentivized risky behavior, impeded the flow of information, and made employees less collaborative.

Finally, there are circumstances in which metric-based reward systems and performance reviews may have unintended consequences because of complexities of human psychology. As Jerry Muller argues in *The Tyranny of Metrics*, people object to being judged by metrics that they believe don't capture, or are at odds with, important aspects of their work. For example, a teacher who frequently challenges students in order to motivate them to do their best may receive low student evaluation scores. Judging the teacher by these scores would misrepresent the quality and value of his or her teaching. The teacher will be in the difficult position of having to choose between teaching in a way that is best for students or teaching in a way that is best for the teacher.[9]

Moreover, as Daniel Pink has documented, attempts to surveil performance often breed resentment and anxiety among employees.[10] People can feel constrained, nervous, or annoyed when their work is constantly scrutinized, diminishing their sense of agency and autonomy. Conversely, the internal analytics team at Google has found that the best managers avoid micromanaging, while extending freedom and trust to employees.[11] Laszlo Bock, the Senior Vice President of People Operations at Google, has gone so far as to argue that people do their best work when they "feel free."[12] Of course, managing software engineers and managing bakery clerks might be different propositions.

So, what is a company to do? The answer is, it depends. Can inputs be measured in a manner that is meaningful and sufficiently comprehensive? If so, it may make sense to reward employees based on those metrics. However, managers need to pay close attention to the strategies that employees use to make their numbers look good, ensuring that they don't involve shortcuts that are unethical or illegal—or simply misleading. Managers also need to consider the overall culture created by review processes, aiming to provide evaluation that is useful and accurate but not patronizing or demeaning. Getting feedback from employees can be a helpful reality check. In certain industries, particularly creative ones in which input is most difficult to monitor, less monitoring may actually lead to better results. Perhaps the most important thing that managers can do is to communicate clear expectations regarding the purpose of a business, what excellence consists of, and which sort of practices won't be tolerated. These provide the parameters within which employees can then optimize their performance.

When inputs are hard to measure and productivity is best served by providing significant autonomy to employees, how else can businesses incentivize performance? The answer is by sharing output, and in most companies this is done through bonuses and stock options. Let's think about the benefits and drawbacks of this approach.

Rewarding Outputs: Stock Options and Profit-Sharing

Metrics may be imperfect, but profits don't lie, at least in the long term. If an employee's work bears a direct relationship to the profits of a firm, then a firm should be able to incentivize employees by sharing profits. This won't completely solve the problem, particularly if an employee's contribution to a company is minuscule. However, if an employee's productivity can have a big impact on a firm—think of top scientists, engineers, and executives—then sharing profits can make it in that employee's interest to do their best and to encourage others to do the same.

The most direct way to share a company's profits is by granting an equity stake in the company (providing an employee with company stock). However, employees can also be rewarded with bonuses linked to the company's performance, or with commissions based on the amount of revenue that an employee brings in.

As compensation contracts have gotten more complex, one of the most popular approaches has been to grant stock options that become valuable if a company's stock increases in price. For example, suppose you join a company whose stock currently trades at $50 and you are provided an option to buy 1,000 shares of stock at $60 once you've stayed with the company for two years. If the company does well over those two years and the stock price rises to $70, then you will receive $10 per share when you exercise your options. This will net you $10,000 ($10 x 1,000 shares). What if the company does really well and the stock rises to $100? Then you'd make $50 per share, and walk away with an extra $50,000. At the end of the day, stock options give an employee a direct share of a business's success, making it in an employee's interest not only for a business to survive (in order to draw a paycheck) but to thrive (in order to collect significant bonuses from stock appreciation).

Why is this alignment of incentives so essential, particularly for a firm's executives and top talent? If a low-level employee takes advantage of a company in order to benefit himself and this is discovered by management, he'll be fired. But if an executive exploits the company that she leads for personal gain, who is going to fire her? She's at the top of the corporate totem pole, with a lot of power and little oversight. A board is better off incentivizing executives to benefit from rises in stock price than trying to police executives to ensure that they are not enriching themselves at the company's expense.

The Nobel Prize-winning economists Paul Romer and George Akerlof explain the temptation that corrupt managers can face in a classic essay, entitled "Looting: The Economic Underworld of Bankruptcy for Profit." Put simply, managers call the shots in the day-to-day operation of a business and can potentially "loot" a company—taking risky bets and paying themselves large salaries—at the expense of owners and creditors who are left footing the bill if the company goes bankrupt.

Managing Conflicts of Interest

At the most general level, owners of a business want to minimize *conflicts of interest* that managers and other employees might face. As a matter of law and ethics, those employed by a company have a *fiduciary duty* to the company. In most jurisdictions, this means that employees have (1) a duty of care, and (2) a duty of loyalty. Care means that when employees make a decision for the company, they must ensure that they are informed of relevant facts. If an employee doesn't bother to gather relevant information before making a decision, he or she would be acting "carelessly." Loyalty means that, when on the job, an employee should act in the best interest of the company, not herself. This prohibits "self-dealing," or using one's office for personal benefit at the company's expense. For example, if a salesperson raided a company's customer database and offered to sell it to a competitor, this would violate the duty of loyalty. If your doctor prescribed you the treatment that made her the most money rather than the treatment best for your health, that would violate the duty of loyalty.

In theory, the law should prevent violations of fiduciary duty, but in practice violations are difficult to monitor and prove. It's much better if owners of a business can prevent conflicts of interest from arising, through stock options or through other means. This is not always easy.

Andy Fastow, the CFO of Enron, held significant amounts of company stock in addition to his salary. However, Fastow was also the architect of "special-purposes entities" that promised to help Enron hedge investment gains by moving certain assets and liabilities off its balance sheet. Without the board's knowledge, Fastow made himself a partner in many of these entities and stood to make enormous windfalls if they were successful, while Enron was on the hook for covering losses if the deals soured. As CFO of Enron, Fastow received $2.4 million in salary, bonus, and other pay, plus an additional $1.8 million in stock-related compensation in 2001.[13]

However, how much do you think he earned from the special-purposes entities that he set up with Enron's backing? One single entity—"LJM"— earned Fastow $45 million. When the board found out, he was fired the next day. By that point, however, it was too late to undo the creative accounting tricks that would lead to Enron's demise.

As a general principle, we should seek to prevent conflicts of interest from arising in the first place. However, that isn't always feasible. If conflicts do exist, there are two ways to prevent them from getting out of hand, beyond simply asking an employee to act with integrity.

The first is disclosure and oversight. When a conflict is disclosed, this gives others the ability to scrutinize a decision-maker's actions and makes it much more likely that self-dealing will be noticed and penalized. Moreover, if you know that you can be caught or criticized, you are less likely to take advantage of a conflict. For this reason, nearly every federal official in the United States goes through a rigorous financial disclosure process, to prevent them from using their office for private gain.

However, note that disclosing information need not always succeed in reducing conflicts of interest. In a large-scale organization, it may well succeed. But sometimes such disclosures backfire. George Loewenstein, Daylian Cain, and Sunita Sah find that when doctors disclose conflicts of interest to their patients, the patients trust the doctors' advice less (as you might expect) but surprisingly are then more likely to take the doctors' advice and less likely to seek a second opinion. The problem: Patients don't want to offend their doctors.[14]

A second way to deal with potential conflicts of interest is to withhold information that could bias a decision-maker. For example, the police in many states have a close relationship with crime labs, and in some states they actually operate a crime lab. Moreover, in at least fourteen states, crime labs receive more money if their analysis secures a conviction.[15] A lab is supposed to provide objective, scientific evaluation of forensic evidence, for example, determining whether the fingerprint of a defendant matches a fingerprint found at a crime scene. However, if a police department tells its crime lab that establishing a particular match will solve a crime, this has the potential to bias the lab's analysis. The lab will be interested in making the police happy and in receiving additional compensation for having secured a conviction. One way to prevent such bias is to withhold all information concerning a case when a forensic sample is sent for analysis. This way, a lab won't know if a match will establish innocence or guilt, or whether it will help or hurt the lab's bottom line. Rather, the lab can only consider the material science, which is all that it should be considering anyway.

The Problem of Gaming

Ultimately, we want the employees of any organization to have strong incentives to help their organization succeed, and providing a share of profits can be a powerful means of doing this. However, we also want to ensure that success is real and honest. A lingering question we have to confront is whether profits and stock prices can themselves be "gamed" in a dishonest manner. If so, they may provide inadequate incentives for good behavior.

By "gaming" we mean concealing or manipulating the underlying economic realities of a company for personal gain in a manner that compromises the long-term profitability of the enterprise. The challenge with gaming is that it may not be illegal but rather lies in a gray zone near the border of the law.

For example, consider a practice that Lehman Brothers employed leading up to its bankruptcy, which helped launch the financial crisis of 2008. One curious fact about Lehman is that it had an "A" credit rating right up to the day it went bankrupt. A number of factors may explain why credit ratings agencies did not do a good job of assessing Lehman's financial health; but on one of the most important indicators that credit agencies examine—net leverage ratio— Lehman looked okay.

The net leverage ratio provides an indication of how much debt a company is carrying compared to its cash and earnings. In early 2018, Lehman reported a net leverage ratio of 12.1 percent, which was close to the maximum that most rating agencies were willing to accept. However, Lehman's real leverage ratio was 13.9, as the company was overstating its cash holdings by about $50 billion. Had ratings agencies and shareholders known this, it would have raised red flags. So, how was Lehman able to fool everyone?

Lehman engaged in some creative account practices using an accounting rule known as Repo 105. This rule governed "repurchase agreements," which banks use all the time to manage liquidity. For example, suppose a bank needs $10 million in cash to settle an account today, but it will take the bank a week to come up with that amount of cash. The bank can go to another financial institution and ask to borrow $10 million immediately. In exchange, the bank provides $10 million of assets as collateral, along with an agreement to "repurchase" those assets from the financial institution a week later, once the bank has assembled the cash. You can think of repurchase agreements as short-term loans that banks make to each other, which are low risk because they are backed by collateral. Indeed, accounting law treats these agreements as loans, and for that reason the underlying assets stay on a bank's balance sheet.

However, Lehman figured out a way to have a repurchase agreement classified as a sale rather than a loan. According to "Repo 105," if the bank put up assets that were worth more than 105 percent of the amount of cash that was being borrowed, it would no longer be classified as a loan because the assets and cash would not be of equal value. No bank had ever tried this before, and it took Lehman awhile to find a law firm and accounting firm willing to sign off on this maneuver, but it eventually did. One reason that no bank ever tried to do this before is that it doesn't make financial sense. Why give up assets that are worth significantly more than the money you are borrowing? So, why did Lehman want to have repurchase agreements booked as sales?

Think about what this did for Lehman's balance sheet. The bank could quickly take assets, park them at another bank, and count the cash that it received on its own books. Even though Lehman would have to give the cash back a week later, and resume ownership of the assets, for the intervening week it appeared that the bank held a lot of cash. This would do wonders for a firm's net leverage ratio.

So, when do you think Lehman engaged in large amounts of repo activity, generating temporary cash holdings as large as $50 billion? It did so just before reporting deadlines in order to make the bank's finances look better to regulators, ratings agencies, and the public. Was this unethical? If you think it's wrong to intentionally deceive investors, then yes. Was it illegal? That is tougher to answer. Lehman found a loophole and had a legal argument for exploiting it. Because of Lehman's bankruptcy, we'll never know if this argument would have held up in court.

In banking, higher leverage leads to higher profits when the economy is growing. However, if the economy contracts, high levels of debt can quickly lead to bankruptcy. Why would executives at Lehman engage in behavior that was so risky that it jeopardized the viability of the firm?

In the wake of the financial crisis and litigation surrounding it, a curious acronym came to light that was often used by Wall Street Bankers when they pondered whether a risky business decision was a good idea: "IGBYBG." These letters were shorthand for "I'll be gone, you'll be gone." This phrase should strike fear in the heart of any stockholder. It suggests that executives were concerned not with the long-term productivity of a firm but in figuring out how to maximize immediate returns and cash out, without having to deal with the full the consequences of their actions. This is not a recipe for accountability.

Lehman's management was not alone in facing incentives to pursue risky strategies that could inflate profits and stock prices in the short term but compromise economic viability in the long term. Indeed, there are many strategies that executives can use to "manage earnings" to make a company's finances look overly positive in the short run. These include cutting back on capital investments and research and development, changing accounting methods, and manipulating how certain assets are valued. You can see why this presents a problem. If executives are compensated with stock options but also have the ability to inflate the value of a company's stock in the short term at the expense of the long term, this will present a conflict of interest.

This kind of thing doesn't simply happen in for-profit firms. Not-for-profit corporations, such as universities and colleges, face the same problem. For instance, an external agency or donor might offer to pay for the first five years of salary and benefits to create a tenured, chaired professorship in their name. Deans often take the deal. They get to count the donation toward their fundraising numbers, which makes them look good and helps them land better jobs at more prestigious colleges. Meanwhile, after they move on, the five years is up, and the university is stuck paying another twenty years of salary and benefits without any funding. Rinse and repeat for hundreds of similar projects, and tuition keeps increasing to cover ever expanding costs.

Before examining what can be done to reshape these incentives, we have to consider one remaining conflict that will recurrently arise in any publicly traded company, namely, insider trading.

Insider trading occurs when someone buys or sells a company's stock based on material, nonpublic information in violation of his or her fiduciary duty. For example, suppose you're a regional manager of a furniture company, and you learn that one of your largest warehouses was just flooded, ruining all of the furniture inside. You immediately sell all the company stock that you own. When word of the flood gets out, the company's stock declines by 20 percent. Have you done anything wrong?

Think about the person who bought your stock. He or she did so believing that the company's inventory was in good shape. However, you knew that a large amount of inventory had been lost and therefore the company wasn't worth as much. If you sold someone a recliner but you secretly knew that the recliner hinge was broken, you would be engaging in fraud. Similarly, if you sell stock in a company that you secretly know has been financially compromised, you've committed a kind of fraud as well. At least, that's the way that law has come to view such transactions.

It is not only an insider who can get into trouble by selling or buying stock based on material, nonpublic information. So, can anyone who is tipped off by an insider, or even anyone who is tipped off by someone who is tipped off by an insider. Martha Stewart was accused of insider trading when she sold her shares in a pharmaceutical company called ImClone after a financial advisor mentioned that ImClone's CEO was selling his shares (because, it turns out, the company's major clinical trial had just failed). Stewart eventually reached a settlement with the SEC in which she neither admitted nor denied the insider trading charge, although she ended up going to prison for lying to investigators in the process of trying to defend herself. However, given the stakes involved, you may be surprised to learn that what exactly qualifies as insider trading remains a gray area because no law has ever been passed in the United States that clearly defines insider trading.

This is not an accident. Although Congress and the Security and Exchange Commission have considered writing laws that lay out a precise definition, they have avoided doing so because of concerns that a clear definition would be easier to game. As one law professor explained, "creating a definition would be a blueprint for fraud. . . . It would allow clever Wall Street types to figure out loopholes."[16] As long as the law is gray, the SEC has more flexibility to go after new types of fraud. In order to ensure that they stay on the right side of the law, executives who wish to sell stock can set up a trading plan with the SEC. These plans outline the parameters of trades far in advance, which prevents real-time trading based on new insider information. The SEC would prefer that executives err on the side of caution, and requiring them to plan stock trades well in advance helps guard against the improper exploitation of insider information.

Improving Compensation Contracts

We've explored why stock options can be a powerful way to encourage talented employees to be productive. However, we've also observed that executives may be able to profit by manipulating stock prices in the short term, in a manner that damages a company's profitability in the long term. Business owners have increasingly searched for ways to improve how stock options and other performance bonuses are granted in an attempt to provide executives with incentives to pursue sustained, long-term growth.

One promising strategy is to lengthen the vesting period of stock options, potentially by many years. This helps address the "I'll be gone, you'll be gone" problem. If an employee's compensation depends on a company's stock performance long into the future, that employee has to care about the trajectory of the company. Cutting back on investment, cooking the books, and taking risky bets for short-term gains will be less attractive if they imperil the company's future profitability. Lengthening the vesting period of stock options and tying bonuses to long-term performance metrics has a second benefit, namely, that it's less likely to reward executives who are simply lucky to be at the helm during good economic times. Rather, those who receive the most compensation will be those who are able to consistently grow a company year after year, in good times and bad.

A second strategy for improving compensation contracts is to include clawback provisions, which can require executives to pay back money if they are subsequently found to have been materially involved in wrongdoing. This is another way to attack the "I'll be gone, you'll be gone" problem. If an executive encouraged and benefited from wrongdoing, why should she be able to keep those ill-gotten gains? Without clear clawback provisions, companies may be limited in how much they can reclaim. Although, if wrongdoing is significant, it may be possible to reclaim recent compensation even in the absence of such clauses.

For example, recall the case of Wells Fargo, whose stock doubled in part because executives pushed aggressive cross-selling quotas that resulted in massive fraud. When John Stumpf, the CEO who presided over the company during this period, stepped down, his total retirement compensation package was valued at $123.6 million.[17] Upon investigation, Wells Fargo's board concluded that Stumpf should be held accountable for those unacceptable sales practices and it asked/forced Stumpf to forfeit $41 million of unvested equity awards. Six months later, the board clawed back an additional $28 million of incentive compensation.[18] Was that enough? Stumpf was undoubtedly displeased to lose $69 million, but if you do the math, you'll notice that he still came out some $54 million ahead.

By codifying expectations and clawback procedures in employment contracts from the outset, companies can set clear boundaries that prevent bad behavior from paying in the long run. Even if executives are long gone, they can be forced to give back rewards that were predicated on bad behavior.

Whistleblower Programs as a Fail-Safe Mechanism

The principal-agent problem that confronts every firm is ultimately a problem of information. At any given moment, owners will find it difficult to know whether an employee is doing what he or she is paid to do or whether an employee is exploiting the company. However, although owners may be in the dark, employees on the inside may not be. Indeed, it's hard for colleagues not to notice if someone isn't pulling their weight on a project, or if someone is engaging in risky or strange behavior. If only there were a way for those with this local knowledge to communicate it to owners. Whistleblower programs aim to make this possible and can serve as a check on the worst forms of bad behavior.

In almost every corporate scandal, plenty of bystanders knew that something wasn't right long before everything blew up. Four months before Enron's bankruptcy, Sherron Watkins, the vice president for corporate development, penned an anonymous memo to the CEO expressing her fear that Enron could "implode in a wave of accounting scandals." Her warning was ignored and not relayed to the board in a meaningful way.[19] Five months before Lehman Brothers bankruptcy, a senior vice president named Matthew Lee penned a memo to the CFO and CRO expressing his concerns that top management had been engaging in misleading accounting and valuation practices in violation of the firm's own ethics code.[20] When Yesenia Guitron began working as a personal banker at Wells Fargo in 2008 she noticed that a large number of fake accounts were being opened up, flagging 300 in a short period of time. As she would later put it, "All the tellers and staff knew." Guitron reportedly "raised concerns on more than 100 occasions, including about a dozen calls to the Wells Fargo EthicsLine, and on no fewer than 37 occasions she provided records that supported her complaints."[21]

This sort of information is invaluable for owners to have, and it is in their interest to find ways to obtain it. However, those who are facilitating and profiting from bad behavior want to prevent this information from getting out. Since they generally stand between employees and owners, being heard is no easy task. What do you think management does to employees who try to expose wrongdoing to owners? Matthew Lee worked for Lehman for fourteen years, rising to the level of senior vice president. He was fired a month after he wrote the memo raising concerns about Lehman's accounting practices. Yesenia Guitron reported that managers at Wells Fargo began to retaliate against her when she drew attention to fraudulent accounts, and she was fired not long after.

Being a whistleblower—someone who exposes unethical behavior within an organization—takes courage. Those whom you expose will be angry, and coworkers may view you as disloyal. However, whistleblowers have unparalleled power to prevent crises and stop wrongdoing before it gets out of hand. The question is whether we can make it in their interest to do so.

Following Enron's bankruptcy, the United States passed legislation referred to as Sarbanes-Oxley, which made a number of changes to corporate governance law. One key provision of the law requires publicly traded companies to have whistleblower procedures, and the law also gives employees significant legal protections against retaliation if they do report wrongdoing. These are attempts to lower the costs of whistleblowing.

More recently in the United States, the Internal Revenue Service (IRS) and Security and Exchange Commission (SEC) have implemented programs that positively reward whistleblowing. If someone has evidence of tax fraud or securities fraud, he or she can fill out a simple form documenting the claim. If the evidence is compelling the IRS or SEC may investigate, and if the IRS or SEC find wrongdoing and recover fines or damages, the whistleblower is entitled to a share. How much? The exact amount depends on a number of factors but generally ranges between 15 percent and 30 percent. If a corporate fraud is large, this could be a lot of money. One of the first whistleblowers with the IRS program was a former UBS banker named Bradley Birkenfeld. He alerted the

IRS to a tax evasion scheme through which UBS helped wealthy Americans conceal assets. Birkenfeld was awarded $104 million for his role in bringing this scheme to light. Now that's a good incentive to be a whistleblower!

There was, however, a peculiar twist in Birkenfeld's case. He was also implicated in abetting the fraud while at UBS and he pled guilty to a felony, which resulted in a forty-month prison sentence.[22] However, $104 million was waiting for him when he was released. Not a bad deal overall. On the SEC side, a whistleblower cannot be materially involved in the wrongdoing that he or she exposes. This is important so as not to incentivize employees to encourage corporate malfeasance for the purpose of turning around to expose it for profit. However, on the IRS side, it is so difficult to obtain insider information concerning tax fraud, but also so valuable, that the agency made the decision to welcome and reward evidence even if it comes from guilty parties.

Perhaps the most important thing to note about the IRS and SEC whistleblower programs is that any member of the public can submit a claim. You do not have to be an employee at the company in question or personally affected by a fraud. Indeed, an attentive analyst who discovers something fishy going on with a company's finances could potentially make a lot of money if she uncovers genuine fraud. So, in addition to providing a large incentive for those within a company to report illegal activity, these programs are a way of "crowdsourcing" fraud detection in the society at large.

Conclusion

Managing humans isn't easy. This is precisely why good managers can be worth the high salary they are often paid. Although successful approaches will have to be tailored to the specific circumstances of a firm and industry, there are some common tools and insights that help solve the collective action problems that arise in any organization.

First, it's important to understand what the existing incentives and norms are in any organization. If either are leading to perverse outcomes, then they can be targets for reform. But if you fail to understand an organization's existing motivational landscape, you can make changes that lead to more harm than good, just like the Boston Mayor's office.

Second, the task in shaping incentives is to reward employees for work that genuinely enables an organization to thrive. Productivity metrics can serve as a useful basis for compensation, as long as they truly capture the kind of activity one wants to promote and they can't be gamed through unethical strategies. Similarly, performance reviews can be helpful for setting expectations and evaluating progress, but a balance must be struck that prevents reviews from becoming onerous, petty, and resented. In some fields, employees may do their best work when provided with considerable freedom, in which case other mechanisms must be sought in order to align their interests with a company's interest.

One powerful way to align interests, particularly when oversight is difficult, is to give employees a share in a firm's output, through stock options, commissions, and performance bonuses. Particularly if an employee is able to make significant contributions to a firm's growth, stock options will provide a considerable source of motivation, making an employee's success conditional on the firm's success. However, this can prove a liability if employees are able to manipulate stock prices, either through outright fraud or through strategies that compromise the long-term viability of a company. Employment contracts can disincentivize this sort of gaming by extending the vesting period of stock options and clawback provisions.

Third, although owners and the public will never have perfect knowledge regarding what is going on inside the firm, plenty of insiders will be aware of bad behavior when it occurs. Whistleblower programs can be an effective way to incentivize those with this critical information to bring it to light before things get out of hand. It is in a company's long-term interest to have communication channels established for employees to voice concerns and for those who investigate these concerns to be sufficiently independent. More generally, firms should aim to limit conflicts of interest and monitor conflicts that are unavoidable.

Finally, although this chapter has focused on incentivizing employees to do their best and creating safeguards to guard against the worst behavior, we shouldn't forget that money isn't the only source of motivation, or the only source of wrongdoing. As we saw in earlier chapters, principals who are able to communicate a compelling vision for an organization and values that employees respect are often able to command the allegiance of employees even in the face of small incentives to shirk or to take ethical shortcuts. Moreover, even well intentioned employees can do bad things, not out of intentional malice but because of blind spots and unconscious bias. Managers have to be concerned about all these factors. At the end of the day, however, it's essential that an employee's interests be broadly aligned with an organization's interests and that employees do not face opportunities to make extraordinary profits at the firm's expense. Only when these temptations are removed through good policies and compensation practices can the more subtle work of managing for excellence begin.

Summary

- Every successful organization has to figure out how to motivate its members to act well and to avoid taking advantage of opportunities to exploit the organization for personal gain. If employees have a strong commitment to an organization's mission and embrace norms against exploitation, this can help solve the "principal-agent" problem. However, it's also important to provide employees incentives to act in the interests of the common good of the organization and the larger society.
- One way to incentivize productive activity is to measure and reward an employee's inputs. However, it is important to avoid metrics that are incomplete or easily gamed, as these can encourage bad behavior. Also, excessive surveillance of work can prove counterproductive when it provokes resentment and anxiety among employees.
- Another way to incentivize productive activity, particularly when it is hard to monitor inputs, is to provide employees a share in a company's output (or profit) through stock options, commissions, and performance bonuses.
- However, profit-sharing can prove a liability if employees are able to manipulate stock prices, either through outright fraud or through strategies that compromise the long-term viability of a company. Employment contracts can disincentivize this sort of gaming by extending the vesting period of stock options and including clawback provisions that require compensation to be paid back if it is later found to have been due to fraudulent practices.
- Overall, firms should try to prevent "conflicts of interest" from arising that pit an individual's interest against the larger good of an organization or society.
- Whistleblower programs that reward those who reveal wrongdoing can help solve the principal-agent problem and prevent bad behavior from starting or getting out of hand.

Discussion Questions

- Would you rather have a job that pays you according to some accurate productivity metric, or one that gives you a share of the company's overall economic value (e.g., stock options)? Why? What are the considerations that led you to your conclusion?

- Think of a job that you'd like to have after you graduate. How would you like to be compensated and managed in that job? Write down a brief description of what your ideal arrangement would look like (how you would want your work would to be evaluated and rewarded). If another employee were given the same arrangement, can you think of any ways that he or she could game it for his or her personal benefit at the expense of the firm or larger society? If so, how could you prevent that?
- Some colleges have a problem with students cheating, and many schools have an honor code requiring students to report cheating that they witness other students engaging in. Should we offer whistleblower rewards for students who report cheating? Suppose a school said that it would pay $500 to any student who exposed serious cheating. Would that be a good idea? Why or why not?
- Suppose you had the option of hiring someone who is very competent but whom you expect will always act in his or her own best interest if it conflicts with the organization's interest, or hiring someone who is a team player committed to furthering the organization's mission, even at some personal expense, but who isn't as competent. Who would you hire and why? Are there certain circumstances, job levels (junior/senior), or industries that would lead you to favor one type of person over another?

Notes

1. Drucker 2006.
2. McLean 2017.
3. Arnold 2016.
4. Reckard 2013.
5. Mehrortra and Keller 2017.
6. Moise 2018.
7. Paine 1994.
8. Healy and Palepu, "The Fall of Enron," Harvard Business School Case 9-109-039.
9. In fact, there is strong evidence that student evaluation scores do not track teaching performance at all; they are closer to be a personality test. See Brennan and Magness 2019: 82–108.
10. Pink 2009.
11. Garvin 2013.
12. Bock 2015.
13. http://articles.latimes.com/2002/jun/18/business/fi-enron18.
14. Loewenstein, Cain, and Sah 2011.
15. Koppl and Sacks 2013.
16. Parloff 2013.
17. Linnane 2016.

18. Independent Directors 2017.
19. McLean 2017.
20. Comstock 2010.
21. McLean 2017.
22. Kocieniewski 2012.

9

The Effect of Incentives

The Problem of Collective Action

Basic Lesson: Even if cooperating will make everyone better off, cooperation won't happen if people lack certain kinds of knowledge and motivation. In group settings, individuals will often have incentives to promote their own interest at the expense of the group, but this can prove disastrous to both the individual and group in the long run. There are two ways to overcome these "collective action" problems: (1) the incentives that individuals face can be changed so that individual and group interest no longer conflict, and/or (2) group members can embrace norms that enable them to exercise self-restraint and forego opportunities to get ahead at the expense of others.

What Can We Learn from Chinese Farmers?

In 1978, farmers in the small Chinese village of Xiaogang were desperate. The previous season had yielded another bad harvest, and the farmers were struggling to feed their families. These were tough people who had survived many horrors of communist rule but now faced the prospect of starvation.

Were they bad farmers? Was their land infertile? Did they not have the right tools? As it turns out, the answer to all these questions was no. Then why couldn't they grow a healthy crop?

China had struggled to feed itself since the communist party came to power in 1949. The government confiscated vast amounts of agricultural land, and people from all walks of life were ordered to work on collective farms. What motivated them? As one historian explains, "People accused of not working hard enough were hung and beaten."[1] Despite these severe threats, agricultural productivity plummeted, and from 1958 to 1962 China experienced a "great famine," which scholars have estimated killed some 45 million people.[2] This led to desperate circumstances and a downward spiral of brutality:

Business Ethics for Better Behavior. Jason Brennan, William English, John Hasnas, and Peter Jaworski, Oxford University Press. © Oxford University Press 2021. DOI: 10.1093/oso/9780190076559.003.0009

One report dated Nov. 30, 1960, and circulated to the top leadership — most likely including Mao — tells how a man named Wang Ziyou had one of his ears chopped off, his legs tied up with iron wire and a 10-kilogram stone dropped on his back before he was branded with a sizzling tool. His crime: digging up a potato. . . .

As the catastrophe unfolded, people were forced to resort to previously unthinkable acts to survive. As the moral fabric of society unraveled, they abused one another, stole from one another and poisoned one another. Sometimes they resorted to cannibalism.[3]

China emerged from the tragedy of the great famine with far fewer mouths to feed. However, by 1978, agricultural productivity was still lower than it had been forty years earlier, before the communists took over.

The way the communist system worked was that the government took all the food that was produced on collective farms and then distributed some back to families (as long as there was some left over from what the government "needed"). Every farmer received the same amount, so working harder didn't pay. If harvests were good, the farmers could generally "steal" some extra food for themselves without raising suspicion or getting caught. However, since everyone farmed the same land and everyone had reason to steal food, again hard work didn't pay. If you did a good job cultivating one corner of the field, what was to stop others from helping themselves to your corner? Ultimately, the farms were supposed to fill certain production quotas defined by the government, and if they didn't produce enough food there would be crackdowns, along with horrific penalties for food theft. The best course of action was thus to do the minimum amount of work needed to avoid sanction and hope that the government provided enough of a food ration to allow you to survive. It's hard to imagine a worse set of incentives for agricultural productivity.

Hungry and desperate, the villagers of Xiaogang had an idea and called a secret meeting. To those working the fields, the problem was obvious. Why work hard or creatively if whatever you produced would be taken away and everyone ended up with the same ration of food? You'd just be exhausting yourself for nothing. However, if your family could keep some of the food you produced, that would change everything. Farmers would go to extraordinary lengths to make their families better off. Of course, farming just for your family was illegal in communist China. The farmland belonged to the government and so did all of the food it produced.

The farmers were certain that if everyone farmed smarter and worked harder they could produce more—likely enough to keep a little extra for themselves without the government noticing. But then there was the secondary problem of ensuring that everyone worked hard. Remember, they all farmed the same large plot of land. How could they be sure that some people wouldn't take it easy, planning to benefit from the hard work that others put in?

The farmers came up with a solution. On a piece of paper, they divided up the farmland and assigned each family a particular plot of land that would be "theirs." They all agreed that the family assigned to that plot could keep whatever a plot of land produced beyond the share expected by the government. This meant that a family could invest effort in their plot of land knowing that they alone would be responsible for ensuring that it was productive. Moreover, if it became highly productive, they alone would have a right to the excess.

In effect, what they created was a system of private property. They couldn't place actual dividers out in the field, as that would draw unwanted attention. However, the piece of paper that they all signed served as both a map and a contract. It confirmed which family "owned" which plot of land, and all the signers agreed that a family would have exclusive rights to any excess that their plot produced. There was also an important addendum. The signers promised that they would take care of the children of any member who was sent to prison or executed by the government. They all understood that this fate would likely await anyone who was discovered to have participated in a conspiracy to circumvent the communist economic system.

With the secret agreement in place, the next season came and went. What do you think happened? Remember, we're talking about the same farmers, the same land, and the same tools.

Not only was the next harvest enormous, it was larger than the previous five years combined. That's a 500 percent increase! How was that possible?

Here's how one reporter, who interviewed members of the village many years later, explained it:

> Before the contract, the farmers would drag themselves out into the field only when the village whistle blew, marking the start of the work day. After the contract, the families went out before dawn.
>
> "We all secretly competed," says Yen Jingchang [one of the original signers]. "Everyone wanted to produce more than the next person."
>
> It was the same land, the same tools and the same people. Yet just by changing the economic rules—by saying, you get to keep some of what you grow—everything changed."[4]

Everything changed, as the village went from living on the edge of starvation to a condition of plenty. But the story didn't end there, and it almost ended very badly.

It was impossible for local officials not to notice the large harvest. Rather than be thankful, they were alarmed. It meant that something had changed—something that they did not understand or control and which might become a threat to their power. So, local officials started interrogating villagers, threatening them with execution, and the truth slowly came out. Although local officials sought to punish the villagers, when word of the agreement and its effects reached the central government, the reaction was different.

Chinese leaders had been searching for ways to reform the country's stagnant economy, and the experience of the Xiaogang villagers revealed something that worked. The government actually decided to adopt the agreement that the villagers forged in secret as official government policy, and within a few years farms across China allowed people to own part of what they grew. Many credit this agricultural reform as being pivotal in China's abandonment of Marxist economics and turn toward markets and private property—reforms that have lifted more than a half a billion people out of poverty in recent decades. By devising an agreement that provided everyone with the motivation and knowledge needed to be productive, the villagers of Xiaogang went from the brink of starvation to a condition of plenty, and they provided China with a model that would change the economic trajectory of the nation. Not bad for some rural villagers.

The real puzzle, though, is why this model wasn't discovered or tried sooner. After all, it only required some paper, ink, and insight into what was preventing people from working together in a productive manner.

The truth is that understanding and changing the "collective action" of a group of people is hard. However, the benefits can be enormous. In this chapter, we're going to explore why individuals so often act in ways that produce bad outcomes for others—and even for themselves—and we're going to identify strategies that can ensure a better outcome for everyone.

Providing the Motivation and Knowledge Needed to Act Well

Friedrich Hayek, the Nobel Prize-winning economist, once described the fundamental economic problem as "how to provide inducements which will make individuals do the desirable thing without anyone having to tell them what to do."[5] Hayek went on to note that this is exactly what the *price system* does in a well-functioning market.

If the weather gets cold, all of a sudden a lot of people want mittens to keep their hands warm. The price of mittens rises. When the price rises, it's as if a loud message is broadcast out to the world, saying: "Make more mittens! People need them, and there aren't enough!" The price system thus disseminates a crucial piece of new information about how one can do good and help others. Moreover, the price system also offers a reward. Higher prices point to a profit opportunity, telling manufacturers: "There is a lot of money to be made if you can produce mittens for less than the high price at which they are now selling." Note that even if manufacturers only care about making money, when they produce more mittens to take advantage of higher prices, they will be meeting an urgent human need and thus doing a good thing. No one had to tell or force manufacturers to do good. Rather, prices provided the motivation (profit opportunity) and knowledge (make mittens!) that manufacturers needed in order to act well.

This is a dynamic that intellectual father of modern economics, Adam Smith, famously noted in his treatise, *An Inquiry into the Nature and Causes of the Wealth of Nations*, in which he described entrepreneurs as being led by an "invisible hand" to act in the interest of society:

> As every individual, therefore, endeavours as much as he can both to employ his capital in the support of domestic industry, and so to direct that industry that its produce may be of the greatest value, every individual necessarily labours to render the annual revenue of the society as great as he can. He generally, indeed, neither intends to promote the public interest, nor knows how much he is promoting it. By preferring the support of domestic to that of foreign industry, he intends only his own security; and *by directing that industry in such a manner as its produce may be of the greatest value, he intends only his own gain, and he is in this, as in many other cases, led by an invisible hand to promote an end which was no part of his intention.* Nor is it always the worse for the society that it was not part of it. *By pursuing his own interest he frequently promotes that of the society more effectually than when he really intends to promote it.*[6]

Indeed, the great virtue of a market economy is that profit opportunities generally lead people to do things that are of value to others. Put another way, prices are a guide to good behavior, providing people both motivation to act well and knowledge about what exactly needs to be done.

This is all good news, but there is a big caveat. We witness the "invisible hand" dynamic when markets are in good order, but what if the structure of a market has serious flaws, or what if we don't have a traditional market at all?

Economists have pointed out that markets function well when:

1. Property rights are well defined (we know who owns what).
2. Contracts are enforced (when you make a deal, everyone has to follow through).
3. Relevant information is accurately represented (there's no fraud).
4. There are no externalities (no hidden costs, like pollution, that are imposed on others).
5. There are lots of buyers and sellers (healthy competition with no monopolies).
6. Transaction costs are low (the cost of exchange aren't prohibitively high).

When these conditions are not satisfied, we say that a market has "imperfections." Consider the following ways in which a mitten maker could profit from market imperfections in ways that are bad for the society as a whole.

If you steal mittens in order to sell them as the price goes up, you would make money, but that would violate property rights (1). If you accept a large payment for mittens, but never ship them to the customer, you would make a lot of money, but that would violate the deal you made (2). If you use inferior materials to make mittens that look nice, but fall apart after the first use, you could make money selling them to unsuspecting buyers, but that would involve fraud (3). If you discover a new way to make mittens that costs less but that involves dumping chemical byproducts into a local stream, you would make more money but you would be burdening other people who have to deal with the cost of cleaning up the stream (4). If the government granted you a monopoly and declared that everyone had to buy their mittens from you, you would make more money, but the lack of competition would be unfair to consumers, who have to pay higher prices, and to competitors, who could do a better job for less (5). Finally, if a customer thought that your mittens might be stolen, or not arrive, or fall apart, or harm the environment, then she might need to spend a lot of time, energy, and resources to check out your factory, test your product, meet up for an in-person sale, and so on. These higher transaction costs (6) would make the entire market less efficient and waste valuable resources.

There's no doubt that imperfections of varying degrees exist in many markets. The question is whether we can do anything to correct, or mitigate, market imperfections when we encounter them. Economists have identified a number of possible mechanisms for dealing with these so-called market failures. Some of these solutions require political or legal action, such as assigning property rights, enforcing contracts, taxing pollution, or breaking up monopolies. Others involve organizational and technological innovations, such as ratings systems that allow customers to report bad actors, payment escrow services, and new ways of measuring and pricing externalities like pollution. Often the best solution is to do nothing, as attempts to fix imperfections frequently introduce even larger problems worse than the imperfections.

You can take entire courses devoted to examining market failures and possible solutions to them, but we want to take a step back and consider a related, but broader, question, namely, how can we ensure that individuals have the knowledge and motivation to act well, regardless of whether they are in a traditional market?

This broader formulation is helpful, because those engaged in business have to deal with two important domains that are not organized as traditional markets and which do not utilize a conventional price system, namely, the internal organization of firms and the political organization of society.

The Firm Is Not a Market

The first of these may surprise you. Consider a typical firm or company. Suppose that you are hired as a summer intern. When you show up for your first day of work, what happens? If the firm operated as a true market, you might begin the day by negotiating exactly what you would do and how much you would get paid for each task that day. Perhaps your boss says, "We'll give you $10 to pick up coffee for the office, $20 to make copies for tomorrow's meeting, and $50 to proofread the latest draft of our quarterly report, with a $10 bonus if you complete it by 6 PM and find at least a dozen typos." You might haggle about the price, but once you agree, then you and your boss would know exactly what you are supposed to do that day, how much you will get paid for each task, and what constitutes satisfactory completion. There's no ambiguity. The next morning, you would enter into a new set of negotiations to figure out what exactly needed done that day and how much you would be paid for each task. Moreover, if the firm thought that you were asking too much for some task, it could consider bids from other vendors. Perhaps Starbucks could deliver coffee to the office for $9, or perhaps the manager's daughter had an appointment that got cancelled, so now she's free to do some proofreading at a discount.

Is this the way that firms operate and interface with their employees? Of course not, but why?

In his famous essay on "The Nature of the Firm," Nobel Laureate Ronald Coase observed that firms don't operate like conventional markets. Quite the opposite. Firms are organized hierarchically. If hired as an employee, you're paid a salary or hourly wage with the expectation that you'll show up each day and do what you're told. Internally, firms are like little islands sheltered from the larger ocean of constantly changing market forces.

Why not operate a firm like a traditional market, with bidding and negotiating for every task and clear criteria for every deliverable? The problem, as Coase saw, and you probably recognize as well, is that this would take a lot of time and energy. You might waste a few hours every morning negotiating tasks and prices and checking bids with outside vendors, and then you'd have to coordinate different payments each day after verifying every task was completed. Put another way, it's more efficient for firms to pay employees a fixed salary with the expectation that they show up each day and do a good job with whatever they are asked to do (within some generally specified boundaries).

Although this arrangement may be more efficient overall, it has dangers as well. How do you know that an employee will do a good job if you're not monitoring and specifically rewarding every task? Economists refer to this as the "principal-agent" problem.

A firm wants to hire employees who will do a good job, often on long-term projects that require not only hard work but countless and subtle forms of creativity, perseverance, and attention to detail. If the employee does a good job, the company will make a lot of money and it will be worth it to pay the employee a high salary. However, what if the company can't easily monitor the work that the employee is putting in? The employee could potentially collect the high salary while neglecting the hard work he or she ought to be doing in order to see a long-term project to completion. In that case, the interests of the employer (the principal) and the employee (the agent) would not be aligned.

In recent years, a lot of work has been devoted to devising employment contracts and oversight mechanisms that better align the incentives of employers and employees. We'll examine some of these in the next chapter.

The principal-agent problem is one major obstacle that firms have to overcome in order to be successful. However, it also points to a deeper question that any cooperative enterprise has to confront, namely, how to ensure that individuals are not motivated to behave in ways that harm others, or even themselves.

How Can It Be in Your Interest to Act against Your Interest?

Now, you might be thinking, why would anyone do anything to harm their own interest?

Well, consider the following game, which you might even try playing in class.

Suppose your professor walks up to you and three other students and hands you each ten one-dollar bills. There would be $40 between the four of you, with each of you holding $10 in your hands. This money is now yours and you can do whatever you want with it. Your professor also passes out an un-marked envelope to each of you and makes the following offer: "Any money that you put in your envelope will be collected, doubled, and split equally between the four of you." The game is illustrated graphically in figure 9.1. What would you do?

At first glance, this might seem like a no-brainer. The professor is giving you a chance to double your money. If each student puts the full $10 into their respective envelope, that would total $40, and this would then be doubled to $80. When split equally, each student would receive $20 back. Not a bad deal—you just doubled your money!

However, is there a way for you to make even more money? Think about it.

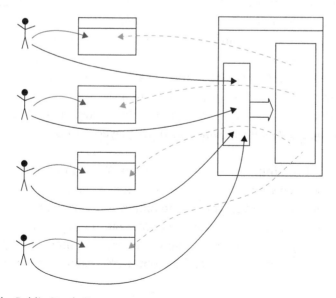

Fig. 9.1 The Public Goods Game.

Notice that you get a split of the money that is doubled, regardless of whether you put any of your own money into the envelope. So, what happens if you keep all of your money out of the envelope while others put all of theirs in? If the three other students all make a full investment, that would mean $30 goes into the envelopes. When doubled, that becomes $60, and when split equally among the four of you, each person will receive $15 (60/4 = 15). So, the three students who invested $10 would each get $15 back, which still isn't a bad return. However, in addition to your $15, you still have the $10 that you didn't invest. Thus, you walk away with $25 total, which is more that you would have received if you had invested all of your money!

Indeed, $25 is the highest amount that you can make in this game, and this occurs when you keep all of your money, while your three compatriots each make a full investment. But why should they make a full investment, if that means they'll earn less than you? Why shouldn't they act like you and keep their money out?

Let's think about the other extreme. Suppose that you invest, hoping to double your money, but the other three players keep all their money out. That means that your $10 will be the only money collected in the envelopes. It will be doubled to $20 and then split equally among the four of you. So, everyone will receive $5. Since the other three players kept their $10s out, they'll all have $15 dollars total. What about you? It turns out you will have lost $5. You would have been better off never investing at all.

The more that you work through the possible outcomes of the game, the more a disturbing conclusion becomes apparent. Whatever the other players do, you will always make more money if you keep your money out. If others make a full investment, you make more by keeping your money out. If others make no investment, you make more by keeping your money out. Even if others make partial investments, you make more by keeping all of your money out. The dominant strategy in this game—the strategy that always yields a higher payoff for you, given whatever other players choose—is to keep your money out.

You should be troubled by this conclusion. You will always make more money if you keep your money out. However, if everyone does this, then no money is put into the envelopes, and no money is doubled. But that would be crazy! You all have an opportunity to double your money. How can it be that when everybody acts in his or her interest to make the most money possible, the result is a missed opportunity for profit, with no one making any money at all?

What would you do? Think about it. Would you put your money in? If the three other students with whom you're paired try to make the most money that they can by keeping their money out, then you're just going to lose half of your money.

Perhaps you know the other three students, and even consider them friends. You all start talking with each other and one of you says, "look, if we all make a full investment, we can double our money, so let's all do that and not try to make ourselves a little better off by not investing." The four of you all nod in approval and make a show of putting all of the money in your respective envelopes. However, as the professor comes around to collect the envelopes, one student—we'll call her Sally—conceals her envelope under the desk and stealthily removes the money.

Having collected the envelopes, the professor proceeds to open them in front of the class. $10 comes out of the first envelope, $10 out of the second, and yet another $10 out of the third. The professor pauses as she opens the final envelope, before turning it over and shaking it to show that it is completely empty. Rules are rules, and this means that you and your two friends will both receive $15, but Sally walks away with $25.

Who made the right choice? Why? Be prepared to present your view and discuss your reasoning in class.

Positive-Sum Games, Zero-Sum Games, Pareto Improvements, and the Problem of Collective Action

By now you can understand why this game—which economists call a "public goods" game—is so challenging. If everyone tries to make the most money possible, no one will make any money. Moreover, if you try to invest on your own but everyone else doesn't, then you actually lose money. So, it seems like the best thing to do is to not invest, but this means that the players will all miss out on an opportunity to double their money.

Economists refer to a game in which the total gains and losses are greater than zero as a "positive-sum game." By contrast, a "zero-sum game" is a game in which the total wealth doesn't increase, and one person's win is another person's loss. Think of dividing a pie. If the other person gets more, then you get less. Zero-sum games are best avoided unless you are confident that you can win.

Notice that if anyone invests any amount of money into an envelope in the public goods game, then the game becomes a positive-sum game because the total amount of wealth generated will be more than the players started with. However, it is still possible for one player to be worse off if he or she is the only one who invests (in which case others each get $15, but the investor gets $5). The overall wealth of all the players combined would have increased from $40 to $50, but one player ends up worse off. The concept of a "Pareto improvement" can help us draw a useful distinction here. Named after the Italian economist, Vilfredo Pareto, a Pareto improvement is an outcome that makes at least one person better off without making anyone worse off.

If at least two players in the public goods game make a full investment ($10 x 2) then the outcome will be a Pareto improvement. The investment of $20 will be doubled to $40, then split among the four players, so the investors end up with $10 each (same as they started with), and the noninvestors end up with $20 each. The total wealth of the combined players will be $60 and no one will have been made worse off.

However, there's a final consideration that is relevant for evaluation this game, namely, the overall amount of wealth produced. If everyone made a full investment, the total wealth could be doubled from $40 to $80. However, if just one player doesn't contribute, he or she will earn more ($25 rather than $20), but the overall wealth produced will be less, only $70 ($25 + $15 + $15 + $15).

In summary, it's possible for this game to be a positive-sum game that makes everyone better off (Pareto improvement) and doubles the wealth of the group. However, individually, each player can always make more by not investing, and if everyone follows this "wealth maximizing" strategy, no one will make anything. Put another way, everyone will miss out on the chance to double both their money and the wealth of the group, if they follow incentives for their own monetary gain.

The dilemma posed by this game is called a "collective action" problem, which occurs when a group of people could benefit from cooperation, but the individual incentives that they each face incline them not to cooperate. Thus, when you face a collective action problem, it is in your immediate interest not to cooperate, even though if everyone cooperated, everyone would be better off.

The million-dollar question is: How can people overcome the incentives of a collective action problem to work together in a manner that increases everyone's well-being? Recall that if you try to be a cooperative person and make a full investment but others don't, you'll just be losing half your money. From the perspective of overall wealth generation, the best outcome would be if everyone invested, which would require each of you to resist attempting to earn a little more by being a noninvestor.

By this point, you may be thinking to yourself: "these are all interesting intellectual points, but this is a strange game concocted by the professor—what relevance does this have to the real world?" Well, think about it. Have you ever been in a situation in which you and others could do well if everyone pitched in, but each of you could do even better by free-riding off the contributions of others?

It turns out that this situation characterizes almost all teamwork, which means that collective action problems are everywhere. The problem that the Xiaogang villagers faced was a collective action problem, and overcoming it meant the difference between life and death. You will face collective action problems as a student, as a businessperson, and as a citizen. It's no understatement to say that the ability to solve collective action problems often determines the success or failure of teams, companies, and even states. So, what are some of the more common forms that collective action problems take and how can we solve them?

Solving Collective Action in the Real World—Change the Game or Change the Players

There are two ways to solve a collective action problem. The first involves changing the incentives of the game such that it pays to cooperate. The second involves getting the players to willingly refrain from profit maximizing because they understand the greater benefits of cooperation and trust others to do the same.

Let's think through how these work in the context of some real-world examples.

The Firm

First, consider the firm. As mentioned, firms aren't organized as markets and this gives rise to the principal-agent problem, which is a kind of collective action problem. Firms will be most profitable if all employees work hard and do their jobs well. However, it's generally difficult to monitor an employee's performance in real time. Moreover, employees will often be working in teams, whose outcomes are only observed in aggregate. An employee will thus face incentives similar to the public goods game. He or she could put in less work without being noticed while still benefiting from whatever contributions others make. What, then, can prevent employees from shirking on their work?

Think back to the public goods game played in a classroom. What would make it harder or easier for people to cooperate in this game? First, there was the suggestion that if the players were all friends who knew each other, then this might provide a basis for mutual trust and a common commitment to cooperate. The same holds true in many cooperative endeavors, and this is why companies often spend significant resources to develop camaraderie among employees and take care to avoid hiring people who aren't "team players." By selecting or cultivating the right kind of people—players who are willing to forsake a small advantage because they all recognize the benefits of cooperation—a team may be able to overcome the incentives of a collective action problem.

Second, think about the role that the envelope played. It provided anonymity, such that players couldn't be sure exactly how much money others were contributing. If contributions were transparent and easily observed, or if people could communicate and signal that they were investing, that could provide the mutual assurance needed for everyone to contribute. Moreover, if a player didn't contribute and others could observe this, then that player could be subject to sanction. The other players might shame that player, or exclude them from future teams. Notice that this would reconfigure the incentives of the game itself. If failing to invest meant that you lost out on other opportunities in the long term, that would be a powerful incentive to put your money in. For companies, the underlying question is: Can the game be changed? Are there ways to make contributions more transparent and measurable, so that work can be rewarded and shirking can be penalized?

Finally, think about the number of players involved. We discussed a game with four players. Suppose your class has thirty students. Would it be easier or harder if the entire class played the game together? Since its less likely that you know everyone well, the social bonds will be weaker and you'll be less certain about whether you can trust everyone to cooperate. It will also be harder to monitor everyone's contribution at the same time. Finally, as the number of players increases, so does the degree to which your contribution will be dissipated if others don't contribute. If there are thirty people in the class and you are the only one who contributes, then your $10 is doubled to $20 and split between thirty, leaving you only 67 cents!

In summary, it's easier for people to work together when groups are small enough that people know each other and/or they share social bonds that run deep. It's also easier if their contributions can be observed and shirkers can be punished. By contrast, when a group is large, people have little knowledge or trust of one another, and contributions are difficult to observe, the collective action problem will be harder to overcome.

These dynamics help explain a common challenge faced by startups as they grow. Initially, most startups attract a core group of enthusiastic founders, bound together by friendship, equity stakes, and a common vision of what their idea can become. Because the group is small, it quickly becomes apparent if someone isn't doing their share, and the founders are often happy to put in long hours with little assurance of additional compensation. If the company does succeed and starts to grow, it goes through a "scale-up" period, which requires hiring many new workers—workers who are not known to the founders or to each other, and who may not share the enthusiasm and vision of the founders. These workers are there for the paycheck, as most workers are. The challenge is for the scaled-up firm to develop methods of incentivizing these workers and overcome the principal-agent problem. Why should employees work long hours on a tough project if it doesn't result in more pay, or if they could get away with doing less? Much of the work that goes into scaling up a successful firm consists of developing mechanisms to measure and reward the contributions of employees. We'll discuss some of these in more detail in the next chapter.

A firm is organized hierarchically, which means that specific people—managers and executives—have a responsibility to understand and shape the incentives that employees face. Firms are constantly searching for ways to improve incentives for productive work. However, it may not always be feasible to design perfect incentives, in which case the selection and cultivation of team players who are willing to cooperate despite opportunities to shirk becomes even more important.

Nonmarket Competition beyond the Firm, a.k.a. Politics

Recall our earlier observation that those engaged in business have to deal with two important domains that are not organized as traditional markets and which do not utilize a conventional price system. The first, which we've discussed, is the internal organization of the firm. The second is politics, which may also surprise you. By politics we mean competition for the power and resources of the state, as well as competition for social legitimacy. This requires some spelling out.

Within a well-functioning market, firms compete with each other by producing better goods and services at lower prices. However, firms can also compete by seeking special favors from the government, such as tax breaks, subsidies, or restrictions on their competitors. These political favors can be extremely valuable, but competing for, and winning, these favors does not produce the same benefits associated with market competition. Indeed, this competition involves collective action problems, like the public goods game, that can lead to bad outcomes.

There's a second reason that businesses need to worry about politics. If a business or industry is widely perceived to be acting badly, then voters and politicians may decide that the business or industry needs to be regulated, sanctioned, or even banned. So, all businesses have to be concerned with whether they are perceived as legitimate in the eyes of the larger public. This, too, presents a collective action problem, because bad actions by one firm in an industry may invite sanction of the entire industry. Moreover, if there is an important role that the government needs to play in correcting a market imperfection or regulating an industry, the firms in the industry will have to figure out how to cooperate to communicate their expertise to policymakers (how to lobby the government), while policymakers will have to figure out how to asses this expertise and prevent it from turning into requests for illegitimate political favors.

This collection of concerns about political favors, public perceptions, regulation, and business-government relations is sometimes called "nonmarket strategy." The idea is that a firm needs to care not only about producing better goods and services at a lower price (market strategy) but also about its larger social and political milieu, which likewise can enrich or destroy a business. However, competition in the nonmarket space does not follow the invisible hand logic. Rather, it is characterized by collective action problems. Let's think through some of these.

Chemical Fishing and Industry Self-Governance

Have you ever heard of "chemical fishing"? Chances are you haven't, but if you lived on an island in Southeast Asia you would have. Chemical fishing refers to the practice of dumping chemicals like bleach or cyanide into the ocean in order to harvest fish. It turns out that this is a highly effective method for catching a lot of fish with little effort. When these powerful chemicals enter the water, they stun fish in the immediate area, suffocating them as the chemicals come in contact with their gills. The immobilized fish float to the surface and can be easily scooped up.

Fishermen using this method can fill their boats with fish in no time. Unfortunately, there's a big downside to this approach, as these chemicals also destroy the coral reefs that they come in contact with. So, within a few years, areas that have been subject to chemical fishing become aquatic wastelands, unable to support the generation of new fish or other marine life. That's bad for the environment, bad for fishing, and particularly unfortunate if communities depended on these fishing grounds, since people will be deprived of their livelihood. On the other hand, the ocean is big, and an ambitious chemical fisher can keep searching out new areas in which to dump bleach and make a quick harvest.

If you lived in a fishing village in Southeast Asia, would you practice chemical fishing? Why or why not?

On the one hand, there are obvious reasons not to. It will destroy the aquatic ecosystem and rob your children and grandchildren of a renewable resource on which your livelihood depends. On the other hand, your family is hungry and needs money, and you can get a lot of fish today by using chemicals. Moreover, there are a lot of people in the same situation. Even if you don't use chemicals to fish, someone else probably will, in which case the aquatic ecosystem will still be destroyed. If the ecosystem is going to be destroyed anyway, then why not at least benefit now from catching some fish with chemicals?[7]

You can start to see the logic of the collective action problem. This particular kind of problem, which involves incentives to overuse a common resource, is referred to as the "tragedy of the commons." Everyone would be better off not destroying the fishery. However, there are huge short-term gains to be made by chemical fishing, and unless you can trust people to restrain from taking advantage of that, you might as well participate yourself. The problem is a lot like the problem the Xiaogang villagers faced. Notice that their solution—assigning property rights—will be difficult to employ because the ocean is harder to divvy up and monitor than an agricultural field.

Governments have made chemical fishing illegal, but this is hard to enforce, in part because patrolling the waters to catch and punish those who use chemicals is costly and the ocean is vast. Another approach is to develop technologies that can detect whether a fish was caught with chemicals, and some progress has been made toward this goal.[8] However, note that it is in the interest of anyone who wants to see these fisheries survive to figure out a way to stop chemical fishing. For this reason, many fishing villages have developed strong norms against chemical fishing. Villagers themselves monitor their local fishing grounds, teach their children that chemical fishing is bad, and penalize anyone caught using chemicals through both the law and social ostracism. That is, participants in the fishing market have developed their own governance mechanisms to help address the collective action problem (some have been more successful than others).

In her classic book, *Governing the Commons: The Evolution of Institutions for Collective Action*, Nobel Laureate Elinor Ostrom documented ways in which different communities from around the world have organized forms of governance to overcome collective action problems. Every industry confronts a related question. Although the firms that are members of an industry all compete with one another, they also have a common interest in ensuring that the industry as a whole is sustainable, well regulated, and socially accepted. In many cases, if one firm wants to do the "right thing" and spend resources to address a problem, then this will put them at a competitive disadvantage if other firms don't also contribute resources. But if a problem goes unaddressed, it can prove disastrous for an industry.

Sadly, sometimes it takes a crisis for an industry to respond. For example, on April 24, 2013, an eight-story building in Bangladesh collapsed, killing 1,134 people, most of them poor garment workers.[9] The building, called Rana Plaza, was filled to the brim with garment factories that made clothes for many internationally known fashion brands. Who was to blame for this terrible loss of life? The building was not designed to house heavy manufacturing equipment, and the top stories were added without permits. The building was also built with substandard materials and lacked many safety features found in developed countries. And the day before the disaster, cracks were observed in the building, which led to a brief evacuation; but managers ordered workers to come back the next day because of pressing deadlines to fulfill orders for companies such as Benetton, El Corte Inglés, and Walmart.[10]

Clearly, the local government did not have that capacity to effectively establish and enforce safety standards and building codes. However, what responsibility did large international clothing companies have to ensure the safety of those who produced their products? Although some companies cared about this question before the disaster and spent resources to address it in their own supply chain, unless a large number of companies acted together the status quo wouldn't change.

The enormous loss of life did provoke public outcry and a reaction from the industry. The outcome was the "Accord on Fire and Building Safety in Bangladesh," which sets safety standards and provides funds to maintain buildings—funds that are paid by all member companies. Although widely praised as an effective way for members of the industry to work together to ensure the safety of garment workers, it came too late for the laborers in Rana Plaza.

One of the enduring questions for any industry is whether it can perceive and address collective action problems prospectively, or whether it takes a crisis for change to happen. An industry should want to prevent a crisis not only for the sake of potential victims but also because once a crisis does strike, an industry may lose the option to self-regulate if public outcry leads governments to step in with their own regulations, which may be less efficient.

Giving Money Away Isn't Easy, and the Challenge of Rent Seeking

In every case that we examine, there is a common criteria of judgment that we need to pay attention to, namely, what is the net effect? Chemical fishing and neglected infrastructure both make money in the short term, but the overall outcomes that they produce are bad. It's possible that forms of collective governance can help us reconfigure or overcome the incentives that produce bad outcomes. However, governing, whether it be done by an industry association or state officials, creates its own challenges and collective action problems. We need to understand these as well.

For example, suppose you want to provide money for someone to do a good thing. What is the best way to award that money? How about a competition? We know that competition in markets produces good outcomes, so why not have a competition for this prize money to determine who can do the most good with it?

This is, in fact, how many governments award grants of all kinds. But this approach has a potential downside.

Suppose that the Department of Housing and Urban Development (HUD) wants to provide grants for large cities to revitalize poor neighborhoods. HUD announces that it will provide ten grants of $10 million each to the ten cities that come up with the best plans for revitalization. Any city with a population above 400,000 is welcome to apply. Given that HUD doesn't know what exactly each city would need to do to accomplish revitalization, it requires cities to prepare detailed proposals with supporting analysis. The best ten proposals will receive funding. Overall, HUD will award $100 million in grant money for revitalization (ten grants of $10 million). Would this competition be a good idea? Let's think about it.

Assume that there are fifty cities with populations above 400,000 that would like to apply for these grants. In order to win, a city not only has to come up with a detailed proposal, but the proposal has to be better than at least forty other cities' proposals. That's going to require a lot of hard work! How much work would it be worth investing in a proposal? Suppose that a city employed twenty-five people in a variety of different positions who all work together to assemble a stellar grant proposal. If each of these people earns a salary of $100,000 for their work, then the overall cost of preparing the grant will be $2.5 million. Is that sort of investment worth it? Well yes—it is if you win. Winning cities will come out $7.5 million ahead ($10 million grant minus the $2.5 million invested to win it). But what about the cities that lose? The receive nothing. Maybe they should have spent more on the grant proposal? Even if they don't, gambling $2.5 million for a chance to win $10 million might still be an attractive proposition.

Are you beginning to see the problem with this competition? If fifty cities each spend $2.5 million preparing grant proposals, that would mean that they would collectively spend $125 million worth of resources (50 x $2.5 million). For what? For HUD to give out $100 million. Put another way, the net effect of this competition is that $25 million of wealth is destroyed! That is not a good outcome. The society would have more resources if the competition never happened in the first place.[11]

This sort of competition is similar to a "Tullock contest" named after Gordon Tullock, who was one of the founders of Public Choice Economics, along with the Nobel Laureate James Buchanan. Tullock's insight was that competition for a fixed resource can incentivize competitors to expend resources in a manner that generates a net economic loss. (Your professor may have you play another kind of Tullock auction in class, but you'll have to wait and see—we're not giving away the details.)

If an agency like HUD wants to make a contribution to society, it has to pay attention to the costs generated by a grant competition. Notice that simply giving grant money away at random would be preferable to a competition that consumes $125 million. However, there might be alternative ways to judge quality and award grants based on objective standards of merit that don't require large, strategic investments by competitors. For example, HUD might look at publicly available statistics that suggest that a city could benefit from a grant and limit the length of proposals to a few pages.

Public Choice Economics also highlights a collective action problem that lies at the heart of democratic government. We've already mentioned that governments can do things to help or harm businesses. Because of this, businesses will often compete for favors from government. This sort of competition is called "rent seeking." The problem with rent seeking is that it resembles a Tullock contest. It involves competition that aims to capture existing resources without creating new wealth. Many compete, but few will win. Those who lose will have expended resources with nothing to show for it. Those who win will profit, but this generally comes at the expense of the larger society.

For example, Public Choice economists have noted that sugar costs about twice as much in the United States as it does everywhere else in the world, costing American consumers an extra $4 billion or so each year.[12] Why? Because sugarbeet farmers in the United States have successfully lobbied the government for protectionist import quotas and tariffs, which decreases competition from foreign sugar. This raises a deeper puzzle—why would American consumers allow this to happen? The United States is a democracy, after all, so how could a policy be put in place that disadvantages the majority of Americans? The answer is: concentrated benefits and diffused costs.

There are about 10,000 farms represented by the American Sugarbeet Growers Association.[13] $4 billion divided by 10,000 yields a benefit of $400,000 per farm. That's big money! You can see why each of these farms would invest a lot of time and resources lobbying for sugar tariffs. As for the rest of us, there are about 325 million people in the United States. If you divide the $4 billion extra we pay for sugar by the total population, it means we're each paying an extra $12.31 each year. That's not big money, and it's hardly worth picking up the phone to call your congressional representative to complain.

Of course, the sugarbeet industry isn't alone. A similar logic of economic interest could drive many companies to compete for profits by lobbying the government; and they have a chance at being successful if the cost will be diffused among a large number of citizens.

Public Choice analysis shows why this sort of competition can be economically profitable for firms but economically destructive for the larger society. We want firms to compete on the basis of quality and price, not by exploiting political power for private gain. Democratic representation alone isn't enough to solve this collective action problem because of concentrated benefits and diffused costs. So, how have successful democracies addressed this challenge?

Before we answer this question, let's consider one final case, which raises the question of how far a business should be allowed to go in order to advance its interest in a court of law.

Collective Action in Politics

In 2002, the A.T. Massey Coal Company was ordered by a jury in West Virginia to pay $50 million in damages for having fraudulently cancelled a coal supply contract with Harman Mining, which caused that company to fail. The Massey Coal Company, led by CEO Don Blankenship, appealed this verdict to West Virginia Supreme Court, where the deciding vote was likely to be cast by Justice Warren McGraw. However, McGraw was up for reelection that year, and his challenger, Brent Benjamin, was perceived to be favorable to the claims of Massey Coal Company. Naturally, Don Blankenship, the CEO of Massey Coal, wanted to see Benjamin elected to replace McGraw. So what could Blankenship do?

West Virginia limits campaign contributions to $1,000 per candidate. Blankenship donated $1,000 to Benjamin, but he didn't stop there. Blankenship also created a nonprofit called "And for the Sake of the Kids," through which he spent some $3 million to run advertisements opposing McGraw. The nonprofit's expenditures were legal because they were uncoordinated with Benjamin's campaign (so-called independent expenditures). However, this was a large amount for a West Virginia race and more than all other expenditures for Benjamin combined. Of course, from Blankenship's perspective, $3 million would be a small price to pay if it would save his company from a $50 million judgment. Benjamin was elected by a small margin.

When the case came before the West Virginia Supreme Court, lawyers representing Harman Mining argued that Benjamin should recuse himself from the case, because it appeared that he was indebted to Blankenship for his victory. Benjamin refused, and he cast the deciding vote (3–2) overturning the judgment against Massey Coal. Blankenship's investment paid off. But should it have?

Do you think it was appropriate for Benjamin to judge this case, given that Blankenship was so instrumental in getting Benjamin elected? Should Benjamin have to recuse himself? Or, was his election just democratic politics at work, with Blankenship exercising his rights as a citizen to advocate for the best candidate? If there was no official agreement with Blankenship, is there also no genuine debt that would require Benjamin to recuse himself?

These were the questions that the Supreme Court of the United States had to answer when the case was further appealed to its nine Justices. By a vote of 5–4, the US Supreme Court found that Benjamin had to recuse himself, not because they believed that he was in fact biased but because Blankenship's expenditures created an "appearance" or "possibility" of bias.[14] The prevailing justices cited an old legal principle—that "no man can be a judge in his own case," . . . that "no man is permitted to try cases where he has an interest in the outcome"—to argue that if "the probability of actual bias" is high, a judge like Benjamin must recuse himself. However, the dissenting Justices objected that it was not clear what exactly constitutes a high probability of bias. So, how are we supposed to know when advocating for your economic interests in judicial elections crosses a line such that a judge you support can't judge your case?

These are all serious questions. On the one hand, we believe that justice should be blind to everything except the relevant evidence in a case and that judges should rule according to the law without any partiality. On the other hand, in a majority of jurisdictions, voters elected judges, and it's in any given voter's interest to elect judges who will be sympathetic to that voter's interests.

This problem is, in fact, a problem with democracy at large. We want a government that advances the common good by being competent, just, and impartial, but most of us support politicians whom we hope will favor our interests. In 1787, James Madison, one of the founding fathers of America, describe the problem in *Federalist 10* as follows:

> No man is allowed to be a judge in his own cause, because his interest would certainly bias his judgment, and, not improbably, corrupt his integrity. With equal,

nay with greater reason, a body of men are unfit to be both judges and parties at the same time; yet what are many of the most important acts of legislation, but so many judicial determinations, not indeed concerning the rights of single persons, but concerning the rights of large bodies of citizens?

Madison pointed out that any society will contain different factions and that most factions will be motivated by economic interests, united by a desire to use the government to benefit themselves. How can this collective action problem be solved? Madison begins by asking whether we can do away with factions, or at least prevent them from trying to influence the government. However, he rejects this approach because it would destroy liberty and take away the right of citizens to engage in political advocacy.

Rather, Madison focuses on trying to control the effects of faction. He argues that the best way to prevent one faction from dominating government is to have an extended republic that includes many factions and to have a system of representation that requires politicians to appeal to a broad base of supporters from different factions. Madison realized that this solution wasn't perfect, and in other *Federalist Papers* he and his compatriots proposed additional measures, such as divided government and checks and balances, meant to ensure that the ambition of some factions will counteract the ambition of others.

At the broadest level, constitutional government is an attempt to overcome a collective action problem and, in so doing, enable a large number of people to cooperate in a manner that produces superior benefits. However, there is always a danger that factions will try to advance their interests through politics in a manner that produces bad outcomes overall. Note that, to the degree that political institutions don't make it in everyone's interest to be a good citizen, something else may be required for people not to exploit politics for personal gain. The political scientist James Q. Wilson has argued that for much of America's history this restraint has been provided by a broad political culture that viewed certain types of economic favoritism by the government as illegitimate. Put another way, if most people believe it's wrong for someone to exploit politics for private gain, then they will refrain from trying to do so themselves and be willing to punish others who do. Finally, a thriving economy also helps prevent any one faction from dominating politics, because new economic interests will continually replace old ones, and citizens will find that it is more profitable to engage in productive business than to try to grow rich by seeking government favors.

In summary, the success of modern democracies is a product both of well-designed political institutions that make it in the interests of factions to keep each other in check as well as widely shared convictions that lead citizens, business leaders, and politicians to avoid certain behaviors that are perceived as illegitimate. However, this is a delicate balance. Just as business leaders need to ask themselves whether collective action problems are holding their firms or their industries back, political leaders and policymakers need to consider the net effect of their actions so that they are not tempted by short-term incentives to undertake actions that undermine the long-term stability and prosperity of their societies. Moreover, although business have to be concerned with non-market strategy, we will all be better off if businesses support policies that preserve competitive markets. Market competition rewards those who find better ways of providing goods and services to others, thus aligning self-interest with the common good.

Summary

- Opportunities for profit can sometimes lead people to take actions that lead to bad outcomes for both themselves and others. When a group of people could benefit from cooperation but the individual incentives that they each face incline them not to cooperate, we call this a collective action problem.
- Collective action problems are all around us. They arise in teamwork, within firms, and in the larger political organization of a society.
- One way of solving a collective action problem is to change the incentives that people face so that it pays for individuals to cooperate. However, this may always not be possible. There may be no entity with the power to change incentives, or the cost of changing incentives may be prohibitively high.
- Another way of solving a collective action problem is for enough individuals to willingly refrain from profit maximizing because they understand the greater benefits of cooperation and trust others to do the same. This, too, can be challenging, particularly as groups become larger and as the rewards for not cooperating increase.
- In practice, a combination of these two strategies is often required in order to successfully overcome collective action problems.
- Ultimately, individuals, businesses, and governments need to evaluate the overall effect of their actions. If existing incentives and behavior are leading to bad outcomes, leaders ought to search for ways to overcome these collective actions problems. If successful, the benefits of collective action can be enormous and mirror the kind of cooperative productivity we find in well-functioning markets.

Discussion Questions

1. Who made the right decision in the public goods game? Was it Sally, who kept her money out and made $25, or her three classmates who made a full investment but only received $15 a piece? Explain your reasoning.
2. In a democracy, why do we sometimes see laws passed that benefit a small number of people at the expense of the majority?
3. Do you think businesses should spend more or less time and resources lobbying the government? Why?
4. Have you ever found yourself in a collective action problem or observed others wrestling with one? Was the problem resolved? If so, how? If not, why?

Notes

1. Dikötter 2010b.
2. Dikötter 2010a.
3. Dikotter 2010b.
4. Kestenbaum and Goldstein.
5. Hayek 1945: 521.
6. Smith 1776: IV.2.9.
7. For an excellent review of this problem and its relationship to property rights, see Schmidtz 1994.
8. Trager 2017.
9. Hoskins 2015.
10. Motlagh and Saha 2014.
11. This example is inspired by the analysis provided by https://www.econlib.org/library/Columns/y2006/Mungerrentseeking.html.
12. http://www.aei.org/publication/u-s-sugar-policy-cost-american-consumers-almost-4-billion-last-year/.
13. https://americansugarbeet.org.
14. https://www.supremecourt.gov/opinions/08pdf/08-22.pdf.

10

The Effect of Incentives

Diffusion of Responsibility

Basic Lesson: *Ethics is everyone's job. But unfortunately, there's a sense in which when something is everyone's job, it's nobody's job. Organizations and groups often create conditions where individual inputs matter very little and in which responsibility is diffused among the many, and so no one has an incentive to do the right thing.*

On January 28, 1986, Mrs. Santigate's first-grade class huddled around the television to watch the first "teacher in space" take off on the Space Shuttle Challenger. About seventy-four seconds after launch, aerodynamic forces tore the shuttle apart. All the astronauts died—though some may have survived all the way until the crew cabin crashed into the ocean at over 300 km/h. Mrs. Santigate now had to comfort twenty-five crying, confused, or dazed children, including Jason.

Subsequent investigations revealed the problem was a defective seal between certain fuel compartments. The shuttle took off in very cold conditions; under such conditions, the rings contract too much and fail to provide a proper seal. Apparently, the Thiokol engineers who helped designed the seal were worried the O-rings might not hold; when the Challenger "exploded," some engineers immediately knew what the problem was.[1]

At least one engineer fought vigorously to stop the launch ahead of time. Apparently, NASA hated the idea of postponing the launch and wanted it to be a success. They demanded Thiokol "put their management hats on" and pressured Thiokol's management to OK the launch They did. The rest is history.

Some of the problems here are familiar: Thiokol's management caved under pressure. NASA's leadership cared more about image than safety. But most analysts think there's an additional problem: Many different people are "in charge" of safety, all at the same time. They can make complaints to others and feel like they've done their due diligence. Some people made complaints but didn't have the power to veto the launch. But when everyone's in charge of safety, then no one really is.

Business Ethics for Better Behavior. Jason Brennan, William English, John Hasnas, and Peter Jaworski, Oxford University Press.
© Oxford University Press 2021. DOI: 10.1093/oso/9780190076559.003.0010

We've seen the same dynamics firsthand at our own university, albeit on a far less dangerous issue. A few years ago, our faculty voted to change the way MBA courses function, including how many students are in each class and how many credit hours a professor would earn by teaching these courses. (Each professor has to teach a certain number of credit hours per year.) The goal was to improve the quality of the MBA courses.

But then a problem arose—it was hard to recruit people to teach the MBA courses. Part of the issue was bad incentives: Not only are undergrads more fun to teach than MBAs, but also the credit hour/student ratio was lower for MBAs than for undergrads. In other words, teaching MBAs was more work for lower compensation. But this incentive problem was created by the faculty themselves when they voted on the program. Why didn't they think the problem through when voting on the design?

Georgetown's Honor System faces problems, too. The purpose of the Honor System is to encourage academic honesty and discourage academic dishonesty, such as plagiarism or data fabrication. But years ago—in an effort to make it easier to prosecute dishonesty—administrators had written overly broad rules, making it so that *any* mistake in citation practices, including technical mistakes, such as using the wrong page numbers in a citation or indenting a paragraph but failing to include all the citation information, counts as a punishable offense. But everyone knows there's a difference between sloppiness and cheating. (One of us has a peer-reviewed book published by this very press which contains an error in a citation by listing the wrong page range; technically, he is guilty of academic dishonesty by Georgetown's rules.) Further, faculty are encouraged to report *all* violations, including such technical violations, to the Honor Council for investigation. In practice, tenure-track faculty use their discretion and don't report such technical mistakes, but adjunct faculty teaching continuing studies courses to adult learners do. The result is deeply unethical: students often get punished as *cheaters* when they are really just sloppy.

The problem here isn't merely that the powers that be made bad choices in designing the rules. It's not just that Honor Council members are conformists who violate Principle 5 and follow rather than question badly designed rules. Rather, the problem is that even though people recognize the rules are bad, no seems willing to fix them. More precisely, two of us, John Hasnas and Jason Brennan, tried to get university counsel to override the rules. Although university counsel agreed the rules were bad, they said they had no legal authority to override them, as students technically consent to the rules by enrolling. Our only hope was to convince the faculty senate and a number of other boards to agree to change them. That seemed hopeless, so we gave up. Many other faculty feel the same. It's a problem, but fixing the problem takes too many steps and requires too many people to agree. So, they shrug their shoulders and move on.

Your Dorm Kitchen, Explained

In the previous chapter, we discussed the tragedy of the commons. It's worth reviewing the problem again, because it presents itself over and over in different forms.

We haven't been in your dorm's kitchens or bathrooms, we promise. We're not creepy and we're not stalking you. But we have a good guess about how they look: disgusting. Maybe they're clean right after the janitor or cleaning people come through, but they turn disgusting shortly after.

You could take it upon yourself to keep them immaculate, but you don't. Why not?

Your dorm kitchen and bathroom suffer from the "tragedy of the commons." The idea here is that when something is held and used collectively, everyone has an incentive to overuse it.

To illustrate, imagine there's pastureland which no one owns. Suppose the pasture can indefinitely sustain one hundred sheep. As long as one hundred or fewer sheep graze on it, the grass will grow back each year. At 101 or more sheep, the pasture starts to die and turn to dust. One hundred sheep is the *carrying capacity* of the pasture—it's the number of sheep the pasture can indefinitely sustain and renew itself.

Right now, ten shepherds each own a flock of ten sheep, for one hundred total sheep. They don't know each other and don't have any ability to control the others. At carrying capacity, the sheep are fully fed and their wool is as lustrous and full as it can be. Let's say each sheep thus produces $200 worth of wool per year. Each shepherd thus gets $2,000 a year in wool sales, and the total economic output of the pasture is $20,000.

However, suppose a shepherd decides to experiment with placing an eleventh sheep into his flock, bringing the total number of sheep up on the pasture to 101. Now there isn't quite enough grass for all the sheep. Their wool is lower quality; let's say it's now worth only $190 per sheep. Now ask these questions:

1. How does adding an eleventh sheep affect that shepherd?
2. What does it do the total output of the pasture?
3. How does it affect the others? How will the other shepherds respond?

The answers:

1. It's a good deal for the shepherd who added the extra sheep. It's better to have eleven sheep worth $190 each than ten worth $200 each: $2,090 > $2,000. So, even though he's starting to kill the pasture, he's happy with his choice.
2. Adding an extra sheep immediately drops the total output of the land. At one hundred sheep worth $200 each, the output is $20,000 per year. At 101 sheep worth $190 each, the total output is $19,190 a year. Exceeding the carrying capacity doesn't just kill the pasture over time; it reduces its value even in the short term.
3. It's a bad deal for the other shepherds. They still have ten sheep each, and now each sheep is only worth $190 instead of $200. Their flocks are now worth $1,900 a year instead of $2,000. Once the other shepherd adds an eleventh sheep to his flock (and the 101st sheep to the entire pasture), he costs each other shepherd $100 a year. Since they can't control what the others do, to make up for the loss, they'll probably add *more* sheep to their flocks. But that will just repeat the problem.

You'd expect the other shepherds to add additional sheep, too, and so the pasture will die and turn to dust.

The shepherds here are responding rationally to the incentives they face. It just turns out that in this case, the background ownership rules make it so that when everyone pursues their self-interest, everyone loses.

You see this kind of problem all around. Why are fishing stocks being depleted in the oceans? Why does climate change happen? Fishers don't want to deplete the oceans and no one wants to cause pollution and ruin the climate. But if an individual fishing company tries to act responsibly and catch less fish, they can't count on others doing so. So, they might as well catch more fish today.

Similarly, if you take two fewer flights a year, drive a twenty-year-old Honda Civic instead of buying a new Toyota Prius or a Ford Mustang, and set your air conditioner up 3 degrees, you'll significantly reduce your carbon footprint.

But who cares? You won't make a difference. You just don't matter than much. Your choice to lead a green lifestyle or to waste as much as you can have a negligible impact on the environment and on the climate. What matters is how *we* act, not how you act.

You can see the tragedy of the commons in action next time you share a dessert with friends. The cake arrives on the table. The spoons come out, and you all chomp down furiously. You'd enjoy the food more if you ate slower and savored each bite. But you can't, because you know others will just eat more while you wait. What's the solution?

In general, there are two ways to deal with this problem:

1. Appoint a dictator. The dictator decides who gets what and is in charge of the cake.
2. Divide the cake up into smaller pieces. Everyone gets their own piece which they can eat as they please.

The first choice often sounds unappealing. Do you want a friend to be in charge? If we made this about climate change instead of cake, do you trust anyone to wield that much power over others? (What if, as inevitably happens, the wrong people win the next election and take over the power you meant to place in different hands? What if they use that power for their own ends rather than the ends you intended?)

The second choice sounds more appealing at first glance. If you gave each shepherd 1/10th of the pasture as her own, she'd no longer have an incentive to add extra sheep. When the pasture is held in common, adding an extra sheep benefits her but hurts the others; she *externalizes* the cost onto others. When the pastures are divided up, adding an extra sheep hurts her rather than benefits her. She internalizes the costs. With ten sheep in her private pasture, she makes $2,000 a year, but with eleven sheep, she makes only $1,919 a year, plus her pasture starts to die.[2] Now her self-interest directs her to preserve her private pasture rather than destroy the common pasture. Further, since she can build a fence, she has the power to ensure others don't intrude much into her property, while before "saving the commons" was everybody's—and thus nobody's—responsibility.

The problem, though, is that this mechanism doesn't work for everything. If everyone had their own private climate, we'd have a strong incentive not to overpollute or cause private climate change. But we don't have any way of dividing the climate up the way we can divide up the pasture. Climate is stuck being everyone's problem.

Why Big Committees Are Dumb and Why Antivaxxers Exist

Georgetown University's business school has a mandatory curve imposed on all of its classes, with a max grade of a B+. In 2018, students and some faculty asked to revisit the curve. They spent months analyzing the curve's effects.

They determined that it undermined collaboration, because it created a zero-sum game. Having a curve means one student can't get a better grade without another getting a worse grade. In a system like that, why would you want to help your fellow students study; their good grades come at your expense. They also determined that it hurt our students' job prospects. We artificially made our students' average grades lower than at other schools. That meant they had a harder time getting good job or getting into good graduate schools, especially since employers wouldn't know that a B+ at Georgetown MSB means the same as an A- at one of our competitors.

So, we recognized what the problems were and knew we should fix them. What did we do? Well, we raised the curve slightly, from a 3.33 (B+) to a 3.5 (halfway between a B+ and an A-). This means we kept the zero-sum aspect of our curve, which means students still have a disincentive to study together or collaborate, and instead to be extremely competitive toward each other. It also means that we continue to artificially deflate our students' grades and make them look worse than their peers at peer universities; we continue to hurt their job prospects, earnings, and graduate school prospects. There was a complete disconnect between the problem we identified and the "solution."

We're smart people as individuals. So why are we so dumb as a group? Some of our faculty are leading experts on management, so why don't they apply their knowledge to make good management decisions?

Part of the problem is that people in general suffer from a cognitive bias called "anchoring and adjustment." People tend to be conservative in their thinking and anchor their decisions and estimates to past ideas and numbers, even if they know these are arbitrary. To illustrate, suppose you ask two hundred experimental subjects to estimate a woman's height. You ask one hundred of them, "How much taller than 5 feet is she?" You ask the other, "How much shorter than 6 feet is she?" The groups will arrive at different average estimates. The "taller than 5 feet" people will have a lower average estimate than the "shorter than 6 feet" people.[3] Feeding them an arbitrary number changes their estimates. (By the way, marketers and political campaigns are well aware of this bias and use it to manipulate you.)

This phenomenon affects how people make decisions. If you place people in arbitrary starting points, they won't so much ask "Where should I end up?" as much as "How far should I move away from where I am?." They treat the status quo as a default from which departures must be justified. Sometimes, this kind of conservativism is pragmatic, especially when we don't understand our situation or the alternatives. But in the case of the curve, we knew we imposed it for shortsighted reasons a decade before, and we all agreed we had strong arguments against it. We wouldn't have picked our new policy if we started from scratch. Nevertheless, as a group, we found it hard to budge.

It's not just that, though. There's another set of problems endemic to group decision-making, especially when large groups when things are put to a vote. Consider two situations:

1. You go to a restaurant. Whatever you order, you eat and pay for.
2. You go to a restaurant along with 1,000 other people. You all have to eat the same meal and split the bill evenly. You get to vote on what meal you eat, but you get only 1 vote out of 1,000.

In which situation, 1 or 2, would you more carefully consider the quality of the meal? In which situation would you think more carefully about what to eat?

Or, consider this parallel:

> You walk into Biology 101, along with 500 other students. On the first day of class, the professor announces, "I am a firm believer in equality. Accordingly, you will take 1 final exam on the last day of class, worth 100% of your grade. However, rather than each student receiving her individual exam grade, I will average all of your grades together. Everyone will receive the same grade.

In this absurd situation, what do you think the average final grade would be? If you guess it would be low—an F—you guess right. The problem here is that each student thinks, "If I work hard, I can't count on others working hard. If I study and learn the material, I'll probably get an F. If I slack off and don't learn the material, I'll probably get an F. So, I might as well slack off." The professor would incentivize the students to remain ignorant of biology. It's not because the students are dumb or lazy but because the rules make them behave that way.

When you put things to a vote in front of a large group, you often get something like the same phenomena. Here's the economics of information in one sentence: People will learn and retain information and reason about that information in a scientific, truth-directed way, only if the expected benefits of doing so exceed the costs. For instance, more than half of what you've learned in school you chose to learn only because a grade depended on it and you needed the grade.

When the costs of learning or retaining information exceed the benefits, most people remain ignorant or let themselves forget the information. (For instance, all four of us once memorized a large number of trigonometric identities, but we don't use them anymore and forgot them.) Economists call this situation *rational ignorance*.

When the costs of reasoning in a scientific or truth-tracking way (the costs of putting in effort to overcome biases and thinking carefully) exceed the benefits of doing so, then people will tend to indulge their biases, allow themselves to follow spurious or silly chains of reasoning, and will not work to overcome their confusion. Economists call this situation *rational irrationality*.[4]

When we make decisions in large groups—such as in big committees, or as shareholders voting with thousands of others on company policy or appointments, or as citizens voting in democracies—the costs of gathering and understanding information, or of reasoning carefully, will usually exceed the benefits. Accordingly, people tend to vote badly or in ignorance in such situations.

This kind of behavior happens outside voting contexts. As we wrote the first draft of this paragraph, around the world, there were outbreaks of measles and other preventable diseases. As we revised it later, we were in the middle of the COVID-19 crisis, with no vaccine yet available. As we examined the copy-edited version, vaccines for COVID-19 were available and we the authors are fully vaccinated. Among some people, it has become high status to be against vaccines, and to hold and express unscientific beliefs about the supposed dangers of vaccines and about "alternative" medicines. The famous article claiming a link between vaccines and autism was not just bad or mistaken science but was *deliberate fraud*—author Andrew Wakefield was being paid to fabricate "evidence" which could be used by lawyers to sue vaccine manufacturers.[5] Yet, many parents around the world trust Wakefield, or model Jenny McCarthy, more than the medical community, with its thousands of papers showing there is no link between vaccines and autism.

Two things are at work here. One is that sometimes *believing* certain things comes with rewards, regardless of whether the things are true. If you live in New England, you can make friends more easily if you loudly proclaim that Tom Brady is the greatest quarterback of all time. If you live outside New England, you can win friends more easily by loudly proclaiming he's a cheater and highly overrated. If you lived in medieval Europe, you would benefit from believing in Christianity and rejecting Islam; if you lived in the Middle East or North Africa at the same time, you'd benefit from believing the opposite. We often use beliefs not to track to the truth but to demonstrate our loyalty to the group.[6] At your own campus, it may be that being a Democrat makes you cool while being a Republican makes you uncool, or vice versa.

The second thing is that, thanks to herd immunity, beliefs about vaccines are partly a collective action problem or a public goods problem (see chapter 9). Imagine, contrary to fact, that that if your kid didn't get vaccines, she'd automatically get all the diseases, but if she does get them, she never will. In that world, parents wouldn't dare indulge mistaken beliefs about medicine or take advice from *Playboy* models; they'd get punished very quickly for being wrong and rewarded for being right. But in reality, if you choose not to vaccinate your kids against measles, pertussis, or polio, they probably won't ever get these diseases. The reason: At least for now, enough other people vaccinate their kids that your kids' chances are low. You can indulge bad beliefs because you free ride on others' responsible behaviors.

The lesson: When groups make decisions, or when individuals make individual decisions but it's the *group's* overall behavior that matters, then people will often have strong incentives to make dumb choices, to reason poorly, to believe misinformation, and to indulge their worst biases. When being smart is everyone's responsibility, it's no one's responsibility.

Short Term and Long Term

For the book *Moral Mazes*, sociologists Robert Jackall did extensive fieldwork interviewing and shadowing managers in corporate bureaucracies, learning what makes them tick and how being part of a corporate web affects their decision-making. One of his primary finds is that the people often saw taking a stand or making big decisions as highly risky. They preferred to wait until a decision seemed inevitable.[7]

For instance, at one large chemical company, a major piece of equipment—a "battery"—showed signs of stress. In 1975, it would have taken $6 million to fix the battery in question. But at the time, the top management preferred to invest the money on other things. Many people were partly responsible for the factory's safety and maintenance, and many people knew the battery needed to be repaired. But sticking one's neck out to argue for it meant risking short-term profits and telling the bosses higher up that their strategies are misguided. Instead, lower-level managers dedicated smaller amounts of money to patching the battery until finally, four years later, it broke entirely. At that point, not only would replacing it in 1979 cost more than properly repairing in 1975, but it caused enough pollution that lawsuits and fines added up to over $100 million in costs. A $6 million fix in 1975 could have stopped over $100 million in losses in 1979. But by then, many managers had moved up or onward, and there wasn't anyone who could clearly be blamed for the mistake. Once the battery collapsed, it was of course risk-free to say the company should pay the fines, settle the lawsuits, and replace it.[8]

Why Professors Don't Stop Student Cheating and Why Tuition Is High

A number of researchers have studied student cheating at American universities. The best available evidence indicates that a majority of students engage in at least one mild form of academic dishonesty, though only a smaller percentage engage in the more serious forms (such as plagiarizing or paying someone to write a paper for them), and only a small percentage habitually or routinely cheat.[9]

Our interest here isn't why students cheat. We've already discussed the trade-offs there. Students have a selfish interest in cheating, but they also want to see themselves as overall decent people (see chapter 7). So, they tend to cheat in small ways, just to the point it's consistent with their sense that they are good people. Further, the more others cheat, the more entitled they feel to cheat. What's the point of being honest when that means you get lower grades than the dishonest?

Instead, ask why most professors do so little to stop cheating. The problem may be that they see cheating as a general problem, not a problem specific to them. They know cheating occurs, but unless they catch it firsthand, they don't know how much occurs in their own classes. (For instance, if students are paying others to write papers for our classes, we have no idea.)

One partial solution may be to make the problem personal. Here's a suggestion from some of Jason's students: Professors usually have the option of adding custom questions to their anonymous course evaluations. They could add a question or two about academic dishonesty—for example, "Did you engage in any form of academic dishonesty in this class?" Even in anonymous surveys, students will underreport bad behavior, but some will admit what they did. If a professor learns that a significant percentage of students cheat in her classes, semester after semester, then she would probably take steps to overcome the problem.

Now consider another problem: tuition. Both private and public universities raise their sticker prices year after year at a rate much higher than the rate of inflation. In all fairness, the *actual price paid*—the amount students really pay after financial aid and scholarships—has risen less quickly. But nevertheless, college is in real terms far more expensive today than in the past.[10] Why?

One reason is that universities expenditures continue to rise at high rates. Most departments spend their entire discretionary budgets and seek to maximize the size of their budgets.[11] Each professor, department, institute, or school (within a larger university) has a separate account and an incentive to grow, but to pass the costs onto others. Although everyone wants the overall budget to be sustainable, they want their own portion of the budget to grow. There's rarely one person in charge who can enforce fiscal discipline upon the separate units, and university rules often make it difficult to cut programs or fire unnecessary administrators and even more difficult to fire unnecessary professors.

Fixing the Problem

In the abstract, some of these problems seem easy to fix. In practice, they are much harder.

Let's start with the abstract:

- For any given issue, problem, or resource, some small body or individuals should have clear ownership of that issue, problem, or resource.
- The people with ownership should also have decision-making authority. They have to have the power to do what they think is right.
- The rules should be set up that people both pay the costs for their bad choices and get rewarded for their good choices.
- If there's no way to parcel the resources up, then someone at the top needs to have clear power to act on the issue and be incentivized to think long term.

For instance, in chapter 4, we discussed how Hasnas worked for a company in which lawyers could veto managers' decisions to ensure legal compliance. Although we noted that putting lawyers on the strategic planning committees was even better than giving them a mere veto, giving them a veto was at least a good idea. Imagine, instead, an organization in which every decision goes through multiple committees and has multiple signoff, but in which no one other than the top officers had actual decision-making power, and in which the legal department merely served in an advisory role but couldn't veto possible criminal decisions. In that case, Jackall's research indicates, the lower-level staff (engineers, managers, etc.) would have a strong incentive to keep their mouths shut rather than criticize the higher-level executives' ideas. The executives might well want to do the right thing, but they'd be taking advice from lower-level staff who lack the incentive to take controversial stands for fear of being killjoys or seen as uncooperative.

In practice, the problems are harder to fix. The issue is that changing the background rules or structures is hard to do, even when one knows what to do. Part of the problem is that just as there is diffusion of responsibility regarding particular problems (like budgets, legal compliance, or safety), there's diffusion of responsibility regarding who's in charge of fixing the bureaucratic structures which cause a diffusion of responsibility.

In chapter 13, we'll discuss how ALCOA's CEO Paul O'Neill overcame problems like this with regard to safety. He recognized that for ALCOA to have a better safety record, safety had to be everyone's problem. But "general safety" can't be everyone's problem—then it's no one's problem. Instead, each group or individual had to know which safety issues it owns and is expected to control.

Some Grounds for Hope

We mentioned that climate change is a good example of the problem caused by the diffusion of responsibility. It looks intractable, too. There's no way to divide up the climate the way we can divide up the pasture. There's no "dictator" who can take charge. (The US government can regulate US corporations, but it can't control what corporations do in other countries.) Your company can go green, but it won't matter unless enough others also do.

So, are we doomed? Probably not. One reason is that while climate change is bad, overall, economic growth will probably counteract its negative effects, at least over the next two centuries. Two, there are some reasons to think that people will start polluting less.

Let's start with the first issue. Suppose you were some sort of god who could create, ex nihilo, one of two Earths:

- *Earth One.* Earth One looks exactly like our current earth, with its current climate, and current levels of poverty around the world. Some people are rich, but most are poor, and many are desperately poor. Many people die of starvation and disease. In the developing world, when a weather disaster strikes, this devastates the economy and the people. But the climate will not get any hotter and less hospitable than it already is.
- *Earth Two.* On Earth Two, gross world product is at least four times larger than it is on Earth One, but the population of Earth Two is only somewhat larger than on Earth One.[12] Per-capita world product is over $50,000.[13] The average per-capita income in the poorest or "developing countries" is about five to six times what is on Earth One. But the average temperature on Earth Two is about 2 to 3 degrees centigrade warmer than on Earth One. As a result, there are more weather disasters. Some parts of Earth One that are arable or livable are not arable or livable on

Earth Two, though some of the colder regions of Earth One are arable and more livable on Earth Two. Thanks to having vastly more wealth and better technology, the people on Earth Two suffer *less*, despite their *worse* climate, than do the people on Earth One.

From a humanitarian perspective, Earth Two looks a lot better than Earth One. That's not to say Earth Two is perfect. A slightly better and more powerful god might prefer to make Earth Three, which combines Earth One's better climate with Earth Two's better economy. But, alas, in our thought experiment, Earth Three is beyond our godly powers.

This thought experiment is meant to illustrate (very roughly) the choice we're confronted with. Ideally, we'd find technological solutions that would allow us to reduce or slow global warming while also allowing for continued economic growth. However, if current trends continue, the world in 2100 will be significantly warmer and less hospitable, but the people living in that world will be vastly richer. They will be better able to deal with their less hospitable climate than we living in 2020 are able to deal with our more hospitable climate.

Think of climate change and economic growth as vectors. Climate change makes us overall worse off. Growth makes us overall better off. What we should do depends on the relative strength of these effects and the trade-offs we face. Poverty is a disaster. Climate change is also a disaster, especially for those very same poor people. After all, rising ocean levels threaten both the Netherlands and Bangladesh, but the two countries have very different prospects. The Netherlands can afford to build extensive flood control infrastructure; Bangladesh cannot.

There is no chance of maintaining Earth One anyway. We're going to get warmer. By all accounts, we're already too late in the game to reverse that. At best, the question is whether the governments of the world should implement policies that keep us closer to Earth One, though there is little political willpower to do that. If current trends continue, we'll move toward Earth Two. The thought experiment above has you imagine creating a world from scratch. It leaves out issues about the distribution of harms that take place during changes, and it ignores the hard questions about who *caused* these harms. In fact, as we progress toward Earth Two, some people will be harmed more by climate change than they will benefit from economic growth, while others will benefit from economic growth more than they are harmed by climate change. We don't all become net winners over the next one hundred years. In fact, the already rich countries are more responsible for climate change than the poor countries, yet the poorer countries will tend to be harmed more by climate change.

So, just how bad will climate be? The 2006 *Stern Review on the Economics of Climate Change* provides very pessimistic estimates.[14] Note that many economists think it is too pessimistic, though some think it's not pessimistic enough.[15]

Stern believes that by 2100, climate change might reduce economic output by 20 percent. But note carefully: Stern does not mean that in 2100, thanks to climate change, world product will be 20 percent lower than it was in 2006. Rather, he means that climate change will reduce world product in 2100 by 20 percent compared to a hypothetical baseline in which carbon emissions and temperatures had not risen. If we *very conservatively* estimate that world product/capita will grow by a mere 2 percent for the next eighty-two years, then by the year 2100, GDP/capita worldwide will be well over $50,000 in today's dollars, while world product will be over $500 trillion.[16]

Stern's pessimistic estimate is that global warming will reduce these numbers by 20 percent. If he's right, that's a tragic loss. Still, this is like picking Earth Two over Earth One. Global warming probably reduces total economic growth, but what this means, even on Stern's account, is that our descendants will be much richer than we are, just not as rich they might have been in a world without global warming.

To be clear, we are not saying that *nothing* should be done to mitigate climate change. We'd prefer instead both (1) to have massive economic growth and (2) to mitigate and reduce the harms of global warming. Further, the problem is that the damage of climate change will not be evenly distributed. The poorest countries are also often the countries that are likely to face the most harm and which have the fewest technological resources to cope with change.

Now on to the second reason. We've witnessed a hopeful trend around the world. The bad news is that as countries develop and industrialize, they initially do more and more damage to their environment for every dollar's worth of output. However, at a certain "turning point," such as $9,000 GDP/capita, countries typically start to pollute less per additional dollars' worth of output.[17] Economists call this the "Environmental Kuznets Curve," which we show in a stylized fashion in figure 10.1.

Take the United States as an example: Carbon emissions in 1900 were 1.8 tons per $1,000/GDP in 2005. Emissions peaked in the 1930s at about 2.8 tons per $1,000/GDP. Since then, they have fallen steadily, to about .4 tons per $1,000/GDP today.[18] As economist William Nordhaus summarizes, "Since 1930, the CO_2-gross domestic product (GDP) ratio has fallen at an average rate of 1.8% per year."[19]

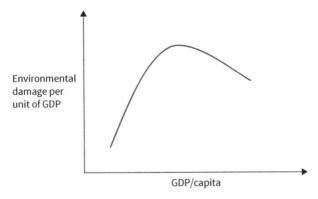

Fig. 10.1 Environmental Kuznets Curve

When people are desperately poor, they focus on meeting their basic needs. When people become richer, they become more willing and able to make trade-offs in environmental quality—they are more willing to forego additional material benefits to instead enjoy a cleaner environment. Few people are willing to let their kids starve to keep the air clean, but most people are willing to pay a little extra for catalytic converters in their cars to reduce their emissions.

This trend provides grounds for optimism. The point is to get the world over the hump. Make people rich enough that they believe their children are safe and secure, and they'll become more likely to support environmental protections and to take measures to reduce long-term climate change.

We invoke this point here because some ethics classes and textbooks encourage a kind of naïveté about the big problems of global poverty and global climate change. They make it sound like to be ethical is simply to have clean hands. Your business should just refuse to deal with sweatshops, lobby for and only do business in countries with stricter government regulations, and unilaterally pay "living wages" even in highly undeveloped countries. Your business should unilaterally choose to reduce carbon emissions and pollution and work toward sustainability.

These kinds of behaviors are well-meaning. But reality is more complex. You can decide to impose certain rules within your company or to lobby for certain regulations. But you don't get to decide how workers or companies might react to your new rules. Maybe the regulation makes the air cleaner, or maybe it induces a company to move overseas to an even less strict regime, and thus makes the air dirtier. Maybe raising wages gives all the poor workers a good life, or maybe it causes the factory to replace the lowest-skilled workers with already better off higher-skilled workers. Further, unilateral actions sometimes make no difference. If you replace your gas-guzzler with a cleaner electric car, you might contribute less to climate change, but it'll make no difference unless enough other people also change their behavior.

We're not recommending you throw up your hands and accept the status quo. We're not recommending you do nothing. But we are recommending that you never rest on platitudes and good intentions. Whatever ideas you have about being responsible with regard to big global problems, make sure you carefully trace the likely consequences of those ideas, and be ready to abandon a well-meaning policy if it doesn't look like it will work. And at some point, you must accept that individual businesses and businesspeople can do very little on their own.

Summary

- The diffusion of responsibility model predicts that when responsibility for an issue is spread among the many, individuals will act less responsibly. They will be more likely to ignore the problem rather than do the right thing.
- Diffusion of responsibility is pervasive in large bureaucracies, including in government, not-for-profit, and nongovernmental organizations (NGOs) and in for-profit firms.
- The tragedy of the commons refers to a problem in which individuals sharing or using a collectively held resource have a strong incentive to overuse it.
- When large groups make decisions and so individuals have little efficacy, individuals have an incentive to remain ignorant and little incentive to think carefully. They are said to be *rationally ignorant* and *rationally irrational*. This explains why large committee decisions are so often badly made.
- The antivaccine movement is a result of the diffusion of responsibility and the problem of rational irrationality.
- In general, the solution is to concentrate responsibility in those who have an incentive and ability to solve the problems at hand. But that can come with its own problems. Sometimes, as in the case of climate change, there's no clear way to do that.
- Many environmental problems are explained by this model.

Discussion Questions

1. If you stop recycling and start using twice as many plastic straws, what effect does that have on local landfills? What does that tell you about people's incentives?
2. What are some examples of problems you see where lots of people could intervene in effective ways but no one does? Why don't they?
3. It's easy to stop bullying at school: When one big kid bullies a smaller kid, three or four medium-sized kids could intervene and stop the bully. Why doesn't this happen more often?
4. The NFL has a problem with too many players getting serious concussions. What steps is it taking to reduce the problem? Why didn't it intervene sooner?

Notes

1. Berkes 2012.
2. Assume the carry capacity of each parcel is the proportional to the total pasture and that adding extra sheep as the same proportional effect.
3. Furnham and Boo 2011.
4. That may sound paradoxical, but it's not. Rational irrationality means it's *instrumentally* rational to be *epistemically* irrational.
5. Godlee, Smith, and Marcovitch 2011.
6. Simler and Hanson 2018.
7. Jackall 1988: 89.
8. Ibid., 86–89.
9. McCabe et al. 2017: 58.
10. Vedder 2019.
11. Ginsberg 2013; Lombardi 2013: 69–95.
12. The 2015 world growth rate was about 3.5 percent. http://www.imf.org/external/pubs/ft/weo/2016/update/01/. If that rate continues, then world product will double approximately every twenty years. By 2100, world product will be over four times as large as it is right now.
13. Nordhaus 2013: 80. Nordhaus assumes a modest 2.5 percent growth rate. Suppose instead that world PPP-adjusted per-capita income (which right now is about $16,200) grows at about 3.5 percent over eighty-five years. If so, then by 2100, world per-capita income will be over $300,000. "World." *CIA World Factbook*. October 6, 2015. Retrieved October 9, 2015.
14. Stern 2007. To our knowledge, the Stern Review is largely seen as too pessimistic and as using improper methods. See here Byatt 2006.
15. Nordhaus 2013.
16. Assume a starting world product/capita of $11,000 and world product of $108 trillion, compound annually at 2 percent for eighty-two years.
17. Grossman and Krueger 1995.
18. Nordhaus 2013: 22.
19. Nordhaus 2013: 23.

11

Psychological Factors

Ethical Fading and Moral Blind Spots

Basic Lesson: The thought that the conflict between self-interest and morality explains most wrongdoing is false. Instead, most of us, most of the time, do morally bad things because we just don't notice that something morally important is at stake.

Moral Character

Recently, a number of management scholars have started to look at which cluster of traits people care the most about in their evaluations of other people.[1] It is still early in this area of impression formation research, so the studies should be taken with several grains of salt. But they do point in a direction that many have suggested repeatedly.

In general, traits associated with good moral character are more important than warmth, and more important than competence, in how we evaluate other people. One way of understanding this is as follows: Consider someone who is in charge of you, and think about their failures along certain dimensions, and think about which ones you are more and less likely to forgive or make excuses for.

- *Grumpy, but good and competent:* Suppose someone is pretty grumpy. Not mean or cruel, just not very pleasant. He is, in your judgment, a morally good person who means well and is competent at what he does.
- *Incompetent, but good and warm:* Suppose someone is not very good at some task or set of tasks. She is a constant bumbler. She is, however, and again in your judgment, a morally good person who means well, and is warm and pleasant to be around.
- *Immoral, but competent and warm*: Suppose someone is morally bad in your judgment. He is a liar and a thief, say. However, he is competent at the job and charismatic and pleasant to be around.

Business Ethics for Better Behavior. Jason Brennan, William English, John Hasnas, and Peter Jaworski, Oxford University Press.
© Oxford University Press 2021. DOI: 10.1093/oso/9780190076559.003.0011

It's easy to forgive grumpiness, provided we think that it doesn't come from a bad place. We'll say that they woke up on the wrong side of the bed, or that their personality makes them very matter-of-fact and to-the-point, or direct. It's not as easy to forgive incompetence, but when we think someone is a good person, we'll at least sometimes try to shore up their competencies and maybe delegate tasks differently. But we will not be so generous to people who we judge to be morally bad people, who cling to the wrong values, who take action without regard for the impact of those actions on others. No matter how competent or warm, we simply don't want to be around people like this, and we definitely don't want them to have positions of power over us.

In fact, competence and warmth might make things worse, not better. Movies that feature competent and charming evil people are the most frightening of all. There are few comedies that depict people like this. There are, however, comedies that depict incompetent evil-doers.

If you've taken a philosophy class, you might recognize a little bit of Immanuel Kant in this explanation. For Kant, competence is not good without qualification. Competence in service of a good will is good; competence in service of a bad will is not. (Consider the competent gulag guard.) So it goes with having a positive and warm disposition. It is, as far as Kant is concerned, the goodness of a person that makes any of these other traits good traits. When the person in question lacks a good will, then that strips the trait of whatever goodness it might otherwise possess.

The research does not support Kant's view as being widely accepted by others, but it does show that what we care about the most in forming impressions of others is that they are a good person. So, again, just as in the case of self-flattery above, it turns out that how we judge others depends mostly and primarily on our moral evaluation of them. If that's true of how we, in general, form impressions of others, then clearly this is what we need to attend to in ourselves if we want to climb the ladder, or be in a position of leadership. People will not put up with us if they think we are morally bad. And they will take every opportunity they can to undermine our leadership position through gossip and other means.

So, you have an extrinsic reason to care about how you behave and whether or not you are being a morally good person: Success appears to depend upon it. And although it is often possible to dupe other people into thinking you are a good person when, in fact, you are deceiving them and others, the simplest way to convince others that you are a good person is still to just be a good person. And this reason is in addition to the intrinsic reason almost all of us appear to already have in being a good and decent person, evidence by the near-universal fact of self-flattery along moral dimensions.

Here's what stands in our way of getting you to plan for ethics: You are already convinced you are a good person, and you are sure that your good moral character will shine through in whatever difficult situation you might be placed in. Whereas others are going to be tempted by power, status, and money, this won't happen to *you*. You are, after all, a good person, who heeds the angel on your left shoulder and disregards the devil on your right shoulder.

If you think this, then you are, once again, engaged in self-flattery. The problem is that everyone thinks this way. Most of us are prone to think we are more competent, skilled, and intelligent than we in fact are. But we are most of all prone to overestimating our moral character.

This chapter is aimed at showing you that you, like everyone else, will, under certain situations, hear nothing but the screams of the devil, failing to recognize that it's the devil, and never even noticing the whispers of the angel. In the opening chapter, we mentioned that most people are pretty good, but they fall into various moral traps and make predictable moral mistakes. This chapter is meant to help you anticipate and avoid some of those traps.

Honesty

People are largely, but not exclusively, motivated intrinsically. They want to do what is meaningful. If you understand this, then you will have a better sense of why some incentives fail, why some backfire, and what makes for good incentives. We discuss this at length in chapter 12, but it will also be important for the DUMB values framework we will discuss in chapter 13.

We tend to think, however, that *other people* are more concerned about money than meaning. We are wrong about that. We are also wrong about how ethical other people are in comparison to us, and how ethical we are, ourselves. Your peers are not as selfishly dishonest as you might think. Not only do your peers say that they want to do meaningful work, and at least some studies show that meaningfulness is motivational, they also hold themselves to a higher moral standard than you might guess.

Suppose you were given a math test, with the number of right answers you get in a limited amount of time corresponds with how much you get paid. Get ten questions right and you get $10. Nine questions and you get $9, and so on. Now suppose that you are doing this test with a room full of other people. Here's the twist: It turns out that the people who are handing out the money shred the tests without checking to see if you actually did get any of the questions right. There's a shredder that everyone can see, and everyone can see that the test gets shredded. Now suppose that, in the time allotted, you got completed six questions, and now it's your turn to shred your test and then tell the people with the money how many questions you got correct.

What would you do? How many questions would you say you got correct? And what do you think other people would do? How many questions do you think they would say they got correct?

We can hazard a pretty specific guess. We guess that you will report having completed two more questions than in fact you did. If you completed five questions, you will report seven. If you completed six questions, you will report eight. But you will guess that your peers will report getting many more questions right than in fact they did. If they answered five, you will guess that they will report having completed eight or nine. If they completed six, you will think they will report nine, or a perfect ten.

We base our guesses in part on the self-flattery research we mentioned that consistently shows that we tend to think that, when it comes to honesty, humility, and other moral character traits, we are better than average, but not perfect. We also base our guess on the research Dan Ariely has conducted.[2]

Ariely is a behavioral economist who is primarily interested in honesty and deception. He has conducted hundreds of experiments to figure out when we are being dishonest, why we are being dishonest, and what might make us more honest than we would otherwise be.

The math test is called a matrix test. You are given twenty numbers (like 7.56, 8.23, 2.44, and so on) each of which is in a matrix on a piece of paper. Your task is to find the pair of numbers that add up to ten, and to try to find as many pairs that have this total as possible. On average, most test takers get about six pairs in the amount of time given for this test. However, when the test takers think that the results are being shredded they will, on average, report that they completed eight.

But what's the "rational" thing to do? If you know you can get away with it, why do anything other than report that you got all of them correct? What stops you from doing this?

The answer appears to be that we care about not just that other people regard us as being "good" people, but that we think this of ourselves as well. Again, much like the self-flattery we discussed above, thinking of ourselves as good and decent and honest people matters a great deal to us. Our ability to flatter ourselves, however, is constrained by at least some facts. So, for instance, if we know that we got six pairs, we can come up with a story for why it is consistent with us being, in general, good and honest people to declare that we got eight right. But not all ten. We could not convince ourselves that we are not dishonest if we just said that we got a perfect score when, in fact, we didn't, and we know that we didn't.

We can report that we got eight correct because we can easily imagine ourselves getting eight correct. We woke up late today, we might think to ourselves. Our mind was taken up thinking about something else—our dinner, our significant other, our grades, whatever—but we would have solved more pairs had we concentrated fully. We were not our best selves when solving the matrix task. If we had been, we would have gotten eight. And so since our best self is still us, then that's the number that seems to make sense to report. We're not cheating and being dishonest, we were cheated by the circumstances of the task. And why should we let the circumstances cheat us out of an extra dollar or two?

This is how we can behave dishonestly but still preserve the thought that we are honest people. If we had reported "ten," however, it becomes more difficult to convince ourselves that we're still being roughly honest when we say "ten," and so we realize that saying "ten" comes at the expense of our being able to think of ourselves as being honest. Since being honest matters to us, we will only "fudge" to the extent that we can preserve our self-image as good people.

We say "fudge" because Ariely calls this the "fudge factor"—we will fudge our numbers, we will fudge a lot, but we will not go beyond fudging. If anything falls in a gray area, we'll give ourselves the benefit of the doubt and fudge, but we won't go beyond it.

Or, at least, most of us won't. Overwhelming majorities of us won't. The number of people who report getting all ten correct when clearly they did not is tiny. It is roughly in proportion to the number of sociopaths out there in the world. And sociopaths don't care about morality.

The conclusion from Ariely's research appears to be that, in general, people are and care about honesty, but they will fudge in their favor. This fudging accounts for most of the dishonesty we are witness to. It is not that people are dishonest, it is that they are imperfectly honest. We fudge. All that fudging adds up to a lot of dishonesty taken together, but we shouldn't overlook the fact that it is fudging, and not outright lying. At least that's true when we are aware of what it is that we are doing. But we are not always aware of what's going on.

See, Judge, Act

We teach at a Jesuit business school. The Jesuits have spent a lot of time thinking about ethics, and thinking about different frameworks for getting people to behave more ethically.

One of their frameworks is called "See, Judge, Act." Sometimes, people add "Reflect." So, we are asked to "See" that a situation calls for ethical reflection, "Judge" the various possible actions we might take in light of our moral convictions, and then "Act" on the basis of those convictions. For those who add "Reflect," the final step is to "Reflect" on what we have done to make sure that we did what we think is the right thing to do, and to think about strategies for improving our behavior if we fell short.

The trouble is that most of the action is in "seeing." If you don't see that you're in a situation calling for ethical judgment, then you won't get to "judge." You'll act, but you'll do so without considering how your behavior impacts other people, and what impact this has on your values.

But that's okay, you'll think to yourself, because you are a good person, with good intentions. You are, after all, motivated by making the world a better place, right? And it's very easy for you to remember all of the times where you were honest despite pressure to be dishonest, and how you are humble and kind and decent. Taking steps to insure against dishonest behavior is what dishonest people need to do, not honest people like you.

Panalba: Roles and Frames

If you don't think you are liable to behave badly, then you probably won't take steps ahead of time to prevent your acting badly later. If you think that all you ever do is fudge a little here and there, and that you are always aware of the situations that call for ethical reflection, then what's the point of spending time and energy on something that won't be of use to you? To convince you that you are liable to do bad things without being aware of it, let us introduce you to a case we use in our classes, and to two famous studies in psychology.

First, here's the case: We call it "Ablanap" when we have students role-play the case in class. Once upon a time, there was a company called Upjohn. Upjohn sold pharmaceutical products, including a drug called Panalba ("Ablanap" is just "Panalba" spelled backward—this is to avoid students finding out about the case by Googling it ahead of time). Panalba was an antibiotic but it also had the side effect of leading to twelve people's deaths at the time. It turns out that a fifth of people are allergic to novobiocin, one of the two ingredients in Panalba (the other being tetracycline). And some people were allergic enough that exposure to it would cause them to die. At the time, there was also a competing drug that took care of all of the same symptoms as Panalba, without the deadly side effect.

A panel of medical experts unanimously recommended that Panalba be removed from the market. The Food and Drug Administration (FDA) also urged that the drug be removed, but did not, at the time, have the authority to command this. Subsequent lawsuits regarding Panalba ended up giving the FDA the authority to remove drugs from the market. We say "subsequent lawsuits," because that's what it took to get rid of Panalba—lawsuits. The company itself did not choose to remove the drug from market voluntarily. Instead, they decided to use all of their financial, legal, and political clout to try to stop the FDA and any other government agencies from banning Panalba. Not only that, but they continued to market Panalba aggressively both through advertisements and through their connections with individual doctors across the United States. They knew their drug was killing people, but they still fought tooth-and-nail to try to squeeze every last penny out of selling it possible.

Profits over people. All they cared about was their bottom line, and if people had to die to maximize profits, so be it.

It's very easy to describe the situation in the above way. It is what most people say when they are told about the case. This makes sense to them. Business people in for-profit companies are motivated by money more than they are motivated by anything else. They are not prosocial, they are proselfish. This response allows us to categorize it, and to see that it wouldn't apply to us. We would never make a decision like that! We would have surely decided to take the drug off the market voluntarily, and refocus on efforts to be profitable from other drugs in our repertoire.

And this is what MBA students said too. Most MBA students, told the above information, expressed outrage, insisted that they, themselves, would never make decisions like that, and would have fought tooth-and-nail not to squeeze out every last penny from Panalba but to save the people who would die from using Panalba.

Unfortunately, it doesn't look like that is what they really would do. This is just another example of self-flattery in action. Instead, the overwhelming majority of them would have done exactly what Upjohn did. The reason we think they would do so is that we've run in-class experiments where this is exactly what students do choose. They are given the case, and they are asked to play the role of CEO, CFO, shareholder, medical director, and so on, of Upjohn. They get forty-five minutes to deliberate about the case, and have to decide between five options:

1. Recall Panalba immediately and destroy it.
2. Stop production of Panalba immediately but allow what's been made to be sold.
3. Stop all advertising and promotion of Panalba but provide it for those doctors who request it.

4. Continue efforts to most effectively market Panalba until sale is actually banned.

5. Continue efforts to most effectively market Panalba and take legal, political, and other necessary actions to prevent the authorities from banning Panalba.

Depressingly, and overwhelmingly, they pick the worst of the options, option 5. The odd thing is that it's not as if the students say, "Profits over people, damn it!" That would require them to acknowledge their action is morally wrong but choose it anyway. Rather, the students generally don't even notice they've acted wrongly.

Now, granted, this is an in-class experiment. Perhaps people are more prone to take the morally worst option when nothing is at stake. Maybe in the real world, when people are really dying, they'd do better. On the other hand, in the real world, they'd also have real money, the health of the company, and perhaps their actual jobs at stake, so they'd be all the more tempted to rationalize their bad behavior.

Of late, we have been keeping one team behind. This small group of students doesn't get to deliberate in their roles, they just discuss the case with us. We tell them all the same things, and ask them what they think the company should do. Instead of landing on the same decision Upjohn did, they typically choose option (1), or (2) at the worst.

Why the difference? One reason why, that we find plausible, is because people playing the case study get roles, while the students who are part of the in-class discussion do not. Being asked to play a role sometimes changes what we think is the right thing to do. We adopt the values that we take to be important for being a good CEO, for example, in place of the values that we take to be important for being a good person. So, we don't ask, "what would a good person do?" but "what would a good CEO do?" instead. And that change in how we frame the question can lead us to make very different decisions than we would just being ourselves.

Of course, there are different decisions that you might make in the different roles that you'll be asked to fill that are compatible with being a good person. A CEO has to consider very many things, while you might have to consider very many, but different, things. So the right approach is not to only ask, "What would a good person do?" but, "What would a good CEO, who is also a good person, do?"

The decision in Panalba is similar to other decisions that were made that you might be familiar with. For example, consider once again the Challenger shuttle disaster. In an article for *Harvard Business Review*, Ann Tenbrunsel explains that, after launch of the shuttle, the O-rings failed, leading to the explosion of the shuttle, and the death of all the astronauts on board. The trouble was with the weather. The O-rings had been tested under different weather conditions, and the engineers did not have good reason to believe that it would be safe to launch. Nevertheless, the launch went ahead. Why?

The launch of the Challenger had been delayed many months. Repeatedly, NASA had set a date for the launch, but the engineers would come back with a verdict of no-launch. They said they could not guarantee the safety of the launch. NASA was frustrated. It had been many years since the general public was excited about anything happening at NASA, and they were worried that all of these delays would dampen public attitudes toward NASA. But the engineers were insisting on safety.

Finally, somebody asked the team in charge of the launch to "make a business decision." According to Ann Tenbrunsel, that was the secret switch that changed how at least some members of the team evaluated the launch decision. While many of the engineers still voted "no," enough had changed their minds so that a majority said, "yes," and the disaster followed.

This is an example of framing. The way we frame a question sometimes pushes us to answer in one way rather than another. Now notice that the roles we fill are also like frames. Questions are asked that we answer as a police officer, as a CEO, as a shareholder, and so on. When asked to make a business decision, some people lowered their guard when it came to safety. They looked at the question from a different pair of eyes than their own. And this framing effect is what happens when we are asked to be in a role.

Authority and Conformity

Here's another role we often fill: that of being a subordinate, and that of being part of a social group, or a team.

If we go in reverse order, think back to high school for a moment. Can you think of times when you did something because you felt pressured to? Can you think of a time when you said that you thought something when, in fact, you didn't, because saying anything else would have made you feel uncomfortable?

Solomon Asch thought to test our willingness to conform not in cases where the right answer was difficult or complicated but in a case where the right answer was obvious and staring us right in the face. He constructed an experiment where people had to look at a line on one piece of paper and then compare it to three different lines on a separate piece of paper and say which one was the same length. There was no trick here. The right answer was obvious. What made it difficult, however, is that three people would report the wrong line as the one that is the same length before it was your turn to speak. So, if the line that was the same length was marked "A," the first person would say, "B," followed by the second person who also said "B," and then one more person before it was your turn would also say "B."

What Asch discovered is that 37 percent of people would say "B," even though "A" was obviously the right answer. He thought they did this either because they became convinced that B really was the right answer (although this is unlikely), or they would just say "B" to avoid rocking the boat or stirring things up even though they knew it was the wrong answer.

The Asch study on conformity is one of the classic psychological studies. It shows us that sometimes we will do or say what others do or say because others do or say them. We are susceptible to social pressures. Sometimes, that's great. When we are surrounded by good and kind and decent people, then this tendency to conform our manner to others promotes goodness and kindness and decency. But when others behave badly, we are more likely to behave badly because it is very difficult for us to behave differently.

Conformity can lead us to behave contrary to our values, contrary to what we think is the right thing to do. So, too, can authority.

In a different classic psychological experiment, Stanley Milgram had people shock others during an experiment. No one was actually shocked, but the subjects who were asked to move progressively to more and more severe and intense shocks didn't know that. They thought the electric shocks were real. They were told that they were testing to see if a punishment, in this case an electric shock, would help improve memory and so be helpful to education in general. For each question the person in the other room, who the subjects could not see, got wrong, they were to administer an electric shock.

The person who they couldn't see was in on the experiment, and was never actually connected to the electric shocking device. Instead, they had a tape recorder that would play certain sounds at preset times. So, for example, one message on the tape recorder was, "Experimenter! Get me out of here. I told you I had a heart condition! Let me out!" At another point, the tape recorder would let out a blood-curdling scream. And then, after a certain point, there would just be silence from the other room. The obvious conclusion was that something had gone terribly wrong, and the person in the other room had either passed out or, as some subjects later reported they believed, had died.

It took some time for Milgram to actually be able to go ahead with the experiment. Not because there were ethical questions about its design (although afterward there were plenty of those!), but because most people thought the experiment would be a failure. No one, people thought, would go all the way in this experiment, except for the tiny minority who were psychopaths. The experiment would only show what we already know—most people are decent and will stop giving shocks at the first sign of real pain, and only a tiny number of people would continue, the same group of people who didn't care about others in the first place.

That is not, as you might by now have guessed, what happened. Instead, two-thirds of people not only continued the experiment, but continued shocking people until they reached the maximum shock possible, which was helpfully marked "XXX Danger."

Milgram explained that the point of the experiment was to see what would cause people to perform horrific acts. He was interested in why apparently ordinary people participated in the atrocities committed in World War II Germany. His experiment suggested that people will obey apparently legitimate authorities, even to the point of harming someone severely. In this case, the apparently legitimate authority was a person in a white coat who would goad the subjects to "please continue" when the subject expressed reservations. "The experiment requires that you continue," the man in the coat would sometimes say. "I take full responsibility for what might happen," he would say if asked about who would be responsible if the other person were to die. And so on.

We sometimes do what others are doing because others are doing it, and we sometimes do what someone tells us to do because we think they have legitimate authority. We obey and we conform. Neither of these are the kinds of behaviors that stereotypically selfish, greedy, and confident people engage in. These are the kinds of behaviors of people who are the opposite of that. People who are meek, lack self-confidence, think themselves subordinate. These are people who fail to act on their own considered values, the values that are acted upon are those of other people.

Failing to Notice

A famous YouTube video is illustrative. You are asked to count the number of times a ball gets passed between people wearing a red shirt. If you're like most people, you focus intently on the task at hand. 1 .. 2 .. 3 .. wait, no, wrong shirt .. okay, now 3 .. 4 .. ., etc. While you're busy doing that, a person in an ape costume walks in the middle of the circle of people passing balls to one another. Did you notice the obvious thing?

Here's what's weird about this experiment: The answer is "probably not." You probably did not notice the person in an ape costume. This is so even though the costumed person is so obvious. In fact, most people fail to notice.

They fail to notice for a number of reasons. Mostly, it's because they are busy focusing all of their energy on a specific task. No one asked them to also notice other things in the video, and so they did not. In your day-to-day life, but also in the world of business, this failure to notice is common. Our claim is that most wrongdoing in business, and in life in general, is not a result of selfish people choosing to be selfish over being morally good. It is not that we look to the devil sitting on our left shoulder and choose him over the angel perched on our other shoulder. Instead, we look straight ahead, never noticing the devil nor the angel at all.

The Panalba role-playing example might be an illustration of such problems. In focusing their attention on what the company should do, and what the expected losses are, and maybe what strategies are available to them to try to keep selling the drug, the students might not even have noticed that they should stop and think outside their role. Perhaps they didn't notice the bigger moral picture. Similarly with the Milgram experiment. Doing what you believe to be a legitimate authority tells you to do might be the focus of all of your attention, failing to take a step back and look at the bigger moral picture.

We fail to notice that we are in a situation that calls for ethical awareness, and ethical judgment. What's worse is that even though we did not consider the ethics, we will often try to deceive others that we really did think it through. Worse still is that this deception will convince us, too.

Ethical Fading and Moral Blind Spots

Ethical fading and moral blind spots are part of what Max Bazerman calls "bounded ethicality." He intends it to be the direct analogue of "bounded rationality."

Bounded rationality tells us more than just that you and I are not perfectly rational all the time; it also tells us that we are irrational in predictable ways. So, for example, we appear to be more loss averse than what it would be rational for us to be. Rather than treat a loss of $20 and a gain of $20 proportionately, we suffer more from losing $20 than we psychologically benefit from a gain of $20. We are also irrationally risk-averse in some contexts. We are more afraid of flying in an airplane than we are of driving in a car, even though, and even if we know this, flying in an airplane is much, much safer than driving in a car. These are examples where we predictably deviate from optimizing as the model of rationality from economics and decision theory would either recommend or predict. Instead of maximizing gains and minimizing losses, and so behaving rationally, we use heuristics or mental shortcuts to make suboptimal decisions. We "satisfice" rather than "optimize."

So, too, with bounded ethicality. The idea is that we do not always act on our own conception of what is morally best (despite, as we talked about before, this being one of the most important things to us). We fail not because we choose to do what we ourselves think is suboptimal from a moral point of view but because we predictably use certain heuristics or mental shortcuts in certain contexts and so don't even notice that we are behaving contrary to what we ourselves think is morally best.

Max Bazerman explains some instances of this as follows: When we think about what we will do in the future, or in some specific future circumstance, we reason in accordance with what he calls our "should" self. We think about what would be morally best, and we predict that we will behave optimally. What would you do, for example, if you were on the board of the Upjohn Corporation and had to decide whether or not to fight the FDA to keep Panalba on the market? Or: What would you do if there was someone in a lab coat telling you to zap a stranger with ever-higher volts of electricity during a test of memory? When we are thinking about what we would do, we engage our "should" self and think explicitly about ethics. "What is the morally right thing to do?" We think to ourselves. "Probably it is to not fight the FDA," and "probably it is to zap them until it is clear that the electricity is painful to the stranger." And so we conclude that that is what we would do. This is what, many times, our students tell us when we are just talking about these two cases.

But this is not what most people actually do. They fight to keep Panalba, and they zap a stranger well beyond the point where they have good evidence that it is doing real harm. Bazerman explains that this happens because, when in those situations, our "want" self emerges and crowds out or silences our "should" self. We are suddenly in a situation where the external pressures, for example, are too much, or where we are laser-focused on some subset of the criteria for making a decision at the expense of other criteria, and we do what our own "should" self would recommend against. Ethics fades from view, morality is in one of our blind spots.

Afterward, however—after we make our decision—our "should" self reappears. Does our should self reprimand us for behaving badly according to our own lights. Far from it! Now our "should" self engages in rationalizing behavior. We use our cognitive abilities to convince others and ourselves that we made the morally best decision after all. This is what actually happens after we play the Panalba role-playing game—the students explain that they were required to prioritize the interests of shareholders. That is, morally speaking, what is best. Yes, it's best that people not die, but people die every day from medications, and this is something everyone knows happens, and people have to decide for themselves whether to take the medication or not. Besides, the job of figuring out what medication is best for a particular patient is up to the prescribing doctor, not the company making the drug. If anyone dies, that's on the doctor, not the company. In fighting for Panalba, we did what morality required of us as board members, namely maximize shareholder value, and if there are deaths that is a problem with the doctors and not with us.

The "should" self reasons ahead of time and convinces us that we would do what we think is best ahead of time; the "want" self emerges in the actual situation and we choose what our should self would recommend against; and then our "should" self re-appears after the decision to rationalize away our behavior, convincing ourselves that we did what was morally best after all. For ethicists like us, this process is frustrating. It is as frustrating for us as irrational, nonoptimizing behavior is to economists.

Self-Deception

Suppose a manager asks you, during a job interview, whether you have a boyfriend, whether people find you desirable, or whether it's appropriate for women to wear bras at work. How do you think you'd react?

If you're like psychologists Julie Woodzicka and Marianne LeFrance's experimental subjects, you'd say that you would refuse to answer the question, demand to know why it was asked, and otherwise stand up for yourself.[3] These questions are inappropriate, sexist, and illegal.

That's what you'd say you'd do, but you're probably wrong. When Woodzick and LeFrance put experimental subjects in actual interviews, nearly all politely answered the questions, and only a few later asked why the questions were asked. There's a large gap between how people think they'd behave and how they would in fact behave. We have mistaken beliefs about our own bravery or integrity.

You can see this any given year. In January, Americans join gyms and buy exercise equipment at high rates. Come May, most of the new members have stopped going and the equipment is no longer used. People overestimate how committed to exercise they will be.

We seem to be experts in self-deception, especially when it comes to moral matters. Psychologists Don Batson and Elizabeth Thompson told experimental subjects they were part of a team of two but would never meet their partner.[4] They would answer skill-testing questions together, and if they answered correctly, they would win a prize. The psychologists also told subjects that the prize could not be divided but had to be awarded to one of the two team members; the other would get nothing. In fact, there was no other partner, and everyone qualifies for the prize.

The psychologists told the real subjects that they would get to decide who gets the prize—them or their unseen partner. Subjects were told the partner wouldn't know the subject got to decide—instead, they'd be told the prize was allocated by chance. The psychologists gave subjects a coin, to use if they wanted to assign the prize by random chance.

Half the subjects did not use the coin. Ninety percent of these subjects allocated the prize to themselves. The other half did flip the coin . . . but then 90 percent allocated the prize to themselves. Regardless of whether they flipped the coin, they gave the prize to themselves 90 percent of the time.

Weeks earlier, the psychologists had given the subjects questionnaires. Subjects who reported being most concerned about morality were most likely to flip the coin, yet no more likely to allocate the prize to their partner.

Psychologist Jonathan Haidt, reflecting on this study, says that although the professed moralists flip the coin, "when the coin flip comes out against them, they find a way to ignore it and follow their own self-interest. . . . Batson's subjects who flipped the coin reported (on a questionnaire) that they had made the decision in any ethical way."[5] Some of the subjects were lying, but Haidt suspects many of them did not know they were lying.[6] They instead lie to themselves. Haidt says we are fairly accurate in our perceptions of others, but our self-perceptions are distorted.[7] We believe ourselves to be more moral than we are.

You may have heard of the Dunning-Kruger Effect, which shows that for any given task, incompetent people tend to overestimate their competence, while highly competent people tend to underestimate themselves. The idea is that ignorant people don't know how little they know, but skilled or informed people know that there are limits on what they know. In related work, David Dunning and co-author Nicholas Epley have measured how people rate themselves compared to others. While people tend to think they are above average on a whole host of positive traits, they are especially inclined to rate themselves favorably compared to others when it comes to moral character.[8]

We mentioned how psychologist Dan Ariely has studied what factors induce people to cheat and lie. In one variation of his "matrix task" experiment, he gave students an opportunity to cheat for money. Afterward, he presented the students who cheated the most with "Certificates of Excellence" for mathematical ability. Surely, you'd think, the students would know they that they cheated, and would know the certificates mean nothing. But he'd then follow up, giving students another chance to play the matrix task game, this time telling them the task would be independently graded and there'd be no chance to cheat. He asked them to estimate how well they'd do on the test. Oddly, the students who cheated the most had the highest estimate of their future scores, even though they knew they couldn't cheat again. It seems the students not only cheated but somehow convinced themselves they didn't cheat.[9]

What to Do

Here's a good summary of the problem: We often fail to see that a situation calls for ethical reflection. We fail to see that values are at stake. Ethics either fades into the background far away from our conscious awareness or is just outside our ability to see, in one of our blind spots. Alternatively, we are tricked by quirks in our psychology to prioritize the wrong things, or to act contrary to the values we reflectively endorse. Is there anything that can be done to fix this?

First, it should be pointed out that this is a hard problem. Evidence suggests that we often fail to notice. It is a predictable failure. If it is a frequent and predictable failure, how can we come up with a way to get people to see something that we are not wired to see?

Second, notice that the most prevalent explanation for wrongdoing is not a failure of inference but a failure of awareness. Many business ethics classes give students a case and ask them to reason from the elements of the case, via one or another moral theory, to a conclusion about what the right thing to do is. So, for example, a question might be, "what would utilitarianism have to say about the Panalba? What decision should executives at Upjohn have made?" That might be followed by a question like, "Now consider Kantian ethics, what decision should executives at Upjohn have made if they wanted to act in accordance with Kantian ethics?"

This approach is fine. Most of us are philosophers, and these are precisely the kinds of questions we are mostly interested in. These questions require an understanding of the various views as premises, and require good inferential abilities to reason from the premises to the conclusion. It requires us to construct valid arguments. These analytic skills are essential not only for a good education but also in helping us to develop our own convictions about what is the right thing to do in a way that we can reflectively endorse. The trouble with this approach is that its application to contexts that call for ethical reflection and reasoning requires us to first be aware that something morally pressing is at stake. If we never notice, we'll never reason, and so we'll never take advantage of the skills we've gathered. So while this approach helps us figure out what the good consists in, helping us to be less bumbling about that question, it does not tell us anything about what to do with the other way in which we bumble: a failure to even notice.

The thing to do, then, is not to engage in more awareness-raising, but in either avoiding situations where we know ethics will be in one of our blind spots or to set up our institutions to fight against these difficulties in the first place. Here are some examples of moral blind spots, or of bounded ethicality, that we have already mentioned:

Conformity: We have a tendency to want to do what everyone else is doing, and to express opinions that are similar to what a group thinks.

Authority: We have a tendency to obey people who we regard as legitimate authorities.

Roles: Sometimes, when we are asked to assume a certain role, we act or reason from values that we think are required by the role we are in, rather than our own values. We narrow our focus to some subset of the values we reflectively endorse as best.

Frames: Sometimes, the way a question is asked can also narrow our focus and get us to answer in ways that conflict with what we really think.

How can we avoid, or at least attenuate, some of the above problems? One method to at least attenuate bounded ethicality is to, for example, give someone the role of being "devil's advocate." That person's job is to object to consensus, and to raise arguments about why the emerging consensus might fail or might be a bad decision. This is a great method since it engages the power of roles against the power of conformity—if your role is to advocate for the devil, then you have a ready excuse for disagreeing: "Hey! I'm just playing devil's advocate over here." Assigning a role like this explicitly can help.

So, too, can a premortem. A premortem is a process during decision-making where you assume that the decision the group has come to has failed somehow (assume that it was the wrong decision). Now your task is to figure out why the decision failed. This is an effort to actively look for disconfirming evidence, to look for things that count against the decision, in an effort to fight against our confirmation bias, our proclivity to find only reasons and evidence that count in favor of whatever decision we would like made.

Conclusion

See, Judge, Act. That's the Jesuit method of moral decision-making. Most of the moral problems occur in that first step. That's the lesson of our bounded ethicality. We simply fail to See. If we fail to See, we will fail to Judge with morality in mind, and so we will Act badly.

The Jesuits have a device, however, that helps them See better. They have a daily ritual that also helps to mitigate the problems of bounded ethicality. Two or three times per day, they go through something called "The Examen." The Examen is, essentially, a kind of prayer, a kind of reflection, and a kind of planning device. It has five steps. In the morning, the five steps go like this: The first step is to look through God's eyes to see the world from His perspective, not merely our own. The second is to express gratitude for what we have. The third is to look back and review the prior day and evaluate how we did from God's eyes. The fourth step is to recognize our failures and shortcomings from the prior day. The final step is to plan ahead for the day, being careful to give ourselves specific directives about what we will do differently. The Examen is part of the Jesuit tradition, but there are secular versions, and there are versions for every major religion. The secular version of The Examen would be as follows:

1. Look at the world from an impartial perspective, from the point of view of morality.
2. Be grateful for the good things in your life, for the good people in your life.
3. Look over your prior day from an impartial perspective, or from the point of view of morality.
4. Recognize our failures and shortcomings from the point of view of morality. And, finally,
5. Plan for the day ahead, with specific goals for how we will be morally better.

Devices like The Examen are effective tools to help keep morality at the forefront of our thoughts. If we get in the habit of going through it in the morning and at night, we will be more likely to not forget about what is most important: Being a good person, and doing the right thing. And maybe, just maybe, we'll be able to see the gorillas in our midst.

Summary

- Most of us think we are more competent, skilled, and intelligent than we in fact are.
- Most of us think we are more honest, fair, and trustworthy than average, but not "perfect."
- We have a tendency to conform, to obey authority, and to allow roles and frames to guide our behavior. We do this even when we ourselves think the behavior we are engaged in is morally wrong.
- We often fail to notice that something morally important is at stake.

Discussion Questions

1. Take a business scandal from the newspapers. Can you explain why that happened by appealing only to ethical fading and moral blind spots, rather than selfishness or greed?
2. What are your blind spots? How do you know? What can you do to safeguard against them?
3. When was a time you conformed to your peers' behavior and regretted it? What could you have to avoid that situation?
4. What are some ways in which you overestimate how you would behave in difficult situations?

Notes

1. See, e.g., Goodwin, Piazza, and Rozin 2014.
2. Ariely 2013.
3. Woodzicka and LaFrance 2001.
4. Batson and Thompson 2001.
5. Haidt 2006: 62.
6. Ibid., 63.
7. Ibid., 66.
8. Epley and Dunning 2000.
9. Ariely 2013: 153–154.

12
Psychological Factors
Meaning and Motivation

Basic Lesson: Most people are good and decent. They mean well, and they try to do the best they can to be morally good. The thought that people are motivated primarily by selfishness, and that most bad behavior is the result of too much selfishness, is probably false. Being a good person is not just important intrinsically but is useful to attain positions of leadership.

Here is a common explanation for wrongdoing: A person does something that is morally wrong because she stands to personally benefit from the wrongdoing. In general, goes this view, people behave badly because they are too selfish. They care too little about others, and too much about themselves.

This selfishness assumption serves us well in many contexts. So, for example, when we are building institutions, it is wise to assume that people are going to behave selfishly and to build institutions in such a way as to carefully limit the amount of damage that selfish people might do.

One such institution is the US federal government. The founders worried a great deal about selfish politicians and administrators seizing power and then wielding that power to enrich themselves at the expense of the country. In order to prevent this, they created checks and balances. Those checks and those balances are supposed to turn the selfishness of politically powerful individuals against one another. So, Congress and the Senate checks the Executive. The Executive checks them in turn. The Judiciary is a check against all of them, and so on. All these checks are a way to balance power in three equally powerful, or at least similarly powerful, institutions.

It's true that people sometimes complain that the government fails to work together in a bipartisan fashion. But that is part of the very design of the system. If they were to work together more often then, maybe, they could accomplish a lot more good—but, on the flip side, the bad they might do might be magnified. So it may, on balance, be better to plan for the worst but hope for the best. This is especially so in cases, as is true of government, where the "worst" is truly, enormously bad.

Business Ethics for Better Behavior. Jason Brennan, William English, John Hasnas, and Peter Jaworski, Oxford University Press.
© Oxford University Press 2021. DOI: 10.1093/oso/9780190076559.003.0012

Think of Japanese internment camps during World War II. The system failed to prevent it, but it was designed in a way to make this sort of event much less likely to occur. It occurred anyway, partly because the pressure to behave this way was too much to bear even for (the few) heroic characters, and also because, in this case, every branch of government and much of the public at large supported it. But if even one branch of government were opposed to interning innocent Japanese, that would have made the bad outcome much less likely to have occurred.

We make similar kinds of assumptions in the business context. We structure our legal system, and the rules and regulations within which businesses conduct their business and compete with one another in a way that accounts for the common explanation of wrongdoing. We assume that businesses behave selfishly, that the individuals that run those businesses are selfish individuals, and come up with rules and systems to check selfishness.

That's a very good idea. But here's an important question: Is the common explanation of wrongdoing correct? Is it true that most of us, most of the time, are selfish? Even if not in general, is it true that most wrongdoing, most of the time, can be explained by people caring too much about themselves and not enough about others?

The answer to both questions is the same, and it may be surprising: No.

Instead, for the most part, we care more about being good people and being perceived as being good people than almost anything else, and when we engage in wrongdoing it is most often a consequence of our failing to even notice that we were in an environment that called for ethical reflection.

We are neither knaves nor saints, we are bumbling do-gooders. We mean well, and we want to be and to do good, but we sometimes don't notice that we are not doing good (or bad), or we don't know what doing good consists of. What compounds this problem is that we often assume that other people are selfish, and so in choosing what to do sometimes make decisions in light of this false assumption.

Extrinsic Incentive Bias

What evidence do we have for the claim that selfishness really is a false assumption? There's plenty. Many scholars delight in repeatedly showing that we are not as selfish as, in their words, economists assume. Some believe that undermining this assumption goes a long way to showing that we can dismiss a great deal of economic analysis. It does no such thing since economists are well aware of the limitations of the Homo Economicus model, and do not need it for much of their work.

But there are still plenty of contexts where the crude assumption of self-ishness rears its head. So, for example, when we are talking about for-profit companies, most of our students assume that the founders of the company are in it "just for the money." It turns out that this attitude is not just restricted to students but is a common assumption made by most people.

Recall the study we mentioned in chapter 1, by Amit Bhattacharjee, Jason Dana, and Jonathan, which found that most people are cynical about the purported prosocial missions of for-profit companies compared with companies that have the same prosocial mission but are not-for-profits.[1] This is puzzling in a business ethics class precisely because we spend a lot of time teaching our students that they should figure out what would make the world a better place first, and then figure out how to build a sustainable business model to deliver that good second. Here, "sustainable" means profitable. There's no point in throwing good money at a problem when those resources could be better spent elsewhere.

The study authors call this "antiprofit beliefs" and conclude that most people have these sorts of beliefs. Given what they are, and given that it is an assumption prior to any evidence apart from the for-profit label, it might better be described as an antiprofit bias. But whether we call it a belief or a bias is neither here nor there. What matters is that, at least in the context of for-profit and nonprofit, people assume that the former is operated by selfish people and that the point of the former is some selfish and antisocial objective, like making as much money as possible.

Another context where we find this assumption is much more intimate. We want to ask you to pause for a moment and consider what you want out of your future career. Think about what you want your career to accomplish. What is driving you? What is most motivational to you? What gets you out of bed in the morning, eager to get to work?

While you're thinking about your own personal mission, see if you can rank-order the following items from most closely resembling your actual motivations to least closely resembling them. Or, put differently, organize the list from what motivates you the most to what motivates you the least:

1. Amount of pay
2. Having job security
3. Quality of fringe benefits
4. Amount of praise from your supervisor
5. Doing something that makes you feel good about yourself
6. Developing skills and abilities

7. Accomplishing something worthwhile
8. Learning new things

Notice that some items on this list describe intrinsic motivation, while others describe extrinsic, or external, motivations. You can think of extrinsic motivations as being basically about money, power, and prestige. The amount of pay, fringe benefits, praise, and having job security are basically extrinsic motivations, whereas learning new things, doing something worthwhile, developing skills and abilities, and doing something that makes you feel good about yourself are basically intrinsic motivations.

We say "basically" because there is some gray area here. So, for example, consider "doing something that makes you feel good about yourself." It might be that your standard for what gets you to feel good about yourself is an external standard. You might think, "This is something I might be praised for." If the standard is "what would get me praised," then that would count as an indirectly extrinsic motivation. "Having job security" might be extrinsic, but perhaps you want job security because what you are doing is worthwhile, and you want to continue doing what is worthwhile. If so, then this would be an indirectly intrinsic motivation.

Nevertheless, some are clearly extrinsic, like the amount of pay, while others are clearly intrinsic, like doing something worthwhile.

Now that you have your ranked list, pause again and think about your peers. If you are reading this book for a class, think about your fellow classmates. If you are reading this book outside a class, just think of people you regularly interact with at work or elsewhere. Now think about what they want out of their careers. What is driving them? What is most motivational to them? What gets them out of bed in the morning, eager to get to work?

Take that same list from above, and organize it from most motivational, to least motivational, for your peers.

Is the order the same, or different?

If you are like most people, you have ordered the list differently. If you are like most people, you have described your most important motives as emanating from yourself, as being motivated by and driven by an intrinsic desire to accomplish something worthwhile. The amount of pay, an extrinsic motivation, is not at the top of your list, but probably second, or possibly even further down. But, and again if you are like most people, you have assumed that your peers are primarily motivated by an extrinsic motivation, the amount of pay, and that intrinsic motivations are either second, or further down the list.

This is the consistent result found by people who work on what is called an "extrinsic incentive bias." According to this literature, we, and you, and just about everyone else, identifies intrinsic motivations as being most motivational to themselves but attribute extrinsic incentives, like money and status and power, to everyone else. We think we are moved by prosocial considerations, but others are moved by selfish ones.

If this is what most people do, however, then there is a puzzle: We are either bad at realizing what we, ourselves, are motivated by, or we are bad at realizing what others are motivated by. Because it cannot be true that most people are primarily intrinsically motivated, by a desire to improve the world, and that most people are primarily extrinsically motivated by money, status, or power. So we are either mistaken about what we want and others see through our self-deception, or we are mistaken about what others want and are deceived about their motivations.

Flattering Ourselves

Figuring out which one it is a bit difficult. There is, after all, plenty of evidence of self-deception. An important example of this is our propensity to judge ourselves to be more honest, humble, fair, just, and so on, than others. We do this consistently. Ask yourself how honest you are compared with the average person. Pretty honest!, you'll think. Definitely more honest than average. This is a self-flattering judgment. We make these judgments in other contexts too. So, for example, most people think that they are better-than-average drivers. That can't be right, of course, since most people will be average (that's how averages work). But it is often easier for us to recollect cases where we have been good at driving than those cases where we were average, or bad, drivers.

The case of driving is illustrative, but these kinds of self-flattering judgments are found most especially in moral contexts. When asked about our actions, and whether they were right or wrong, and when we are asked about our moral character, whether we are honest and humble or dishonest and boastful, we consistently flatter ourselves. We flatter ourselves about things that matter to us. We are less self-flattering about things we don't care about. So, if you don't care about bowling, and if someone asks you to tell them how good you are at bowling, you'll give an answer that is less self-flattering. You might be wrong about just how good you are, but, if you really don't care, you won't try to make yourself out to be better than you are.

When it matters to us, we preserve our ego and self-identity by focusing on the good and downplaying, rationalizing, or ignoring the bad. We do this by attributing the good actions we have done to our intrinsic motivations and character while downplaying the bad we have done by highlighting external pressures. And we also do this by being more able to recollect and remember the good that we have done, forgetting or ignoring the bad more easily.

This is evidence of self-deception in morally tinged contexts. But it also highlights something very important: It must be the case that being a good person matters a great deal to us. This is, after all, how we explain self-flattery in the first place. If it didn't matter to us, we wouldn't make an effort to lie to ourselves about it. So even though we have evidence for self-deception, that evidence also tells us that being a good person matters a great deal to us. But you might still think that self-deception is not just true of small things, but is true of the big things too—we are mistaken in a deep and global way about what makes us tick.

Meaning

If that's where you are, then consider the following. There are now a number of studies that show that meaningful, purposive work generates more productivity and effort than nonmeaningful work, at the same level of extrinsic incentive. Here's one example: Researchers went online and used Amazon M-Turk to recruit workers. The workers were tasked with looking at images of brain scans and identifying "anomalies" in the images—bumps or lumps or weird patterns. They would be paid based on how many images they worked through. The workers were randomly assigned into three different groups (or "treatments"). One group was told nothing at all apart from the task itself. A second group was told that the results would be discarded, treated as garbage. A third group, meanwhile, was told that this was part of a project to try and see if crowdsourcing the identification of brain tumors would be more effective than having doctors try to do it alone.

Guess which one people spent the least amount of time on? And guess which one got people to look at more images, for a longer period of time per image (at the expense of earnings)?

When they were told their work would be treated like garbage, people spent the least amount of time on it. When told it might lead to improving the identification of brain tumors, people spent more time per image, and went through more images. Identifying brain tumors is meaningful work, and doing meaningful work is more rewarding to us. Since people do, in fact, take on meaningful work and do it at the expense of possibly higher financial rewards, it appears as though people really are, perhaps not exclusively but at least significantly, intrinsically motivated.

Finding Meaning

One of the tortures the Communist regime came up with in Soviet Russia played on meaninglessness. They would make one group of prisoners dig ditches and then make another group fill those ditches back up. And they would repeat this process. The fact that it was utterly pointless was very much part of the torture.

David Graeber, an anthropologist, calls tasks like these "bullshit." He describes at least some jobs as being "bullshit." What he has in mind is that at least some jobs are nothing more than digging a ditch and filling it back up again. These kinds of jobs are pointless, are meaningless, and are harmful to those who perform them. They are "a form of employment that is so completely pointless, unnecessary, or pernicious that even the employee cannot justify its existence.[2]"

He distinguishes these kinds of bullshit jobs from what he calls "shit jobs." Shit jobs are just difficult jobs or are bad for other reasons, but they are not pointless. They are still necessary, and so must exist. But bullshit jobs are the kinds of jobs that shouldn't exist, says Graeber.

Graeber thinks more and more of our work life is filled with these kinds of jobs. In 2015, YouGov ran a poll in England asking about whether or not respondents thought the work that they do made "a meaningful contribution to the world." There were 37 percent who said "no," while 13 percent said that they weren't sure.

We disagree with Graeber's claims about current jobs in places like England. Unlike Graeber, we can't find a time in the history of the world that is better than now when it comes to opportunities for meaningful tasks, jobs, and pursuits than ever. That YouGov poll did find that 50 percent thought their job was "making a meaningful contribution to the world."

But our disagreement is only about the empirical facts about how many jobs are, as he would put it, bullshit, and whether we are seeing more or fewer of them. We don't disagree with the other claim that Graeber makes, which is that bullshit jobs are demotivating, dispiriting, and depressing. It doesn't matter if you can get a promotion, and have an entire career digging ditches and filling them back up, those kinds of jobs are to be avoided.

But whether or not a particular job is bullshit is at least sometimes up to us, and not up to others. How we regard our job, how we conceive of it, can impact whether or not we find meaning in it.

In the Myth of Sisyphus, Sisyphus was punished by having to roll a rock up a hill. He would push and push the rock up, and then it would fall back down again. He would then have to go down and push the rock back up the hill. He would never accomplish the task, the rock would always roll back down. The pointlessness of the task was the punishment. It wasn't that it was hard to do, it was that it made no difference whatsoever, since the same task would have to be repeated again and again.

In writing the story of Sisyphus, Albert Camus insisted that, despite the apparent pointlessness of the task given Sisyphus, it was, in fact, meaningful. Camus, a kind of existentialist, thought that all of our lives were Sisyphean in a way—our lives are just us pushing a rock up a hill, and then it rolls back down again and we have to push it back up. Like other existentialists, Camus did not think that there was some transcendent point or meaning to be discovered out there in the universe. Meaning comes from us, not from the world. Sisyphus's task was meaningful because it was his, Camus thought.

There's a lot of profundity in what Camus has to say. But for all that profundity, and even giving him a great deal of poetic license, it is hard not to conclude that Camus is wrong about Sisyphus. No matter how we reconceive the task put to Sisyphus, it really does seem not just pointless but utterly meaningless too. Camus may be a bit too generous about how we might discover or find meaningfulness in even the most apparently meaningless tasks. But his being overly generous does not license us to ignore a kernel of truth in what he says: We really can reconceive of at least some tasks and discover them to be meaningful even though many or most people have a hard time finding it so.

Take the story of a president, a janitor, and a rocket to the moon. John F. Kennedy, who was president of the United States, visited NASA a few times. The story we are told is that he noticed a janitor who was very energetic and enthusiastic at fulfilling his janitorial duties. Kennedy had seen him a few times and, each time, the janitor did not seem to be anything but excellent at his job. Finally, Kennedy approached him and asked him what the janitor thought he was up to, with all that vim and vigor.

"I'm helping to put a man on the moon," is what the janitor told Kennedy.

That's a profoundly meaningful way of looking at a task that many of us might dismiss as just "cleaning." It is, after all, important that NASA be clean. And a dirty workplace would go a long way to slowing the mission of NASA to get a man on the moon. The janitor could have regarded what he did at NASA as an unimportant part of what NASA does, but he did not.

And thinking of his task as being part of a process that led to the spectacular outcome of putting a man on the moon made him excited to come to work, and gave him all the incentive he needed to excel at it. It was intrinsically motivating to him.

That does not strike us as an overly generous way of discovering meaning in a job. It strikes us as perfectly appropriate for people to find this kind of meaning. It's just that it's rare and striking, and perhaps it shows that we are too conventional and narrow about what sorts of professions and tasks really are meaningful.

Understanding the important role of intrinsic motivation to productivity and performance is vital for not only how we think about our various jobs but also for how we reward and recognize performance at work. If you want more out of employees, you need to find people who already think the task you need accomplished is meaningful, or find a way of organizing the task so that it is more meaningful. Discovering that we suffer from an extrinsic incentive bias when it comes to other people means that we should be careful about how we construct and wield incentives. People are not primarily moved by carrots and sticks, they are moved by meaning too.

Backfire Effect

Not only do we want to engage in work that is meaningful, we also want to have meaningful control over when and how we engage in it. In psychology, there is a view called self-determination theory. According to this theory, we place a great deal of value on being self-determined or self-directed. Philosophers would say that what we value is autonomy—self-directed action. We don't like it when others make us do something we don't want to do, or try to manipulate us into doing what we would not otherwise do. This is why sometimes, and to the surprise of many, financial incentives can backfire. Instead of getting more productivity from people by waving money in front of them, we sometimes get less productivity.

When a task is robotic, increasing the amount that you pay someone for, say, laying a certain number of bricks will increase their productivity. They will lay more bricks. However, when a task requires more creativity or cognitive skill, a financial incentive on performance can result in less productivity.

Imagine you were asked to write short stories. And now imagine that we will pay you $20 for every short story you write. Do you think you would write more or fewer short stories than if we paid you a salary, and gave you time to write as many short stories as you would like? At least sometimes, the evidence suggests that paying people in the latter way promotes productivity more than giving them incentives to perform specific tasks.

Consider the following example: People were asked to look at brain scans. They were going to look for abnormalities in the scans. But they were put into three different treatment groups. One group of people were told that they were looking for brain tumors. Another group was told their results would be discarded, treated like garbage. A third group was told nothing additional. The results should not be too surprising: The first group looked at more scans and were more careful. Since they were being paid on the basis of how many scans they looked at, people in the first condition chose to be paid less to do a more thorough job. The worst performers were the ones who were told their work would just be garbage. The study authors concluded that the first condition was meaningful, and that it was the fact that it was meaningful that led to increased motivation and so greater productivity.

According to self-determination theory, we sometimes interpret financial incentives as an attempt to short-circuit our autonomy, and so rebel against this attempt to manipulate us. We want to choose to do something, we don't want to be pushed or prodded into doing it.

Economists call this the "crowding effect." More precisely, it is the "motivational crowding effect"—when the offer of an extrinsic incentive crowds out, reduces or eliminates our intrinsic motivation. This is a surprising finding. We "should" see the offer of money as additive—you want to write a short story, plus someone will pay you for it as well! That gives you two reasons to write the story; you like writing stories, and you'll get money. But sometimes we have found that instead of the offer of money adding to our motivations, it instead subtracts from them.

These findings, however, require interpretation. That is, people offered money have to interpret that offer as, for example, an attempt to manipulate us, or to push us to do something. Or, we have to interpret the offer of money as communicating that the person offering it to us thinks we wouldn't otherwise do it. Or, finally, the offer of money may be interpreted by us as signaling to other people that we are really doing it because of the money, and not for other reasons.

We can change how we offer money to short-circuit the crowding effect. So, for example, consider blood donations. Ever since Richard Titmuss wrote his famous book, *The Gift Relationship*, in 1971, people have thought that paying for blood donations might lower the total amount of blood donations. They thought this because the payment was a way to push people to donate blood, and communicated that the donor was only doing it for the money. But there are plenty of people who would be willing to donate if only they were asked.

And so, overall, Titmuss (2018) and others have argued that paying for blood would crowd out blood donations.

The evidence for this effect appears only sometimes, and the most recent and most rigorous studies by people like Nicola Lacetera and Mario Macis (2010) appear to show that payment for blood donations increases overall blood donations. But there are still some people who, when offered money, reject donating altogether. There is, however, a difference between saying, "you'll get $5 if you donate blood," and "to thank you for your time, we'll reward you with $5." Changing how we frame the incentive can change how people respond to it. After all, we do pay nurses and doctors and teachers, and hardly any of us think that this means that they are only doing it for the money. How people are incentivized, how they are paid, matters.

When we are busy thinking about how to promote productivity at work, we have to keep in mind that people care about meaning, and they care about how they are incentivized. Sometimes, it may be best to avoid having performance bonuses, for example, and to focus on meaningfulness instead.

Summary

- Most people report being intrinsically motivated, and say they want to do something meaningful.
- Sometimes, what is meaningful depends on your perspective.
- Most people care about extrinsic rewards, like amount of pay, very much.
- Sometimes, extrinsic rewards can backfire, and generate less productivity.
- We flatter ourselves, especially in morally relevant contexts.

Discussion Questions

1. Consider the way you are or were evaluated in college. Do you ever do things "just for the grade"? If so, what effect does that have on your motivation? Are there classes that you can think of where you were motivated by more than just the grade? How much work did you put into the former class, and how much for the latter?

2. Think about a boring job that you have had (a "bullshit" job). How would you describe it? What is the most meaningful way of describing it? How would you motivate someone else to perform that job with gusto?

3. Think about your future or current career. How would you describe it? What is the most meaningful way of describing it? When you describe the jobs or career you want to have, do you find yourself describing it in a more meaningful way than those jobs or careers that you don't want to have?

4. Why do you think we describe other people as being mostly motivated by extrinsic motivations? Why do we think of for-profits in that way? Is there an explanation for this persistent attribution of motivations that makes sense to you?

Notes

1. Bhattacharjee, Dana, and Baron 2017.
2. Graeber 2019.

13

Psychological Factors

Avoid DUMB Values

Basic Lesson: *Companies sometimes make predictable mistakes when formulating their mission, vision, and values statements. They fail to have values that are clearly connected to their company, they fail to understand how to incentivize or motivate people to act in accordance with the values, they fail to measure the values, and they too often rely on clichéd or otherwise boilerplate values.*

Business people often talk about SMART objectives. SMART is an acronym for Specific, Measurable, Achievable, Relevant, and Time-bound. The idea is that to have objectives that are easily understood and can get accomplished, you need them to meet these criteria. If it isn't specific, but too general, then you either might fail to meet the objective or others might fail to understand exactly what the objective is. Similarly with "measurable." We want to measure things so that we have a good sense of whether we are making progress toward the objective or not. We want to know if we're headed in the right direction. Achievable means that the objective is something that we know can be accomplished. There's no point in setting objectives that are not achievable, that are unrealistic. To be relevant means that the objective has to relate to the current market and market conditions. And, finally, for an objective to be "time-bound" is for it to have a deadline. As you might already be aware, a goal or an objective without a deadline is often put aside and never actually accomplished.

SMART objectives were very popular a few years ago. Even now, in MBA classes, plenty of professors teach the importance of having SMART objectives. While there are critics and alternatives, it is a good rough guide when you are assigning tasks for others, or when you are setting tasks for yourself.

People are aware of the need to set SMART objectives. What they too often don't know is that their value documents need to be "SMART" as well. Or, at least, they should avoid being DUMB.

In what follows, we'll take you through a framework for evaluating values documents, from corporate social responsibility (CSR) statements to company values and purposes. As you might have guessed, the framework's

Business Ethics for Better Behavior. Jason Brennan, William English, John Hasnas, and Peter Jaworski, Oxford University Press. © Oxford University Press 2021. DOI: 10.1093/oso/9780190076559.003.0013

acronym is DUMB, and its mission is to show you what you should avoid when constructing or thinking about company values.

Too many companies treat values, from CSR to values statements, as ornaments and baubles. They are not there to do any real work, to guide the actions of employees and management. They are there because it's what you're supposed to do, it's what most companies have, and you don't want to be out of step with what everyone else is doing—having vague values and looking good but not demanding much of you.

That's why the task of determining core values, putting together a CSR, and other values-related materials, so often falls to the marketing department. Marketing is about communicating with people in a way that makes you, your service, or your product look good.

In our classes, there are always at least a few students who are skeptical about values and ethics. They come to our classes thinking that values are, at bottom, little more than marketing slogans. Unless they work for some branch of the US armed services, they don't know their own company's values.

Values and Success

Values drive success; value statements don't.

Meaningful and sincere values improve employee engagement, increase retention, reduce turnover, and motivate commitment and loyalty to your brand by customers. They help with recruitment. But perceived inauthenticity, disingenuousness, can hamper or even torpedo success. How can you avoid being perceived as being inauthentic? How can you ensure that your team is on the same page? And exactly how do you go about putting together excellent values documents that accomplish all of those goals? By avoiding DUMB values:

- Disconnected
- Unincentivized
- Measureless
- Boilerplate

Or, if you want to be a bit cheeky, replace "Boilerplate" with "Bullshit."

Safety at ALCOA

Let's begin with a story about ALCOA, the aluminum company, under the leadership of Paul O'Neill.

O'Neill was tapped to be CEO of ALCOA in 1987. He ended up being a very good choice for ALCOA, as measured not just by the financial performance of ALCOA during his tenure but also by measures like employee retention and employee satisfaction. It didn't look that way at first, however. It looked like choosing O'Neill to run ALCOA was a big mistake.

His very first address to shareholders, as the newly minted CEO, did not go the way most people expected. It is often expected of CEOs to tell shareholders about the company's financial situation, where it has been, and what the CEO plans on doing in order to improve the bottom line. O'Neill did none of that. Instead, his first address to shareholders was about safety.

That's right, safety. He told shareholders that he was going to improve ALCOA's safety record, that ALCOA was going to be the kind of place that would have no—zero—safety incidents. The new slogan would be "Zero is possible." And he walked them through all of the ways in which he was planning on improving ALCOA with respect to safety.

The room was stunned. Some shareholders left the meeting calling their stockbroker to sell their shares of ALCOA. This new CEO, they thought, is focused on the wrong thing, and doesn't understand that what shareholders want and care about is increased profits. Instead, all this new CEO seemed to care about was safety. Who does that?

Shareholders were not the only ones who thought O'Neill had something else up his sleeve. Employees did not immediately buy in, and managers of the various aluminum plants under ALCOA didn't either.

But O'Neill was consistent. He instituted a system for measuring safety incidents, and made those numbers public. He insisted that each of his reports be as familiar with the safety numbers as they were with the stock price. He released a manager of a plant in Mexico, a rising star, for repeatedly failing to give O'Neill the safety numbers at the beginning of their phone conversations. He gave employees on the floor of the plants his personal phone number in front of the management team and asked them to call him directly as soon as an injury occurred. He started all of his speeches by pointing out the fire exits. He wore safety equipment when he toured the plants. And when injuries did occur, as of course they did, O'Neill would spare almost no expense to try to figure out why it happened and what they could do to avoid it happening in future.

Despite the rocky start, O'Neill stayed on as CEO, and stayed true to his commitment to safety. By the time O'Neill stepped down as CEO, ALCOA had lowered workplace safety incidents to below that of all competitors. ALCOA became a leader in safety. They never did hit "zero," but they came close. Also, ALCOA improved the bottom line significantly, with consistent increases in the value of ALCOA shares, and lower employee turnover than competitors, but O'Neill rarely talked about that. It seemed as though all he ever talked about was safety.

Admittedly, ALCOA under O'Neill is a significant outlier, and is something of an exceptional case. But it is a very good illustration of the framework. Let's go through it.

Disconnected

First, there is no disconnect between the value, safety, and why this company chose to emphasize it. Working at an aluminum plant is dangerous. Employees who work there don't need an explanation for why the company would choose "safety" as a value—it is the top of their mind for each of them. There is a simple and obvious connection between the type of work that is expected of employees and the value of safety.

At other companies, it is not always clear what the connection is between a particular value—like honesty or safety—and the product, service, company, employees, or customers. For example, many companies tout their environmental bona fides, or give 1 percent for the planet. Sometimes, it makes sense for a company to do that. But other times, it's just not obvious why they do it. And when it isn't obvious why they do it, then, for at least some of us, we get this creeping skepticism, and begin to think that there is some kind of manipulation being attempted here.

This is exactly what happened with hotels and their sudden interest in being environmentally friendly. In the 1990s, some hotels started putting a door hanger on your bed that said, "help save the planet. Put this door hanger on the door to let us know that you plan on reusing your towels and bed sheets. That helps us use less water, less energy, and fewer laundry detergents, and helps make the environment better for all of us."

It doesn't take a complete cynic to wonder about what the real motivation here is. This is especially so when you realize that the hotel you're staying at doesn't have a recycling bin (as sometimes happens), or doesn't carry over its apparent commitment to the environment in other parts of the hotel. It doesn't help that your choosing not to have your towels cleaned helps the environment, yes, but also (coincidentally?) helps lower costs for the hotel and improves its bottom line.

Many critics have dubbed this practice an instance of "greenwashing"—a proclaimed interest in the environment that was actually an interest in lowering costs or increasing revenues. As you saw in chapter 9, most people care very much about what your real intentions are, and they don't only focus on the outcomes. If they judge you to be insincere, they will sometimes think that they are being manipulated, and so will not comply in order to boost their sense of self-determination.

Consider Wendy's, the hamburger chain, for a moment. One of their commitments is to the Dave Thomas Foundation, which is the charitable arm of the hamburger chain. The Dave Thomas Foundation is dedicated to helping orphans and promoting adoptions. Here, there is no obvious connection between a fast-food restaurant that makes delicious hamburgers and adoptions. But all you need to know is that Dave Thomas, the founder of Wendy's, was himself an orphan to immediately understand why Wendy's chose to dedicate some of their revenues to help others in this specific way. It's clearly connected.

To avoid "disconnected" values, you need clear answers to questions like, "Why are you doing this?" in order to get an answer to a related question, "What are your motives?" There should be a strong connection between what you do and the values you insist on. It makes sense for a sports team to value teamwork. Working well together is what helps teams succeed. It makes less sense for a hotel chain to value environmental sustainability. Environmental sustainability is a great value; it's just far from obvious why a hotel should prioritize that over other values.

The connection between your values and your product or service need not be about the product or service itself. Many founders have personal histories and stories that might make a sensible connection to some value, as is true in the case of Wendy's and the Dave Thomas Foundation.

There must be some story, a narrative, either connecting the product itself to the value, some significant event in the company's life and the value, something personal about the founders or the employees and the value, and so on. The tighter the connection, the more it adds to our understanding of the brand as a coherent whole rather than a disconnected grab bag of random nice-sounding platitudes.

One reason why this matters is because your customers are not as interested in your company as you are. Your opportunity to inform them about what you do and why it matters is limited. If your product and your company values tell a coherent narrative, that is more likely to make us associate good things with what you do.

More importantly, values that are disconnected from the product or the people give rise to the suspicion that the values are simply dishonest, or deceptive—that you don't really mean it. Lots of fly-by-night operations put together values statements. They don't care what is in them or what they might mean. It's an effort on their part to help hoodwink their customers.

Values like "communication," "respect," "integrity," or "excellence" give off a warm glow. When you read a values statement that includes concepts like "integrity" you might let your guard down a little bit. A company that values integrity is not going to try and hoodwink me, we think.

But these were the values that Enron claimed to uphold. They sounded good, but they were just lying. Management didn't believe it, and employees didn't either. It was a way for Enron to try to dupe the rest of us into thinking that they were something they were not. In principle, the values were connected to the products and services Enron was offering, it's just that they didn't mean it.

Unincentivized

Second, Paul O'Neill ensured that safety played a role in promotion, hiring, firing, onboarding, and other decisions within ALCOA. Being a leader in safety at ALCOA was one way to move up the ranks. Being a laggard in safety was a good way to be shown the door.

How are you motivating people to comply with and live the values that you purport to care about? What incentives are you using to get people to not only accept but to embrace your values? Instead of having systems in place that motivate values uptake, too many companies ignore the need to have good incentives in place for values. Failing to provide motivation may lead to the suspicion that you don't mean it, or that you don't care about it. Again, if people think you don't mean it, they won't consider it.

Incentivizing people to act in accordance with some value does not have to take the form of a financial incentive. Chapter 9, on meaning and motivation, explains when and why some kinds of incentives sometimes backfire, but there are some nonfinancial incentives to consider.

When looking for new hires, are you insisting on values fit? That's motivating. If the people you select are selected, in part, based on their alignment with your core values, that sends a strong signal that you do care about these values. Are values an important part of the onboarding process? Again, if so, that's a signal that you care. When moving people up the organization to higher levels of responsibility, are you using values metrics to make that decision? If so, that's motivating. During monthly meetings, are you highlighting team members who lived the values of the company? That kind of social recognition is motivating.

To emphasize, motivating people to think about the values of the company does not require crude pay-for-values kind of thinking. A pat on the back for doing something based on the values we purport to care about around here serves as a good reminder of those values, as well as a good way to show that you really mean it.

Incentives at Wells Fargo

While we're talking about incentives, it would be worth our while to pause for a moment and look at the disastrous case of Wells Fargo. Wells Fargo is a bank, the oldest still-running bank in America.

Wells Fargo was a leader in values and ethics. They were the first bank to put together a comprehensive set of values documents. Their vision and values documents would become a model for other banks to emulate. They had special meetings where values would be discussed, and, during onboarding, all employees receive a slick pamphlet that touts Wells Fargo's commitments to "What's right for customers," "People as a competitive advantage," "Ethics," "Diversity and Inclusion," and "Leadership," as the Values section of their Vision, Values, and Goals document says.

On paper, these values look great. They are values that customers looking for a bank want their bank to possess. But in practice, those values were not what drove the day-to-day mission of many branches. Instead, very many Wells Fargo branches operated in direct contravention of those values. Among the abuses, perhaps the most significant one was signing up customers for new accounts and credit cards and other instruments without the customer knowing about it, or asking for it. Clearly not "What's right for customers."

Why would someone do this? There may be a number of answers to this question, but at least part of the answer has to do with what Wells Fargo incentivized, how they incentivized it, and what they didn't incentivize.

Internally, Wells Fargo called accounts "solutions" and had a slogan that the CEO and others were fond of: "Eight is great!" That's the number of "solutions" that they wanted each customer to carry at Wells Fargo—eight accounts. A credit card is a "solution," as is a checking account, and a savings account, a mortgage, an investment vehicle, and so on. The average banking customer doesn't even carry half that many accounts at their banks, but that was the goal at Wells Fargo.

Of course, on its face, there is nothing wrong with a "big, hairy, audacious goal" or a "BHAG" as some management consultants like to call these. In fact, setting one of these kinds of goals is often motivational. ALCOA's "BHAG" was no workplace injuries captured by their preferred slogan, "Zero is possible." Zero may very well be possible, but ALCOA has never managed to hit that target. And eight really may be great, but exceedingly rare is the customer who wants or even needs that many "solutions." This, then, is the first relevant difference between ALCOA's and Wells Fargo's audacity: It is good for the employees at ALCOA for the firm to strive for zero workplace injuries. It is not good for the customers of Wells Fargo for that bank to strive for eight solutions. The second relevant difference is all about incentives: ALCOA incentivized safe behavior, and made safety a part of how you succeeded at ALCOA. Wells Fargo did not incentivize the values in their values documents but, instead, incentivized getting to eight solutions, revealing that what they actually valued was very different from what appeared in their values documents.

The audacity of eight resulted in a culture within some branches that was described as "cutthroat" and a "pressure cooker." Employees were fired for failing to meet eight solutions. Promotions were determined based on performance in meeting the targeted eight solutions. Employees were publicly embarrassed if they failed to meet those targets at meetings. And managers would be routinely asked about one thing, the great eight, often to the exclusion of other metrics and performance indicators.

What is incentivized—what gets you hired, promoted, fired, and recognized for—is what people will conclude is valued. If your values document expresses wonderful sentiments but what is rewarded is performance along something else, then people will ignore the former and pay attention to the latter. You get more of what you reward or, to use a common expression, you get what you pay for.

Measureless

If you're going to reward it, you're going to have to know how much of it you have. If it's a value that matters, then you need a way to track whether or not you or your team, or your employees, are doing more or less of it, acting in conformity with it or not. Instead of being measurable, too many companies' values are unmeasured or, worse, unmeasurable. Exactly what is the point of insisting on something that no one bothers to track? If you're not measuring, you're not evaluating.

At ALCOA, safety was measured. It was measured every day. The numbers were updated regularly. Safety was meticulously tracked. One way of knowing that ALCOA sincerely cared about safety is precisely because they measured it. At Wells Fargo, the number of "solutions" per customer was the defining metric. What did they care about? Was it the fine sentiments expressed in their purpose, vision, and mission documents? Was it the wonderful values contained in the document containing their core values? They didn't actually bother to measure any of those. But they did measure solutions. You would be forgiven if you concluded, just on the basis of what got measured, that at Wells Fargo they cared about the values underpinning getting more solutions per customer rather than the values in their values documents.

Failing to measure, failing to have a metric that permits you to gauge how you are doing with respect to something is very close to failing to care about it at all. If it matters, as values should, measure it.

Boilerplate

Finally, at ALCOA, safety was memorable. It wasn't unique (just about every aluminum plant says that they value safety as one of their core values), but the way it was implemented, and the slogan attached to it, met the key requirement of ensuring that your values aren't easily forgotten and easily overlooked.

For something to be "boilerplate" is for it to be standard or uniform or, essentially, the same. Like a standard method or a standard document. The word's current connotation comes to us from nineteenth-century journalism. Some news stories had elements that were the same, regardless of the specific story you were writing. Those elements were cast out of metal for use in the printing press, and were used repeatedly. Since they resembled literal boilerplate (a plate attached to boilers identifying the brand of the boiler), they started calling these "boilerplate."

In the world of values documents, you sometimes see the same core values used over and over, and similar language used for the purpose and mission of a company. An analysis of Fortune 100 companies' values statements shows that x percent have x as a value. x percent have y as a value. And x percent have z as a value. That's an awful lot of duplication. You will have to forgive the rest of us if we look at your values and suspect that you just picked your values from among the popular ones at the moment, taking no time to discover the ones that really matter to you, the ones that are yours, uniquely.

The values do not have to be unique. Honesty and integrity are meaningful, significant, and important values. It's just that your team may suspect that you put no thought into it at all if it appears as though you just looked at your competitor's values and took them as your own. You don't want to give off the impression that your values documents are copies of other firms' values documents, that they are nothing more than boilerplate.

There are many ways to avoid having boilerplate values. You can use a synonym, come up with your own word for it, use a slogan like "Zero is possible," and so on. You can make the values uniquely yours, or use some method or system that keeps the values top-of-mind, as it should. So, for example, Uber has a value called "super-pumpedness." That's unique and memorable. It suffers from failing to have a clear definition, and so it is difficult to measure whether you are more or less "super-pumped," but it illustrates the point that you can make it unique. "Do no evil" is uniquely Googlian. There is nothing bland or boilerplate about it. At Amazon, the value is that the customer comes first. That's not a unique value, but Amazon often leaves an empty chair at meetings which is supposed to represent the customer. Having an empty chair like this is a good way to remind yourself of a key—or, in Amazon's case, *the* key—value. Hilton, the hotel chain, uses the name of their company as an acronym for their values: Hospitality, Integrity, Leadership, Teamwork, Ownership, and Now.

Avoiding boilerplate values is important because the values need to be memorable to fulfill the function of guiding decisions. You want the values to be memorable, to be the kind of thing that people think about before they make decisions, and while they are making decisions. If people have a difficult time remembering the values, then those values will fail to be included in decision-making.

It is also important to avoid the suspicion that the values are just "bullshit." The philosopher Harry Frankfurt wrote an article, later turned into a small book, called *On Bullshit*. In *On Bullshit*, he identified "bullshitting" not with lying but with saying something that one is not committed to, something whose truth value is up in the air. When we are "bullshitting," we're just tossing things out there, without committing to its being true. And whatever else is true, we should avoid even giving the impression that our company's values are boilerplate, lest people think we're just piling on the bullshit.

Conclusion

SMART objectives give you a clear idea of some important elements of good objectives. DUMB values give you a clear idea of what you need to avoid when constructing all your values documents—from purpose to mission to the core values and so on. These documents should avoid being Disconnected, Unincentivized, Measureless, and Boilerplate. In summary, you should connect it, measure it, motivate it, and make it yours. Together, these are the keys to the "I mean it" door.

Summary

- Often, what is incentivized is what people will conclude you value.
- Choosing the right values requires that they "fit" with the organization by being clearly connected.
- Measuring values is possible, and it is important since it helps communicate sincerity and authenticity.
- The suspicion that an organization is being insincere is often a result of using boilerplate values and descriptions of values. These should be thoughtfully chosen and described.

Discussion Questions

1. Find two organizations that you believe are sincere in their values. Do they follow the advice in this chapter? If not, what is it about them that makes you believe that they are being sincere?
2. Find two organizations that you believe are in it just for the money, and are insincere in their values statements. What is it about them that makes you think they are being insincere and inauthentic?
3. Can you think of an example of an incentive system that could be or was "gamed"? How was it gamed? Can you come up with a different way of incentivizing the activity or behavior that might avoid gaming?

Conclusion

How to Run an Unethical Business

We've spent thirteen chapters trying to give you good advice for getting better behavior. We've talked about why ordinary people of goodwill sometimes act badly. Sometimes they suffer from moral confusion, so we've helped clarify the moral issues. Sometimes they face bad incentives, so we've discussed how to incentivize good behavior. Sometimes the problem is that we suffer from various psychological dispositions—such as a tendency to conform to others' norms or a tendency to suffer from blind spots—so we've discussed how to reduce the problems these cause.

We're going to turn the tables here and give you bad advice, advice for how to ensure you and your employees act *badly*.

Of course, we don't want you to take this advice. Our goal instead is to help summarize the lessons of the last thirteen chapters by offering you the lessons in negative form. If you wanted to induce bad behavior, here's how to do it. The upshot: If you want good behavior, here's what to avoid.

We're putting this advice in negative form in part because that can help you understand the positive advice better. But we also want you to ask yourself, do you, or does your organization, actually seem to *follow* this bad advice? If so, that's a red flag, and a sign you need to change.

Prime People for Bad Behavior

- Make people's performance reviews based on one or two high-stress, high-stakes activities, assessed only once or twice a year.
- Overwork your employees. Ensure they get little rest. Make them feel stressed and anxious.
- Give people more to do than they could reasonably do in a normal work-week. Make sure the only way to succeed is to cut corners.
- Stress that people disagree about ethics. Make sure to say "It's all just an opinion, anyways."

Business Ethics for Better Behavior. Jason Brennan, William English, John Hasnas, and Peter Jaworski, Oxford University Press.
© Oxford University Press 2021. DOI: 10.1093/oso/9780190076559.003.0014

Signal You Think Ethics Is a Joke

- Don't put your money where your mouth is. Use lots of high-falutin' moral language, but devote few or no resources to ethical management.
- Create a CSR campaign which uses vague language and makes impossible-to-assess claims about the good you do.
- Constantly congratulate yourselves for your charitable work but ignore questions about whether your actions harm or exploit anyone, or whether you are keeping your word.
- Lobby the government for regulations which harm your competitors, but use moralistic language when you do so. Claim you're really serving the common good rather than yourself.
- Discuss how you care about ethics but refuse to find a way to measure it.
- Wait until bad things happen to put in an ethical compliance program.
- Be reactive rather than proactive. When you have bad press, act. Don't do the right thing if no one is looking.
- Think of ethics as a PR and marketing problem, to be solved by good advertising and slick photography.

Conflate Ethics with Other Things

- Have ethics training seminars where you only discuss the law.
- Find the latest abstract slogan, phrase, or platitude. Put that platitude in all your moral marketing materials. Make sure it has no real meaning so an employee can't easily judge whether you're living up to your values.
- When your business is accused of doing something wrong, point out all the good you do elsewhere.

Create Bad Incentives

- Create a system where employees can generate benefits for themselves but push the costs onto others.
- Share resources but put no constraints on who can use it.
- Only reward short-term profit maximization. Don't have any part of performance reviews or raises depend on measured ethical behavior.
- Make pay raises zero-sum. Your gain is someone else's pain. You can get a good score only if someone else gets a proportionately bad score. Ensure employees have a personal stake in their coworkers *failing*.

- Ensure that if employees save the company money, they don't see any reward.
- If employees show a willingness to go above and beyond the call of duty, punish them by loading them with extra responsibilities but no extra pay or status. Reward slackers by giving them less work and less responsibility for the same pay.
- Make sure everything is everyone's responsibility. That way, no one can be directly blamed for anything.
- Give employees a stake in increasing their department's budget and the number of people in their division, independently of the value to the organization.
- Encourage short-term thinking. Reward immediate gains. Ensure that when the long-term costs come due, the employees responsible will have moved on.
- Let bosses take credit for employees' successes but make sure underlings take the blame for bosses' failures.
- Reward people for signaling how moral they are. Watch them get into an arms race of self-righteous *talk* but not actual good behavior.

Create a Bad Culture

- Hire bosses who think they are always right and can't take criticism.
- Encourage employees to see each other as enemies or direct competitors.
- Make sure employees have multiple bosses with different agendas.
- Put all the problematic employees together in the same group. Give them a lot of responsibility.
- Place new employees with the worst employees or the worst performing division.
- Rather than firing bad or problematic employees, keep them on the payroll in sinecures.
- If someone challenges the firm's decisions or the "Way Things Have Always Been Done," humiliate him publicly.
- Ensure that people who say yes to every order get rewarded and promoted.
- Make sure employees know their job is to do what they're told, not to think for themselves.
- Hire "a-holes," especially as bosses.
- Hire employees with a history of high-risk and irresponsible behavior.

- Instead of keeping your word and honoring your contracts, ask employees to think about how profitable it would be to fudge on the contracts, just a little. For instance, if you deliver 90 percent of what you promised, your customers probably won't sue.
- Make sure your employees are scared to ask for help, lest they be seen as incompetent.
- Make sure employees feel like they have an arm's-length, transaction relationship with the business and their other employees. Don't let them think of the business as something more.
- Don't explain to employees how your product or service directly makes the world a better place and makes other people's live better.
- Hire outside consulting firms to make the hard choices and then say your hands are tied. Encourage employees to think firm leaders can't think for themselves.
- If your organization has systematic problems, encourage employees to think of themselves as passive spectators or victims who need to be saved. Don't encourage them to ask what they could *do* about it.
- Encourage employees to think being ethical is about *having the right beliefs* rather than doing the right thing. Purge people who disagree.
- Encourage employees to think that unethical behavior is widespread and that most wrongdoers are getting away with it. They'll feel resentful and will feel that they might as well act badly too.

Encourage Moral Blindness

- Avoid using moral language.
- Use euphemisms such as "competitive advantage" rather than moral terms such as "fraud."
- Use vague moral language and obscure slogans.
- Separate ethical analysis from strategic planning. Tell employees they should first think about strategy, and only afterward assess the ethics of their proposals.
- Better yet, create a separate ethical oversight board. Give them the job of reviewing ethical proposals, but tell regular employees it's not their job to worry about ethics. The Ethics Oversight Board can take care of it.
- Encourage employees to leave legal compliance to the experts.
- Tell people to "stay in their lane" and "just do their job."
- When making strategic decisions, don't ask tough questions such as "Who might this harm?" or "Are there any unseen costs to what we do?" Instead, assume everything will work out exactly as intended.

Encourage Moral Confusion

- Teach employees to think as follows:
  - It's someone else's problem.
  - You agreed to follow orders, so do as you're told.
  - If you can get away with it, it's not really wrong.
  - It's okay to coerce people to get what you want.
  - Little lies never hurt anyone. Everyone cheats anyway.
  - What matters is whether it *sounds* good.
- Teach employees the crudest versions of major theories of business ethics or major ethical theories. Ask them to apply them on the job. They probably can't think the issues through, and, as a bonus, the theories are too abstract to be useful.
- Give employees impossible-to-fulfill standards, such as "balancing every stakeholder's interests" (How? What counts as the proper balance? How do we resolve conflicts?) or "Managing the triple bottom line."
- Spend your time thinking about *hard questions and dilemmas* rather than training them to deal with the most common problems that actual arise.

Putting It All Together

There is no magic pill that will make you immune to temptation. There is no simple algorithm or decision procedure you can use which will guarantee you make the right choice in every situation. There is no management style which ensures employees do the right thing for the right reason without fail.

Ethics is too complex for that.

However, over the course of this book, you've had a crash course in understanding the fundamentals of business ethics—including understanding why so many people confuse business ethics with something else, such as law or corporate social responsibility marketing campaigns. You've gotten a crash course in understanding how different rules create different incentive structures, some of which reinforce good behaviors and some of which reinforce negative behaviors. You've gotten a crash course in understanding the various psychological impediments people face—from moral blind spots to self-deception to a bias toward conformity—which induce people to act badly. We've offered you advice for how to reduce, if not quite overcome, these problems as best you reasonably can.

Putting it all together:

1. Human nature is complicated. Lots of things contribute to good and bad behavior.
2. A good corporate social responsibility campaign is no substitute for primary business ethics. Ethics is fundamentally about how your company makes its money, not what it does with its profits after it's made them.
3. The main way a business serves society is by ensuring its core products and services make the world a better place.
4. The core principles of business ethics are refrain from coercion and fraud, honor your contracts, respect the personhood of all participants in the market, and remember that personal responsibility is inalienable.
5. Compliance with the law is no substitute for ethics. Although the law and ethics sometimes overlap, the law sometimes requires unethical behavior, and many unethical behaviors are nevertheless legal.
6. From a self-interested point of view, being ethical is a good bet. Your ability to make future trades depends upon your reputation for ethics. The most reliable way of having a good reputation is to deserve it.
7. Managing for ethics requires creating incentive structures which measure and reward good behavior but which cannot easily be gamed.
8. Ethics must be part of strategy. Every strategic decision should involve explicit discussions of the ethics of that decision, including who might be harmed by it, who might be helped, and what dangers or downsides the decision may pose.
9. When something is everyone's responsibility, it is no one's responsibility. Good management requires avoiding the diffusion of responsibility.
10. In particular, individual decision-makers need to bear the consequences of their actions, or they will likely promote their own interest at the expense of the company's.
11. People suffer from moral blind spots. Integrating ethics into strategy can help overcome that.
12. Most people are conformists. This means putting all the bad apples together will reinforce bad behavior. Having bad or unethical bosses means having bad and unethical employees. But the good news is that ethical people will reinforce each other's good behaviors.
13. Most people are intrinsically motivated to make a positive difference. Helping employees see how they make a positive difference can help produce better behavior. However, we have to be careful to avoid moral accounting, where employees give themselves permission to act badly to balance when the act well.

14. A company's values need to be connected to its core product, incentivized, measured, and meaningful. Otherwise, mission statements, CSR campaigns, and the like will backfire.

Appendix: Some Heuristics for Making Ethical Decisions

Recognize the Problem

- Is this a legal problem? A strategy/management problem? A public relations problem? An ethics problem? Or a mix of the four?
- Look for signs of moral disengagement: Does the issue make you feel uncomfortable? Do you find yourself not wanting to talk or think about it? Do others seem uncomfortable or unwilling to talk about it? If so, it's probably an ethical issue.
- Look for problems: Could this decision harm someone? Does it involve breaking a promise or lying to someone to whom you owe the truth? Is there some reason to think it would impede one of your duties? Is the decision coercive? Are you manipulating someone or taking advantage of someone's ignorance or bad luck?

Get the Relevant Facts

- What are the relevant facts of the case? What facts are not known? Can I learn more about the situation? Do I know enough to make a decision?
- What individuals and groups will be affected by the outcome? Are some of their concerns more important? Why?
- What are the options for acting? Have all the relevant persons and groups been consulted? Have I identified creative options?

Consider These Questions

- Does the decision involve coercing or defrauding anyone?
- Will the decision induce others involved to act in ways contrary to their best interests? (People don't usually choose to do that, so it's a warning sign that you may be acting deceptively.)
- Are you subjecting people to a risk they did not adequately understand and would not willingly assume?
- Have I elicited trust from someone who legitimately should expect to trust us? If so, am I acting in a way consistent with that trust?
- Is this action the kind of action someone I admire would undertake?
- Is this action consistent with my previous agreements and promises?
- Does this action violate anyone's moral rights?
- Are the people with whom I'm dealing particularly vulnerable in some way? Should I treat them with extra care?
- Am I following orders? If so, is this the kind of thing the people making the orders have the authority to command? Would I do this if I were my own boss and not being ordered to do so?

- What are my values? Is this action consistent with my values?
- What are my company's values? Is this action consistent with those values?

Other Heuristic Devices

- Would I be comfortable defending my decision in front of my friends? On TV? To my pastor? To my grandchildren?
- Would I want people to know why I made this decision the way I did?
- Would I want to live in a world where people acted like this?
- Given what we know about human psychology, what are my likely biases? Will I be tempted to analyze the case incorrectly? How should I counteract these biases?
- Do I trust that I am in a good position to make this decision? Should I seek out guidance from a third party?

Bibliography

Acemoglu, Daron, and James Robinson. 2013. *Why Nations Fail*. New York: Penguin.

Achen, Christopher, and Larry Bartels. 2016. *Democracy for Realists*. Princeton, NJ: Princeton University Press.

Adler, Jonathan. 2000. "Clean Politics, Dirty Profits: Rent-Seeking behind the Green Curtain." In *Political Environmentalism: Going behind the Green Curtain*. Edited by Terry Anderson, 1–30. Stanford, CA: Hoover Institute Press.

Ainslie, Elizabeth K. 2006. "Indicting Corporations Revisited: Lessons of the Arthur Andersen Prosecution." *American Criminal Law Review* 43: 107–142.

Al-Ubaydli, Omar, Daniel Houser, John Nye, Maria Pia Paganelli, and Sophia Xiaofei Pan. 2013. *"The Causal Effect of Market Priming on Trust: An Experimental Investigation Using Randomized Control"[https://doi.org/10.1371/journal.pone.0055968]*. *PLoS One* 8(3): e55968.

Ariely, Dan. 2013. *The Honest Truth about Dishonesty*. New York: Harper Perennial.

Arnold, Chris. 2016. "Former Wells Fargo Employees Describe Toxic Sales Culture, Even at HQ." *Morning Edition*. Aired October 4 on NPR. https://www.npr.org/2016/10/04/496508361/former-wells-fargo-employees-describe-toxic-sales-culture-even-at-hq.

Axelrod, Robert. 1984. *The Evolution of Cooperation*. New York: Basic Books.

Batson, C. Daniel, and Elizabeth R. Thompson. 2001. "Why Don't Moral People Act Morally? Motivational Considerations." *Current Directions in Psychological Science* 10: 54–57.

Begley, Sharon, and Janet Roberts. 2012. "Insight: Komen Charity under Microscope for Funding, Science." *Reuters*, February 8. https://www.reuters.com/article/us-usa-healthcare-komen-research/insight-komen-charity-under-microscope-for-funding-science-idUSTRE8171KW20120208.

Berkes, Howard. 2012. "Remembering Roger Boisjoly: He Tried to Stop Shuttle Challenger Launch." *All Things Considered*. Aired February 6 on NPR. https://www.npr.org/sections/thetwo-way/2012/02/06/146490064/remembering-roger-boisjoly-he-tried-to-stop-shuttle-challenger-launch.

Bever, Lindsey. 2019. "Censorship or Social Responsibility? Amazon Removes Some Books Peddling Vaccine Information" (blog). *Washington Post*, February 15. https://www.washingtonpost.com/business/2019/03/18/censorship-or-social-responsibility-amazon-removes-some-books-peddling-vaccine-misinformation/?noredirect=on&utm_term=.33bc8923623e.

Bhattacharjee, Amit, Jason Dana, and Jonathan Baron. 2017. "Anti-Profit Beliefs: How People Neglect the Societal Benefits of Profit." *Journal of Personality and Social Psychology* 113: 671.

Bloom, Paul. 2010. "The Moral Life of Babies." *New York Times Magazine*, May 5. https://www.nytimes.com/2010/05/09/magazine/09babies-t.html.

Bock, L. 2015. Can Google's Rules Transform Your Workplace? Knowledge@Wharton. Accessed September 25. http://knowledge.wharton.upenn.edu/article/ow-google's-rules-can-work-in-your-office/.

Bond, Chris, and Bella DePaulo. 2011. *Is Anyone Really Good at Detecting Lies?*. CreateSpace Publishing Platform.

Bovard, James. 1995. "Archer Daniels Midland: A Case Study in Corporate Welfare." *Policy Analysis 241*.

Brennan, Jason. 2012. "For-Profit Business as Civic Virtue." *The Journal of Business Ethics* 106: 313–324.

Brennan, Jason. 2016. "Argument: Trump Won Because Voters Ignorant, Literally." *Foreign Policy*, November 10. https://foreignpolicy.com/2016/11/10/the-dance-of-the-dunces-trump-clinton-election-republican-democrat/.

Brennan, Jason, and Peter Jaworski. 2016. *Markets without Limits*. New York: Routledge.

Brennan, Jason, and Phillip Magness. 2019. *Cracks in the Ivory Tower*. New York: Oxford University Press.

Britschgi, Christian. 2018. Starbucks Bans Plastic Straws, Winds Up Using More Plastic. *Reason*, July 12. https://reason.com/blog/2018/07/12/starbucks-straw-ban-will-see-the-company.

Byatt, Ian. 2006. "The Stern Review: A Dual Critique, Part II. Economic Aspects." *World Economics* 7: 199–225.

Caplan, Bryan. 2007. *The Myth of the Rational Voter*. Princeton, NJ: Princeton University Press.

Carig, David. 2017. "Breast Cancer Charities: Where to Give—And Where to Avoid." *USA Today*, October 3. https://www.usatoday.com/story/money/personalfinance/2017/10/03/breast-cancer-charity-ratings-julia-louis-dreyfus/714899001/.

Carroll, Archie B., Kenneth J. Lipartito, James Post, and Patricia Werhane. 2012. *Corporate Responsibility: The American Experience*. New York: Cambridge University Press.

Carter, Evan C., Lilly M. Kofler, Daniel E. Forster, and Michael E. McCullough. 2015. "A Series of Meta-Analytic Tests of the Depletion Effect: Self-Control Does Not Seem to Rely on a Limited Resource." *Journal of Experimental Psychology: General* 144: 796.

Cohen, G. A. 1995. *Self-Ownership, Freedom, and Equality*. New York: Cambridge University Press.

Cohen, Laurie P. 2004. "Prosecutor's Tough New Tactics Turn Firms against Employees." *Wall St. J.*, June 4.

Comstock, Courtney. 2010. "Read the Letter Lehman Brothers Whistle Blower Wrote." *Insider*, March 19. https://www.businessinsider.com/read-the-letter-a-lehman-employee-sent-out-saying-lehmans-books-are-cooked-2010-3.

Corvino, John. 2015. "The Fact/Opinion Distinction" (blog). *The Philosophers' Magazine*, March 4. http://www.philosophersmag.com/essays/26-the-fact-opinion-distinction.

Cowen, Tyler. 2002. *Creative Destruction*. Princeton, NJ: Princeton University Press.

Cowen, Tyler, and Alex Tabarrok. 2015. *Modern Principles of Economics*. New York: Worth.

Danzinger, Shai, Jonathan Levav, and Loira Avnaim-Pesso. 2011. "Extraneous Factors in Judicial Decisions." *Proceedings of the National Academy of the United States* 108: 6889–6892.

Darley, John, and C. Daniel Batson. 1973. "'From Jerusalem to Jericho': A Study of Situational and Dispositional Variables in Helping Behavior." *Journal of Personality and Social Psychology* 27: 100–108.

Deci, E. L., and R. M. Ryan. 2010. Intrinsic Motivation. *The Corsini Encyclopedia of Psychology* (pp. 1–2). https://onlinelibrary.wiley.com/doi/abs/10.1002/9780470479216.corpsy0467.

de Soto, Hernando. 2000. *The Mystery of Capital*. New York: Basic Books.

Dikötter, Frank. 2010a. *Mao's Great Famine: The History of China's Most Devastating Catastrophe, 1958–62*. New York: Walker & Company.

Dikötter, Frank. 2010b. "Mao's Great Leap to Famine." *New York Times*, December 15.

Dorfman, Jeffrey. 2016. "Price Gouging Laws Are Good Politics but Bad Economics." *Forbes*, September 23. https://www.forbes.com/sites/jeffreydorfman/2016/09/23/price-gouging-laws-are-good-politics-but-bad-economics/#1084ec4464d3.

Drucker, P. F. *The Effective Executive*. 2006. New York: Harper Business.

Epley, Nicholas, and David Dunning. 2000. "Feeling" Holier Than Thou": Are Self-Serving Assessments Produced by Errors in Self- or Social Prediction?" *Journal of Personality and Social Psychology* 79: 861–875.

Erickson, Angela C. 2016. "Barriers to Braiding: How Job-Killing Licensing Laws Tangle Natural Hair Care in Needless Red Tape" (press release). Arlington, VA: Institute for Justice. https://ij.org/wp-content/uploads/2016/07/Barriers_To_Braiding-2.pdf.

Foot, Philippa. 1957. "Abortion and the Doctrine of Double Effect." *Oxford Review* 5: 5–15.

Footer, Alyson. 2017. "MLB Unites to Honor Mom, Raise Awareness." *mlb.com*. https://www.mlb.com/news/mlb-goes-pink-for-mothers-day-good-cause/c-230097814.

Frishberg, David. 1973. I'm Just a Bill. ABC Publishing, 1973.

Furnham, Adrian, and Hua Chu Boo. 2011. "A Literature Review of the Anchoring Effect." *The Journal of Socio-Economics* 40: 35–42.

Garvin, D. A. 2013. "How Google Sold Its Engineers on Management." *Harvard Business Review* 91: 74–82.

Gibney, Alex, Jessie Deeter, Erin Edeiken, Lincoln Else, Antonio Rossi, Andy Grieve, and Will Bates. 2019. *The Inventor: Out for Blood in Silicon Valley.*

Gilligan, Carol. 1983. *In a Different Voice.* Cambridge, MA: Harvard University Press.

Ginsberg, Benjamin. 2013. *The Fall of the Faculty.* Princeton, NJ: Princeton University Press.

Gintis, Herbert. 2012. "Giving the Economists Their Due." *Boston Review.* June 25. http://www.bostonreview.net/gintis-giving-economists-their-due.

Godlee, Fiona, Jane Smith, and Harvey Marcovitch. 2011. "Wakefield's Article Linking MMR Vaccine and Autism Was Fraudulent." *British Medical Journal* 342: c7452.

Goodwin, G. P., Jared Piazza, and Paul Rozini. 2014. "Moral Character Predominates in Person Perception and Evaluation." *Journal of Personality and Social Psychology* 106: 148–168.

Graeber, David. 2019. *Bullshit Jobs.* London: Penguin, p. 3.

Grossman, Gene, and Alan Krueger. 1995. "Economic Growth and the Environment." *Quarterly Journal of Economics* 110: 353–378.

Haidt, Jonathan. 2006. *The Happiness Hypothesis.* New York: Basic Books.

Hamlin, J. Kiley, Karen Wynn, and Paul Bloom. 2007. "Social Evaluation by Preverbal Infants." *Nature* 450: 557.

Hart, Stuart, and Susan Svobada. 2008. *McDonald's Case (B1): The Clamshell Controversy.* Ann Arbor: William Davidson Institute, University of Michigan.

Hayek, F. A. 1945. "The Use of Knowledge in Society." *American Economic Review* 35: 519–530.

Henrich, Joseph, Robert Boyd, Samuel Bowles, Colin Camerer, Ernst Fehr, Herbert Gintis, and Richard McElreath. 2001. "In Search of Homo Economicus: Behavioral Experiments in 15 Small-Scale Societies." *American Economic Review* 91: 73–78.

Hoffman, Mitchell, and John Morgan. 2011. *Who's Naughty? Who's Nice? Social Preferences in Online Industries.* Berkeley: University of California Press.

Holcombe, Randall G. 1994. *The Economic Foundations of Government.* London: Macmillan Press.

Hollier, Rod. 2021. "Physical Attractiveness Bias in the Legal System." *The Law Project.* http://www.thelawproject.com.au/blog/attractiveness-bias-in-the-legal-system.

Holusha, John. 1990. "Packaging and Public Image: McDonald's Fills a Big Order." *New York Times*, November 2. https://www.nytimes.com/1990/11/02/business/packaging-and-public-image-mcdonald-s-fills-a-big-order.html.

Hoskins, Tansy. 2015. "Reliving the Rana Plaza Factory Collapse: A History of Cities in 50 Buildings, Day 22." *The Guardian*, April 23. https://www.theguardian.com/cities/2015/apr/23/rana-plaza-factory-collapse-history-cities-50-buildings.

Independent Directors of the Board of Wells Fargo & Company. 2017. Sales Practices Investigation Report. https://www08.wellsfargomedia.com/assets/pdf/about/investor-relations/presentations/2017/board-report.pdf?https://www.wellsfargo.com/assets/pdf/about/investor-relations/presentations/2017/board-report.pdf.

Isidore, Chris. "Walmart Ups Pay Well above the Minimum." *@CNNMoney.* February 19. https://money.cnn.com/2015/02/19/news/companies/walmart-wages/index.html.

Iyengar, Shanto, and Sean J. Westwood. 2014. "Fear and Loathing across Party Lines: New Evidence on Group Polarization." *American Journal of Political Science* 59: 1–18.

Jackall, Robert. 1988. *Moral Mazes*. New York: Oxford University Press.

Jambeck, Jenna R., Anthony Andrady, Roland Geyer, Ramani Narayan, Miriam Perryman, Theodore Siegler, Chris Wilcox, and Kara Lavender Law. 2015. "Plastic Waste Inputs from Land into the Ocean." *Science* 347: 768–771. https://jambeck.engr.uga.edu/landplasticinput.

Kestenbaum, David, and Jacob Goldstein. 2012. "The Secret Document That Transformed China." *All Things Considered*. Aired January 20 on NPR. https://www.npr.org/sections/money/2012/01/20/145360447/the-secret-document-that-transformed-china.

King, Martin, Jr. 1963. *Letter from a Birmingham Jail*. Stanford University, The Martin Luther King, Jr. Research and Education Institute. http://okra.stanford.edu/transcription/document_images/undecided/630416-019.pdf.

Kline, John M., and Edward Soule. 2014. *Alta Gracia: Four Years and Counting* (Research Results Report). Reflective Engagement Initiative. https://ignatiansolidarity.net/wp-content/uploads/2014/08/AltaGracia-LowRes-1.pdf.

Kocieniewski, David. 2012. "Whistle-Blower Awarded $104 Million by I.R.S." *New York Times*, September 12. https://www.nytimes.com/2012/09/12/business/whistle-blower-awarded-104-million-by-irs.html.

Koppl, Roger, and Meghan Sacks. 2013. "The Criminal Justice System Creates Incentives for False Convictions." *Criminal Justice Ethics* 32: 126–162.

"KPMG in Wonderland." 2005. *Wall St. J.*, October 6, p. A14.

Krugman, Paul. 2001. "Reckonings: Hearts and Heads." *New York Times*, April 22, p. 17. https://www.nytimes.com/2001/04/22/opinion/reckonings-hearts-and-heads.html.

Krugman, Paul, and Robin Wells. 2012. *Microeconomics*. 3rd ed. New York: Worth.

Lacetera, Nicola, and Mario Macis. 2010. "Do All Material Incentives for Pro-social Activities Backfire? The Response to Cash and Non-cash Incentives for Blood Donations." *Journal of Economic Psychology* 31(4): 738–748.

Latané, Bibb, and John M. Darley. 1968. "Group Inhibition of Bystander Intervention in Emergencies." *Journal of Personality and Social Psychology* 10(3): 377–383.

Lichtblau, Eric, and Katie Benner. 2017. "Apple Fights Order to Unlock San Bernardino Gunman's Phone." *New York Times*, February 17. https://www.nytimes.com/2016/02/18/technology/apple-timothy-cook-fbi-san-bernardino.html.

Linnane, Clara. 2016. "Ousted or Not, Wells Fargo CEO John Stumpf Will Enjoy a Comfortable Retirement." *MarketWatch*, September 23. https://www.marketwatch.com/story/ousted-or-not-wells-fargo-ceo-john-stumpf-will-enjoy-a-comfortable-retirement-2016-09-23.

List, John A., and Fatemeh Momeni. 2017. *When Corporate Social Responsibility Backfires: Theory and Evidence from a Natural Field Experiment* (No. w24169). Cambridge, MA: National Bureau of Economic Research.

Loewenstein, George, Daylian M. Cain, and Sunita Sah. 2011. "The Limits of Transparency: Pitfalls and Potential of Disclosing Conflicts of Interest." *American Economic Review* 101: 423–428.

Lombardi, John. 2013. *How Universities Work*. Baltimore: Johns Hopkins University Press.

MacAskill, William. 2014. *Doing Good Better*. New York: Oxford University Press.

MacDonald, Chris. 2009. "Down with CSR! Up with Business Ethics" (blog). *The Business Ethic Blog*, February 14. https://businessethicsblog.com/2009/02/14/down-with-csr-up-with-business-ethics/.

Maddison, Angus. 2007. *Contours of the World Economy, 1-2030 AD*. New York: Oxford University Press.

Mankiw, Gregory. 2008. *Principles of Economics*. 5th ed. New York: Southwestern College Publishers.

"Market." 2000. *Oxford English Dictionary Online*, December. http://www.oed.com/view/Entry/114178?rskey=Iv7RKy&result=1#eid.

McCabe, Donald, Kenneth D. Butterfield, and Linda K. Treviño. 2017. *Cheating in College: Why Students Do It and What Educators Can Do about It*. Baltimore: Johns Hopkins University Press.

McCloskey, Deirdre. 1991. *If You're So Smart: The Narrative of Economic Expertise*. Chicago: University of Chicago Press.

McCloskey, Deirdre. 2006. *The Bourgeois Virtues*. Chicago: University of Chicago Press.

McLean, Bethany. 2017. "How Wells Fargo's Cutthroat Corporate Culture Allegedly Drove Bankers to Fraud." *Vanity Fair*, May 31. https://www.vanityfair.com/news/2017/05/wells-fargo-corporate-culture-fraud.

Mehrotra, Kartikay, and Laura J. Keller. 2017. Wells Fargo's Fake Accounts Grow to 3.5 Million in Suit" (blog). *Bloomberg*, May 12. https://www.bloomberg.com/news/articles/2017-05-12/wells-fargo-bogus-account-estimate-in-suit-grows-to-3-5-million.

Meyerson, Allen R. 1997. "In Principle, a Case for More 'Sweatshops.'" *New York Times*, June 22, sec. 4, p. 5. https://www.nytimes.com/1997/06/22/weekinreview/in-principle-a-case-for-more-sweatshops.html.

Milanovic, Branko. 2007. *Worlds Apart*. Princeton, NJ: Princeton University Press.

Minter, Adam. 2018. "Plastic Straws Aren't the Problem." *Bloomberg Opinion*, June 7. https://www.bloomberg.com/view/articles/2018-06-07/plastic-straws-aren-t-the-problem.

Moise, Amani. 2018. "Wells Fargo Will Pay $575 Million to Settle Claims Stemming from Sales Scandal." *Reuters*, December 28. https://www.businessinsider.com/wells-fargo-sales-scandal-575-million-settlement-2018-12.

Motlagh, Jason, and Atish Saha. 2014. "The Ghosts of Rana Plaza." *Virginia Quarterly Review* 90: 44–89.

Navasky, Victor. 1980. *Naming Names*. New York: Viking Press.

Nichols, Shaun. 2014. "Process Debunking and Ethics." *Ethics* 124: 727–749.

Nordhaus, William. 2013. *The Climate Casino*. New Haven, CT: Yale University Press.

Orlitzky, Marc, and John D. Benjamin. 2001. "Corporate Social Performance and Firm Risk: A Meta-Analytic Review." *Business & Society* 40: 369–396.

Orlov, Alex. 2018. "Budweiser Spent a Ton of Money on a Super Bowl Ad That's All about Its Charitable Efforts." *Mic*, January 26. https://mic.com/articles/187623/budweiser-spent-a-ton-of-money-on-a-super-bowl-ad-thats-all-about-its-charitable-efforts#.6w1zZnkVc.

Paine, Lynn Sharpe. 1994. "Managing for Organizational Integrity." *Harvard Business Review*, May. https://hbr.org/1994/03/managing-for-organizational-integrity.

Parloff, Roger. 2013. "The Gray Art of Not Quite Insider Trading." *Fortune*, September 2. http://fortune.com/2013/08/15/the-gray-art-of-not-quiteinsider-trading/.

Phelps, Glenn, and Steve Crabtree. 2013. "Worldwide, Median Household Income about $10,000." *Gallup*, December 6. https://news.gallup.com/poll/166211/worldwide-median-household-income-000.aspx.

Pink, D. H. 2009. *Drive: The Surprising Truth about What Motivates Us*. New York: Penguin.

Pinker, Steven. 2012. *The Better Angels of Our Nature*. New York: Penguin.

Post, Leonard. 2006. "Deferred Prosecution Deal Raises Objections." *National Law Journal*, January 30, p. 4.

Powell, Benjamin. 2013. "Sweatshops in Bangladesh Improve the Lives of Their Workers, and Boost Growth." *Forbes*, May 2. https://www.forbes.com/sites/realspin/2013/05/02/sweatshops-in-bangladesh-improve-the-lives-of-their-workers-and-boost-growth/#551ef7c774ce.

Powell, Benjamin. 2014. *Out of Poverty: Sweatshops in the Global Economy*. New York: Cambridge University Press.

Prichard, H. A. 1912. "Does Moral Philosophy Rest on a Mistake?." *Mind* 21: 21–37.

Read, Leonard E. 2015. *I, Pencil*. Atlanta, GA: Foundation for Economic Education. https://fee. org/resources/i-pencil/.

Reckard, Scott. 2013. "Wells Fargo's Pressure-Cooker Sales Culture Comes at a Cost." *Los Angeles Times*, December 21. https://www.latimes.com/business/la-fi-wells-fargo-sale-pressure-20131222-story.html.

Ritchie, Hannah, and Max Roser. 2019. "Natural Disasters." In *Our World in Data*. Oxford: Oxford University Press. https://ourworldindata.org/natural-catastrophes.

Roser, Max. n.d. "Light at Night." In *Our World in Data*. Oxford: Oxford University Press. https://ourworldindata.org/light.

Roser, Max. n.d. "War and Peace." In *Our World in Data*. Oxford: Oxford University Press. https://ourworldindata.org/war-and-peace.

Saad, Gad. 2011. "How Often Do People Lie in Their Daily Lives" (blog). *Psychology Today*, November 11. https://www.psychologytoday.com/us/blog/homo-consumericus/201111/how-often-do-people-lie-in-their-daily-lives.

Schmidtz, David. 1994. "The Institution of Property." *Social Philosophy and Policy* 11: 42–62.

Schmidtz, David, and Jason Brennan. 2010. *A Brief History of Liberty*. Oxford: Wiley-Blackwell.

Schwitzgebel, Eric. 2009. "Do Ethicists Steal More Books?." *Philosophical Psychology* 22: 711–725.

Schwitzgebel, Eric, and Joshua Rust. 2009. "The Moral Behavior of Ethicists: Peer Opinion." *Mind* 118: 1043–1059.

Schwitzgebel, Eric, and Joshua Rust. 2014. "The Moral Behavior of Ethics Professors: Relationships among Self-Reported Behavior, Expressed Normative Attitude, and Directly Observed Behavior." *Philosophical Psychology* 27: 293–327.

Simler, Kevin, and Robin Hanson. 2018. *The Elephant in the Brain*. New York: Oxford University Press.

Smith, Adam. 1776. *The Wealth of Nations*. London: Metheun and Co.

Stern, Nicholas. 2007. *The Economics of Climate Change: The Stern Review*. New York: Cambridge University Press.

Stevenson, Betsey, and Justin Wolfers. 2008. "Economic Growth and Subjective Well-Being: Reassessing the Easterlin Paradox" (Brookings Papers on Economic Activity). *The Brookings Institution* 39(1) (Spring): 1–102.

Strazzella, James A., and American Bar Association, Task Force on Federalization of Criminal Law. 1998. *The Federalization of Criminal Law*. Washington, DC: American Bar Association.

Stringham, Edward. 2015. *Private Governance*. New York: Oxford University Press.

Story, Louise, and Jo Becker. 2009. "Bank Chief Tells of U.S. Pressure to Buy Merrill Lynch." *New York Times*, June 11. https://www.nytimes.com/2009/06/12/business/12bank.html.

Strom, Stephanie. 1996. "A Sweetheart Becomes Suspect; Looking behind Those Kathie Lee Labels." *New York Times*, June 27, p. D1. https://www.nytimes.com/1996/06/27/business/a-sweetheart-becomes-suspect-looking-behind-those-kathie-lee-labels.html.

Titmuss, Richard. 2018. *The Gift Relationship: From Human Blood to Social Policy*. Policy Press.

Tosi, Justin, and Brandon Warmke. 2018. *Moral Grandstanding*. New York: Oxford University Press.

Trager. Rebecca. 2017. "Sensing Illegal Cyanide Fishing." *Chemistry World*, April 6. https://www.chemistryworld.com/news/thiocyanate-detector-aims-to-end-illegal-cyanide-fishing/3007092.article.

van der Vossen, Bas, and Jason Brennan. 2018. *In Defense of Openness*. New York: Oxford University Press.

Vandivier, Kermit. 2002. "The Aircraft Brake Scandal." In *Ethical Issues in Business: A Philosophical Approach*, 7th ed. Edited by Thomas Donaldson, Patricia H. Werhane, and Margaret Cording, 323–335. Upper Saddle River, NJ: Prentice Hall.

Vedder, Richard. 2019. *Restoring the Promise*. Oakland, CA: Independent Institute.

Velasquez, Manuel. 2012. *Business Ethics: Concepts and Cases*. Boston: Pearson.

Verschoor, Curtis C., and Elizabeth A. Murphy. 2002. "The Financial Performance of Large US Firms and Those with Global Prominence: How Do the Best Corporate Citizens Rate?." *Business and Society Review* 107: 371–380.

Voltaire, de, Francois Marie Arouet. 1961. *Philosophical Letters*. Macmillan: New York.

Waddell, Kaveh. 2016. "Why Google Quit China—And Why It's Heading Back." *The Atlantic*, January 19. https://www.theatlantic.com/technology/archive/2016/.

Weil, David. 2009. *Economic Growth*. 2nd ed. New York: Prentice Hall.

White, Gillian B. 2017. "The Tiny Dominican Factory That Disproves the Need for Sweatshops. *The Atlantic*, November 24. https://www.theatlantic.com/business/archive/2017/11/factory-apparel-industry-ethical/546419/.

Woodzicka, Julie A., and Marianne LaFrance. 2001. "Real Versus Imagined Gender Harassment." *Journal of Social Issues* 57: 15–30.

Yager, Jordy. 2007. "Chiquita Fined for Colombia Payments." *Los Angeles Times*, September 18. http://articles.latimes.com/2007/sep/18/nation/na-chiquita18.

Zak, Paul. 2008. *Moral Markets*. Princeton, NJ: Princeton University Press.

Zak, Paul, and Stephen Knack. 2001. "Trust and Growth." *Economic Journal* 11: 295–321.

Zwolinski, Matt. 2007. "Sweatshops, Choice, and Exploitation." *Business Ethics Quarterly* 17: 689–727.

Zwolinski, Matt. 2008. "The Ethics of Price Gouging." *Business Ethics Quarterly* 18: 347–378.

Index

Printed in the USA/Agawam, MA
June 23, 2021

776766.013